Teaching the Nuts and Bolts of Physical Education

Building Basic Movement Skills

A. Vonnie Colvin, EdD
University of Kentucky

Nancy J. Egner Markos, MEd
Broadus Wood Elementary School
Earlysville, Virginia

Pamela J. Walker, MEd
Red Hill Elementary School
North Garden, Virginia

Human Kinetics

Library of Congress Cataloging-in-Publication Data

Colvin, A. Vonnie, 1951-
 Teaching the nuts and bolts of physical education : building basic
movement skills / A. Vonnie Colvin, Nancy J. Egner Markos, Pam
Walker.
     p.   cm.
 Includes bibliographical references.
 ISBN 0-88011-883-0
 1. Physical education for children.   2. Movement education.
I. Markos, Nancy J. Egner, 1949-   . II. Walker, Pam, 1953-   .
III. Title.
GV443.C59   2000
372.86--dc21
                                              99-38507
                                              CIP

ISBN: 0-88011-883-0

Acquisitions Editor: Scott Wikgren; **Developmental Editor:** C.E. Petit, JD; **Managing Editor:** Laura Ward Majersky; **Copyeditor:** Patricia Fortney; **Proofreader:** Pamela S. Johnson; **Graphic Designer:** Stuart Cartwright; **Graphic Artist:** Kathleen Boudreau-Fuoss; **Cover Designer:** Jack W. Davis; **Photographer (cover):** Tom Roberts; **Illustrators:** Roberto Sabas (line art) and Tom Roberts (Mac art); **Printer:** United Graphics

Printed in the United States of America   10 9 8 7 6 5 4 3 2 1

Human Kinetics
Web site: http://www.humankinetics.com/

United States: Human Kinetics, P.O. Box 5076, Champaign, IL 61825-5076
1-800-747-4457
e-mail: humank@hkusa.com

Canada: Human Kinetics, 475 Devonshire Road Unit 100, Windsor, ON N8Y 2L5
1-800-465-7301 (in Canada only)
e-mail: humank@hkcanada.com

Europe: Human Kinetics, P.O. Box IW14, Leeds LS16 6TR, United Kingdom
+44 (0) 113-278 1708
e-mail: humank@hkeurope.com

Australia: Human Kinetics, 57A Price Avenue, Lower Mitcham, South Australia 5062
(08) 82771555
e-mail: humank@hkaustralia.com

New Zealand: Human Kinetics, P.O. Box 105-231, Auckland Central
09-523-3462
e-mail: humank@hknewz.com

We would like to dedicate this book
to the many students we have been privileged to teach.
Our students of all ages
have helped us become better teachers
and enabled us to write this book.
Thank you.

Contents

Preface

"People rarely succeed at anything unless they have fun doing it."
—Anonymous

As educators, we should strive to create a fun and successful learning environment for our students. While the main goal of all education—including elementary physical education—is improved skill, we believe fun can serve as both a means and a motivation for students. When motivated children receive sound instruction, they are more focused on learning. In physical education, this learning may result in students continuing to be physically active throughout their lives.

Early movement success is crucial to later skill acquisition. The ages between three and nine represent a critical time for children to learn physical skills (Pangrazi, Chomokos, and Massoney 1981). In the early grades, children are able to master basic movement skills with less difficulty than at any other time in their lives. Initial movement experiences with locomotor and manipulative skills are the foundation for later sport performance. These building blocks are essential for individuals to cross the "proficiency barrier" into successful sport and recreational participation (Seefeldt 1979).

In the past, many programs focused on playing games that had no instructional focus. The games of Red Rover and Duck, Duck, Goose are enjoyable, but do nothing to develop basic skills. According to the National Association for Sport and Physical Education's (NASPE) Outcomes Project (Franck et al. 1992), "The greatest emphasis during the preschool and early elementary grades should be upon movement skill acquisiton" (p. 9). The challenge for individuals who teach elementary-age children is clear: basic skills should be at the heart of a successful physical education curriculum.

However, knowing what children should be able to do at each grade level can be a difficult task for the teacher to keep up with. In its report, the NASPE Outcomes Project Committee defined what students in physical education should know and be able to do. This report also established benchmarks for student accomplishments at various grade levels; these assessment points were designed to serve as guides for physical education teachers. NASPE's suggested benchmarks are included in the appropriate chapters in this book. This information can serve as a guide in making decisions about your curriculum and your students' progress.

While current research clearly indicates *what* should be taught, few resources are available to provide detailed activities and methods for teaching these skills. The purpose of this book is to provide individuals who work with elementary-age children a sequence of information and activities that will serve as the foundation or the building blocks of successful movement experiences for children. These building blocks include mastering the components (or parts) of the basic locomotor and manipulative skills.

To assist the reader in building this foundation, we have organized this book to be user-friendly, with similar ideas and skills combined. Chapter 1 provides an overview of how to use this book. Chapter 2 specifically deals with eight basic locomotor skills: run, hop, vertical jump, horizontal jump, gallop, slide, skip, and leap. Locomotor skills are an integral part of sports participation and should not be overlooked when planning a complete physical education experience for all students. The chapter describes and then breaks down each individual skill into teachable components that are then combined in a variety of practice activities. When practice time is engaging and skill-specific, students are able to master the skill.

Chapter 3 is perhaps the most crucial chapter of this book. Here we explain activities that stress learning the essential parts of each skill. Any or all of these nine activities will help students master the components of any of the 13 manipulative and eight locomotor skills detailed in this book. Creating a fun and exciting learning environment while stressing correct performance of the skill provides your students with practice opportunities in which they will want to participate.

Chapters 4 through 10 are devoted to the manipulative skills. While some chapters discuss just one manipulative skill (e.g., chapter 4 is devoted to the underhand roll and chapter 6 contains information exclusive to the catch), other chapters pertain to groups of similar manipulative skills. For example, the underhand throw and the overhand throw are distinct skills, but both involve throwing an object with one hand. Therefore, they are found in the chapter on throwing (chapter 5). Other chapters that include combinations of manipulative skills are chapter 7 (the bounce pass and chest pass), chapter 8 (the basketball dribble and soccer dribble), chapter 9 (the strike, side-arm strike, and two-hand side-arm strike), and chapter 10 (the kick and the punt).

Our focus as physical educators should be on skill mastery and lifetime fitness and sports participation. While there are many sport-specific manipulative skills, the ones we have chosen to cover provide a basic foundation for the acquisition of other skills. For example: a tennis serve uses several of the components required for mastery of the overhand throw; a serve in volleyball requires the understanding of the components needed for mastery of the underhand throw; and a bowling ball roll uses the basic components of the underhand roll. The list is endless but the outcome is the same: when students can master some fundamental manipulative skills, they can apply that knowledge to other skills that use similar actions.

We feel that the skills covered in this book are the nuts and bolts essential to building successful physical education curricula for children. This book is a collection of teaching strategies and ideas that we have developed over our combined 70+ years of teaching experience. The activities are "kid tested" and are very successful in our elementary schools. It is our hope that individuals who teach elementary-age children will use our ideas, create some of their own, and most of all, experience fun and success with their students.

Acknowledgments

This exciting project would not have been possible without a great many people's assistance. We would like to specifically acknowledge the efforts of Jim Nance from the University of Kentucky. He willingly shared his insights on and experiences in writing a book. We are very grateful for his guidance and encouragement. We also would like to extend our appreciation for the time commitments and efforts of Jenna McLane and Logan Ripley, who served as models for the photo drafts that were submitted to the artists at Human Kinetics.

Vonnie Colvin:

I would like to thank my parents, Alice and Dixie Colvin, for their encouragement, love, and support. Also, a big thank you to other members of my family—Nancy, Terry, Mike, and Alan—for being the supportive, wonderful people they are. Professionally, I have been fortunate to work with such outstanding mentors as Barb Call and Jim Nance from the University of Kentucky and Ann Boyce from the University of Virginia. Thank you. Other educators who have assisted me with this book and deserve a lot of thanks are Marilyn Basham, Lynn Crotts, and Mary Hipes from Trevilians Elementary in Louisa County, Virginia; Scott McAtee from Veterans Park Elementary in Lexington, Kentucky; and Janet Stone and Greg Laber from the University of Kentucky.

Nancy Markos:

I would like to thank my husband, Artie, for the love and support he has given me over the years. A thank you to my children, Lance and Wendy, for making my life complete. A special thanks to my parents, Bob and Betty Egner, for their constant love and support. They taught me that anything in life is possible. I would like to thank my sister, Barbara Stansfield, who is always there when I need a laugh, and Chris Egner for becoming an important part of my family. Also, I would like to thank my friends—especially Diane Brownlee—for their encouragement, support, and friendship.

Pam Walker:

I would like to thank my parents, Sue and Jim Walker, for their constant love and support and for teaching me that anything is possible. A big thank you to Deb, Kim, Howard, Tracy, and the kids for keeping me from taking myself or life too seriously. Thank you, Gwen, for cooking, reading, questioning, and encouraging me to take time out for myself. I would also like to thank my friends for their encouragement, humor, and support.

chapter 1

Ready, Set, Read This Before You GO

Primary-age children bring an excitement to the physical education environment that is contagious. This book capitalizes on that student excitement by providing fun and motivating ideas to promote successful learning experiences. When children are motivated to learn, when they want to keep practicing because they enjoy it, and when they are provided sound, sequential instruction, then success and achievement will follow.

While fun and success are important components of the teaching/learning process, quality instruction requires that detailed lesson plans be developed and implemented to meet the needs of all children, regardless of skill level. This book provides those resources.

How to Use This Book

We have attempted to provide a wide variety of materials on each of the eight locomotor and 13 manipulative skills covered in this book. Our goal is for you to be able to easily locate and implement a multitude of activities that will enhance instruction and promote student learning. Regardless of the topic, the skill chapters are organized in the following manner:

1. *Introduction:* Depending on the skill, this general introduction may include teaching suggestions, safety precautions, equipment modifications, and suggested ages at which the skill or a part of the skill should be mastered according to the 1992 NASPE Outcomes Project. Please note that the NASPE outcomes are only suggestions, not absolute dates at which the skill must be mastered.

2. *Components and Cue Words:* Next, we identify the basic components of each skill and appropriate cue words. Each skill is separated into the four to five components that are necessary for the skill to be performed correctly. To assist the student in remembering each component, cue words are emphasized and interwoven throughout instruction.

The cue words are part of a start phase (ready position), an action phase (which may have two or three parts), or an ending phase (stop). Your choice of cue words will depend on your areas of emphasis and the characteristics of the students you are teaching. Younger students should be given cues that are short and descriptive of the action they are to perform; older students may be able to use longer, more specific cues. You should be sure that the cues you use contain only a few words and that they don't become sentences. When a skill is introduced for the first time, you will want to emphasize just one or two crucial elements or cues.

It may be necessary to adapt cues for children with disabilities. For example, when teaching the underhand roll to a child in a wheelchair, the teacher may omit the STEP cue, but maintain the other cues (READY, ARM BACK, ROLL, and FOLLOW THROUGH).

3. *Partner Skill Check Sheets:* To help the students master each skill's component parts, partner skill check sheets are included for each of the 21 skills. The partner skill check sheets allow partners to assess each other's progress in learning the selected skill. You may also use the sheets as assessment supplements and/ or send them home as a report of student progress.

We have designed two versions of the skill check sheets so that all children may benefit from their use. The first version contains drawings that relate to the designated cue words. This version may be used by young children who do not know how to read or by children who do not speak English. The second version contains written descriptions of the skill components and appropriate check boxes. This version should be used by older children who are able to read.

4. *Success Builders:* In the manipulative skill chapters (4 through 10), following the partner skill check sheets, we have included a section on success building activities. If the partner skill check sheet reveals that a student is experiencing difficulty with one or more components of the skill, specific activities are explained in *success builders* to help the student correct the problem.

At each success builder station, regardless of the skill being taught, we suggest using an unbreakable mirror and a poster showing each component. The mirror is particularly helpful because it allows the child to see what she is doing. Making the posters can be accomplished easily by photocopying and enlarging the partner skill check sheet drawings from this book (an opaque projector works well for enlargements). Laminating each poster will ensure its use for many years.

5. *Activities:* To reinforce the *entire* skill, not just isolated components, we have included numerous activities for individuals, partners, and groups. Each activity contains extensions to add variety to the lesson or to make the tasks easier or more difficult. Whenever possible, we have integrated other academic areas (e.g., language arts, math) into the performance of physical skills in the practice activities. For example, the Color Targets activity suggests using colors, shapes, numbers, or words, depending on the age and abilities of the students. In Create-A-Word, students use letter targets to spell out words. After students have achieved mastery of a particular skill, the activities in these sections may be duplicated and used during recess.

6. *Troubleshooting Charts:* We have included troubleshooting charts to describe typical problem areas and suggest remedies. While the partner skill check sheets and success builder activities examine *how* the student performs the skill, the troubleshooting charts describe problem areas in student performance, that is, *what happened* or the resulting action.

Specifically, each chart includes two headings. The first heading, *If you see,* details problem areas. The second heading, *Then try this,* offers solutions. For example, in a lateral slide—like you might see used defensively in basketball— you may see the student's body turned in such a way that his side does not lead the slide. In this situation, a possible solution would be to have the student stand with his back to a wall and slide along the wall at a slow speed. Once he understands the movement, the speed of the skill can be increased and the student can practice away from the wall.

7. *Lesson Plans:* For all of the manipulative skills, we have included a sample 30-minute lesson plan. This plan focuses on an aspect of the skill that can be the most challenging to teach and the most difficult for children to learn. To guide the teacher through the instructional sequence, each lesson is deliberately overplanned and described in detail. Within each plan are warm-up activities, detailed directions for the entire lesson, and exactly what to watch for when the students are practicing.

Change Is Good

Since movements are never the same each time they are executed, we encourage you to combine skills with other activities as soon as possible. This method is embedded in chapter 2, where we use the various movement concepts (e.g., pathways, levels) throughout the skill instruction for each locomotor skill. We also include challenges in chapters 4 through 10 that encourage students to combine each manipulative skill with other movements. These challenges include the use of force, level, speed, and pathways. Using any of the moving concepts will not only add to the challenge of the activity, but will also make the practice sessions more exciting for your students.

Assessment

Assessment is an essential part of the teaching and learning process. The information obtained through assessment may help you modify instructional strategies, identify areas of student strength or weakness, and serve as a motivational tool. It may also be used to communicate such observations to students and parents (Smith 1997).

Assessments may be done by students, teachers, or both. They may be informal, as when the teacher observes the students to determine what part of the skill the students need to continue practicing or if they are ready for an increased challenge. Or the assessments may be more formal, where there is a specific evaluation tool (such as the partner skill check sheets) used and findings impact grades. *How* you choose to assess your students will depend on many factors including time, resources, personal philosophy, and expectations. Whether you use informal or formal assessments, it is important to evaluate the skill development of your students. These assessments will help you focus on student needs and develop your lesson plans to better meet the instructional needs of your students.

This book provides several activities that can be used to assist you and your students with assessment. Sections devoted to specific skill components, skill check sheets, success builder activities, and troubleshooting charts are included in each manipulative skill chapter. Each of these sections can be used as they are or adapted to fit your specific assessment needs.

We strongly recommend using ongoing peer observations in which the students are asked to examine one another's skills. Learning can be enhanced when students use the partner skill check sheets *and* when they observe a partner without the check sheets to determine if he has mastered one or more targeted parts of the skill. In either setting, a student can tell his partner what parts of the skill are being performed correctly and what parts need improvement. This specific feedback will improve the student's understanding of the skill.

You may also use the partner skill check sheets to highlight individual students' areas of strength or weakness or as a method of student evaluation to be shared with parents. When used as a pretest and later as a posttest, the sheets can clearly show specific areas of student improvement and skill acquisition.

Information from this book will help you in planning subsequent lessons. The partner skill check sheets and troubleshooting charts will help identify potential problem areas and suggest ways to correct the problems. Once you have a clear idea of what needs to be "fixed," a lesson plan can be specifically designed to meet the needs of your students. Skill mastery will be enhanced with this procedure.

Organizational Tips

Becoming a successful teacher requires training in sound pedagogical practices. While this book is designed as a resource for teachers, it is not a replacement for an elementary physical education methods class. As you use the ideas in this book, however, we recommend that you minimize class management time and maximize instructional time. Following is a list of strategies we have used to reduce management time and increase instructional time.

Management tips:

- Always preplan the lesson.
- Establish rules and procedures for class behavior.
- Have a predetermined start and stop signal.
- Maximize student participation by avoiding any activity that eliminates a child from participation.
- Minimize student wait time by having equipment for every child, if possible.
- Bring students in close for direct instruction.

Instructional tips:

- Make sure your day's lesson is well-planned, and follow it.
- Have equipment set up and ready for use.

- Use a tape recorder/CD player with a remote control for music.
- Use visual cues such as pictures.
- Use a chalkboard, poster board, some butcher paper, etc., to write out the appropriate cue words.
- Use a video camera for skill analysis, if your school district allows.

We hope you will find this book a valuable tool in helping you to create rewarding and successful movement programs for your students. HAVE FUN!

chapter 2

Locomotor Skills

Children begin performing locomotor skills early. They learn to crawl, then to creep, and finally, with much family excitement, to walk. In this chapter we will examine eight other methods of movement—running, hopping, vertical jumping, horizontal jumping, galloping, sliding, skipping, and leaping. Some of these locomotor movements relate directly to sport skills (e.g., running, jumping, and sliding). Others will assist students with dance skills and in becoming skillful movers (e.g., galloping and skipping).

About This Chapter

This chapter is divided into eight sections, one for each locomotor movement. In each section, we have included a brief description of the specific locomotor skill, the components or parts of the movement, and selected cue words that may be used when teaching that particular skill. We have included at least two cue sets for each skill. You may use each set individually or mix and match the cue words as needed. We have found it beneficial to have the students say the cue words out loud as they practice.

In addition, to facilitate your students' skill mastery, we have included partner skill check sheets and specific troubleshooting charts in each section. The partner skill check activity allows partners to assess each other's progress in learning the locomotor skills. If the students cannot read or do not speak English, the picture version of the partner skill check sheet may be useful.

To use the partner skill check sheets:

1. One partner observes the other to see if she has the correct form for the first area of concern, for example, the eyes and body position.

2. If the eyes and body position are correct, then the partner places a *Y* in the first box. If the eyes and body position is not correct, the partner places an *N* in the first box. Nonreaders can put a smiling face if the eyes and body position is correct or a sad face if the eyes and body position is not correct.

3. This evaluation continues until each of the components has been assessed five times.

4. A partner skill check sheet is used for each student.

You may elect to use the partner skill check sheet yourself to assess the skill development of each student. In addition, to keep the parents informed of student progress, you may elect to send these sheets home with report cards or after individual students master specific skills.

While we highly recommend using the movement concept approach (Graham, Holt-Hale, and Parker 1998) to teach the locomotor skills, we have included a few specific ideas to reinforce the acquisition of selected locomotor skills.

The final section of the chapter describes activities that can be used to reinforce any or all of the locomotor movements. These may serve as culminating activities or warm-up ideas.

How to Teach Locomotor Skills

We highly recommend that you begin each school year teaching or reviewing the basic movement concepts (location, pathways, force, levels, and relationships). Their addition will provide the necessary variety to the skill performance and thus promote skillful movement. You should plan to devote at least one class period to each topic and then revisit these concepts often throughout the year. These movement concepts lay the foundation for future skills. The NASPE Outcomes Project suggests that the kindergartner should be able to move in a large group without touching others (outcome K-1), move forward and sideways (outcome K-2), demonstrate both fast and slow speeds (outcome K-3), distinguish the pathways of straight, curve, and zigzag (outcome K-4), and demonstrate directions such as over and under while moving (outcome K-6). Table 2.1 provides a brief list of the basic movement concepts and possible ways to describe the skills to your students (Buschner 1994, 26).

When a foundation for movement concepts is established, you can begin to reinforce specific locomotor skills by integrating the concepts into your lessons. You may, for example, challenge the children to practice jumping, running, and skipping in pathways.

Linking the concept of pathways with another concept, such as force, allows for more complex combinations. For example, you might challenge your students to run along a curvy pathway with light force, or along a straight pathway with medium force. Adding a third movement concept further increases complexity and variety. For example, you might add relationships to the combination and challenge your students to run along a curvy pathway with light force while leading (or following) a partner. Table 2.2 organizes these movement concepts to clarify possible combinations (Graham, Holt-Hale, & Parker 1998).

Once the basic movement concepts and a specific locomotor skill have been taught, you can provide limitless challenges to your students by selecting a challenge from one or two or even three columns of the movement concept chart (table 2.2). This variety of combinations will provide countless opportunities to reinforce each of the locomotor skills.

You may elect to make a bulletin board or poster display of the movement concepts. With either visual aid, you may try the following:

1. Allow students to select the movement concept that will be used with the locomotor skill being taught.

2. Place the students in small groups and challenge them to find ways to combine the targeted locomotor skill with two or three movement con-

Table 2.1 Basic Movement Concepts and Suggested Ways to Describe the Skill

Location	Direction
Personal space—an area where you can move and not touch anyone else. General space—the overall play area.	In place—stay where you are. Forward—walk the direction your toes point. Backward—walk the direction your heels point. Sideways (left and right)—put your two hands in front of you with the thumbs together and fingers straight. Notice that the thumb and fingers of one hand make an L. That is your left hand. If you move in that direction, you will move to your LEFT. The other way is your RIGHT. Over—move so you are above. Under—move so you are beneath. Around—move so you are circling an object. Up—move at a high level. Down—move at a low level.
Pathways	
Straight—move in a straight line. Curvy—move in a line that curves. Zigzag—move in a pathway that has many turns with obvious "points." There are no rounded turns.	
Force	**Relationships**

Light—move like a mouse.
Medium—move like you are walking to the cafeteria.
Heavy—move like an elephant (or T-Rex).
	With people:
	    Leading—be in front of a partner.
	    Following—be behind a partner.
	    Mirroring—move together with a partner so that when she raises an arm, you raise an arm; when she is on tiptoes, you are on tiptoes. You move together. It usually works better to practice at a slow speed.
	With partners—Two people together.
	With groups—Three or more people.

Levels	
Low—move in the area closest to the floor, low like a turtle. Medium—move at your normal walking level. High—pretend you are a giraffe and be as tall as you can when you move.	
Speed	
Slow—move like a turtle. Medium—move like you are walking to the cafeteria. Fast—move fast like the wind.	

Table 2.2 Basic Movement Concept Chart

Location	Pathways	Force	Levels	Speed	Direction	Relationships
Personal space	Straight	Light	Low	Slow	In place	With people:
General space	Curvy	Medium	Medium	Medium	Forward or Backward	Leading or Following
	Zigzag	Heavy	High	Fast	Left or right	Mirroring
					Over, Under, or Around	With partners
					Up or Down	With groups

cepts. These skills may be demonstrated to a nearby group or to the remainder of the class.

3. Place the descriptions of the movement concepts (e.g., light force, medium level) in a container and have students randomly select one, two, or even three concepts. Students then perform the locomotor skill as the movement concept directs.

Younger students will be very successful with one or two concepts. Combining three or more concepts with a locomotor skill should be reserved for older children or those "extra special" classes that seem to be able to do anything.

Plan ahead for movement concept combinations that may be very difficult or even impossible to perform. For example, if a student draws the combination of skipping at a low level with heavy force, you may decide to change the challenge to skipping at a high level with light force in order to make it an achievable task.

Run

After a child learns to walk, he wants to move faster and that naturally progresses to the run. The young child will move intuitively in a way that maintains balance. To keep from falling, the young runner may have his arms outstretched and use a much wider running stance than an adult would (Gabbard 1992). This is a natural adaptation that occurs after several falls. Unfortunately, many of these extra movements become permanent motor patterns unless instruction is provided.

Proper skill performance can be established at an early age with proper instruction. According to the NASPE Outcomes Project, a kindergartner should be able to demonstrate a mature running form (outcome K-15).

Components of the Run

Eyes and Body
—the eyes focus in the direction of travel, and the body moves in an upright position with a slight forward lean.

Flight
—both feet are temporarily off the ground in a stride position.

Arms
—arms are bent at about a 90-degree angle and move in a forward and backward direction without crossing the midline of the body.

Knees
—knee is bent to bring the heel up behind the body and parallel to the ground.

Cue Words

EYES FORWARD—eyes focus in the direction of travel.

PUMP YOUR ARMS and ARMS BENT—arms are bent at about a 90-degree angle and move in a forward and backward direction without crossing the midline of the body.

BIG STRIDE—legs extend farther than they would in a walking step with a temporary flight phase.

FEET STRAIGHT—feet are parallel to each other throughout the running motion.

Cue Set 1: EYES FORWARD, PUMP YOUR ARMS, BIG STRIDE

Cue Set 2: ARMS BENT, FEET STRAIGHT

Partner Skill Check

Skill: **Run**

Runner's name: _____ Watcher's name: _____

 **1.**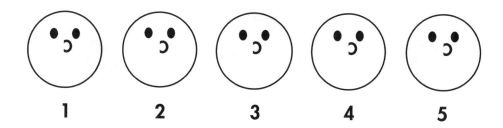

Body lean

 **2.**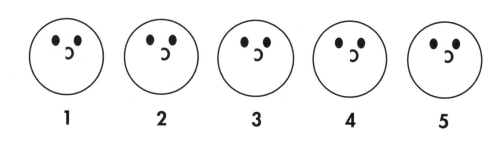

Fly

 **3.**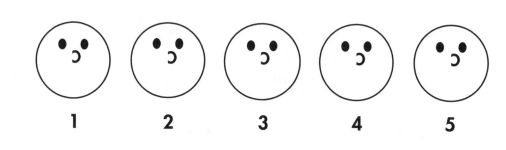

Arms

 **4.**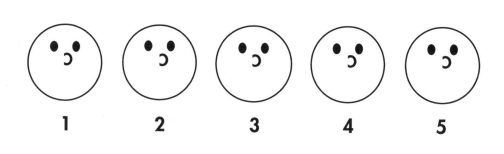

Leg bent

Partner Skill Check

Skill: **Run**

Runner's name: _____ Watcher's name: _____

Watch your partner and mark each component of the skill. Let your partner do the skill 5 times. Each time your partner does it right, mark a **Y** in the box. If your partner doesn't do it right, mark an **N** in the box.

RUN SKILL COMPONENTS

TRIALS

Eyes and body

Eyes look in the direction of travel, and body moves in an upright position.

☐ 1 ☐ 2 ☐ 3 ☐ 4 ☐ 5

Body

There is a slight forward lean of the body.

☐ 1 ☐ 2 ☐ 3 ☐ 4 ☐ 5

Flight

Both feet are temporarily off the ground.

☐ 1 ☐ 2 ☐ 3 ☐ 4 ☐ 5

Arms

Arms move in a forward and backward swinging motion.

☐ 1 ☐ 2 ☐ 3 ☐ 4 ☐ 5

Arms do not cross the midline of the body.

☐ 1 ☐ 2 ☐ 3 ☐ 4 ☐ 5

Knees

Knees bend to bring the foot up behind the back parallel to the ground.

☐ 1 ☐ 2 ☐ 3 ☐ 4 ☐ 5

Run Troubleshooting Chart

IF YOU SEE	THEN TRY THIS
1. No forward body lean	• Use a mirror or flashlight (reflection or shadow) to let the student see his body position. The student should have his side to the mirror or wall. • Videotape the student performing the skill. Using a remote to start/stop the action, show the student the tape.
2. No flight phase	• Encourage the student to run at a faster speed. • Place footprints or tape along a straight pathway approximately 40 feet long. The footprints or tape should be far enough apart to create a comfortable stride length for the student. As the student increases the stride length and speed of the run, periods of flight will result.
3. Arms crossing the midline of the body or not swinging with the run	• Have the student work with a partner. The partner must stand about 30 feet in front of the student. The student does a fast walk toward the partner, demonstrating the arm swing. The partner tells the student whether the arm swing is correct and lets the student know if the arms crossed the midline of the body. • Videotape the student performing the skill. Using a remote to start/stop the action, show the student the tape.
4. Foot not coming up behind the body	• Have the student run in place and try to kick her heel up near her body. • Have the student work with a partner. The partner watches the student run 30 feet and counts the number of times the student's foot does not come up near her bottom. The object is to score a zero.

Hop

Proper performance of the hop involves taking off from one foot, having a brief period of nonsupport, and landing on the same foot. While the hop is an integral part of many children's games (e.g., hopscotch), it is also crucial to such advanced skills as the layup in basketball.

Unfortunately, the term *hop* is often used to describe a jump. For this reason, some children may be confused when you first begin instruction in the proper hopping technique. You may need to solicit their help in enlightening their teachers about proper terminology. After all, that very popular kindergarten dance should really be called the "Bunny Jump."

Learning the hop involves an orderly progression. Before a child can begin to hop, she must be able to balance on one foot. Once the child can balance, she may proceed to the skill of hopping by holding onto a support. The child can then advance to hopping without assistance (Gabbard 1992). According to the

NASPE Outcomes Project, a second grader should be able to demonstrate a mature hopping pattern (outcome 2-18).

Besides using the movement concepts to reinforce the hop, we have found the following ideas to be helpful:

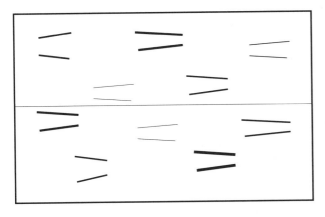

When teaching the hop, it is helpful to make 10 or more learning stations. These stations are composed of nonparallel lines that are at least six feet long and are positioned one inch apart at the closest point and two feet apart at the widest point (see figure). The lines may be taped to the floor, or jump ropes may be used.

Students can be challenged to hop across these imaginary "creeks." They may be further challenged to go to the widest part and hop across without "getting their feet wet." Small "stepping stones" (taped lines or floor spots) can be placed within wider "creeks" to assist in hopping.

Encourage your students to play hopscotch. A variety of hopscotch designs can be found in many activity books; they can be traditional (straight), spirals or circles (curvy), or you can make up your own (zigzag is a possibility). All you really need are connecting shapes with spaces large enough for a child's foot. The type of pattern is limited only by the imagination!

Extensions:

1. Provide sidewalk chalk for small groups of students. After showing them the traditional hopscotch design, allow them to make up their own. The students can practice hopping on each other's diagrams.

2. Make copies of these diagrams and use sidewalk chalk to mark them during recess. When the hopscotch diagrams are made smaller and include numbers, they can become math lessons. Challenge the students to hop on only even numbers, or hop on the answer to 2 + 1.

Components of the Hop

Eyes and Body
—the eyes look forward in the direction of travel, and the body moves in an upright position.

Foot and Take-Off Leg
—take off and land on the same foot, bending the knee on landing.

Swing Knee
—the swing knee is bent and swings forward.

Arms
—the elbows are bent, and the arm opposite the swing leg moves forward.

Glide
—the body moves with a smooth, rhythmical motion.

Albemarle County Physical Education Curriculum Revision Committee, 1996, 2-1.

Cue Words

SPRING—take off and land on the same foot, knees bend on landing.

SWING—the swing knee is bent and swings forward.

UP—the eyes look forward in the direction of travel, the body moves in an upright position, the swing knee is bent and swings forward, and the student takes off and lands on the same foot.

DOWN—the knee bends on landing, and preparation begins immediately to take off again.

STEP AND SWING—step forward on the hopping foot, bend the other knee, and swing that knee up and forward; there is a brief period of nonsupport, and the body moves with a smooth, rhythmical motion.

Cue Set 1: SPRING, SWING

Cue Set 2: UP, DOWN

Cue Set 3: STEP AND SWING, STEP AND SWING

Partner Skill Check

Skill: **Hop**

Hopper's name: _____ Watcher's name: _____

1.

   1   2   3   4   5

One foot

2.

   1   2   3   4   5

Knee up

3.

   1   2   3   4   5

Arm

4.

   1   2   3   4   5

Fly

Partner Skill Check

Skill: **Hop**

Hopper's name: _____ Watcher's name: _____

Watch your partner and mark each component of the skill. Let your partner do the skill 5 times. Each time your partner does it right, mark a **Y** in the box. If your partner doesn't do it right, mark an **N** in the box.

HOP SKILL COMPONENTS

TRIALS

Eyes and body

Eyes look in the direction of travel, and body moves in an upright position.

☐ 1   ☐ 2   ☐ 3   ☐ 4   ☐ 5

Foot and take-off leg

Take off and land on the same foot; knee bends on landing.

☐ 1   ☐ 2   ☐ 3   ☐ 4   ☐ 5

Swing knee

Swing knee is bent and swings forward.

☐ 1   ☐ 2   ☐ 3   ☐ 4   ☐ 5

Arms

Elbows are bent, and arm opposite the swing leg moves forward.

☐ 1   ☐ 2   ☐ 3   ☐ 4   ☐ 5

Glide

Body moves with a smooth, rhythmical motion.

☐ 1   ☐ 2   ☐ 3   ☐ 4   ☐ 5

Hop Troubleshooting Chart

IF YOU SEE	THEN TRY THIS
1. Hopping foot not coming up off the floor or landing knee not bending	• Using floor spots (or carpet squares if outside), have the student hop over the squares. The student will need to bend the knee on the hopping leg to generate more force. • Videotape the student performing the skill. Using a remote to start/stop the action, show the student the tape.
2. Two feet touching the floor	• Use a wall or partner for support. • Using a scarf, pinny, Dynaband, etc., have the student hold the nonhopping foot up off the ground. The student tries to hop while holding the foot. The student has control of when she can put the nonhopping foot down.
3. Swing knee not moving or arms not swinging during the hop	• Have the student stand stationary on one foot next to a wall. The hand opposite the hopping leg side holds the wall for balance. The student swings the swing knee while swinging the arm opposite the swing knee. • Once the student can successfully hop holding onto the wall, have him practice without the wall, swinging each arm in opposition to the legs.
4. Student not hopping with a smooth pattern	• Review the components of the skill. Being able to perform any locomotor skill smoothly requires the student to use the components of the skill correctly. You will need to review the components to create a smooth, rhythmical motion.

Jump

The locomotor skill of jumping is fairly complex. A jump may technically involve a one- or two-foot takeoff with a two-foot landing. A jump may also involve a two-foot takeoff with a one-foot landing (Gabbard 1992). The NASPE Outcomes Project suggests that a second grader should be able to "jump and land using a combination of one- and two-foot takeoffs and landings" (outcome 2-4). Technically, a leap and a hop both are variations of the jump—but we have found these explanations to be very confusing for young children. Therefore, in the vertical jump and horizontal jump sections we will take the more universal approach of defining a jump as taking off from two feet and laxnding on two feet.

Vertical Jump

A rebound in basketball and a spike in volleyball are two obvious examples of the vertical jump. Children enjoy learning to jump because it is "measurable," meaning they can see a result from their movement. For example, being able to touch the net on a basketball rim is a major accomplishment for many elementary school students.

While children generally enjoy jumping, several safety concerns must be addressed. Jumping up to touch a spot on a wall can cause injuries if it is not done properly. The preliminary run may provide too much momentum and the child may run into the wall. Children perform more safely when an object is suspended from an overhead structure. However, students should be taught to touch the object, not pull it. Pulling down an attached overhead object may cause injuries to the student.

In addition, you should be sure to clearly mark the starting point for the running approach to a jump. Often children believe that if a 10-foot approach is good, a 1,000-foot approach is *much* better. If a student moves back too far, the run becomes more important to him than the jump. This can cause the student to be out of control on his takeoff, thus interfering with mastery of the skill. Carefully marking the starting point for each practice will eliminate this problem. Challenge your students to touch objects suspended from an overhead structure at varying heights and/or work with a partner to execute a proper "high-five" jump. These activities, in addition to using the movement concepts (see page 7), will help reinforce the vertical jump.

Jumping instruction can begin in kindergarten. However, the NASPE Outcomes Project suggests that a mature pattern for both the vertical and the horizontal jump may be expected in the fourth grade (outcome 4-11).

Components of the Vertical Jump

Knees and Arms
—knees are bent and arms are back to begin the jump.

Feet
—feet are shoulder-width apart.

Arms
—arms begin to swing forward and up toward the sky.

Legs
—legs forcefully thrust the body upward.

Landing
—knees are bent and shoulder-width apart.

Albemarle County Physical Education Curriculum Revision Committee, 1996, 1-1.

Cue Words

SWING—knees are bent and arms are back to begin jump, feet are shoulder-width apart, and arms swing forward and up toward the sky.

EXPLODE—forcefully thrust body upward and land with knees bent and feet shoulder-width apart.

SWING HIGH—knees are bent and arms are back to begin jump, feet are shoulder-width apart.

TOUCH THE SKY—arms swing forward and up toward the sky, legs forcefully thrust body upward, and student lands with knees bent and feet shoulder-width apart.

Cue Set 1: SWING, EXPLODE

Cue Set 2: SWING HIGH, TOUCH THE SKY

Partner Skill Check

Skill: **Vertical Jump**

Jumper's name: _____ Watcher's name: _____

1.
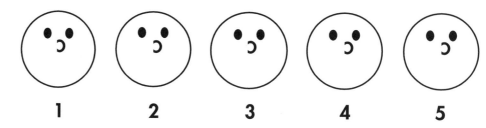

    1   2   3   4   5

Knees and feet

2.
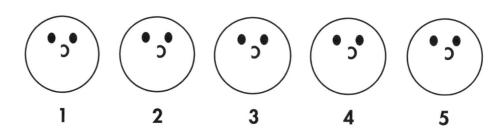

    1   2   3   4   5

Arms

3.
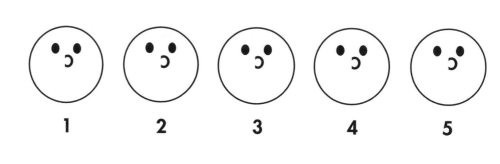

    1   2   3   4   5

Legs push

4.
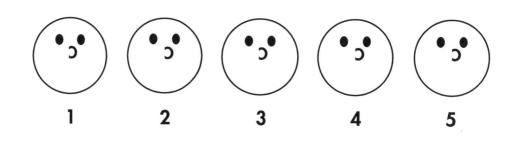

    1   2   3   4   5

Landing

Partner Skill Check

Skill: **Vertical Jump**

Jumper's name: _____ Watcher's name:_____

Watch your partner and mark each component of the skill. Let your partner do the skill 5 times. Each time your partner does it right, mark a **Y** in the box. If your partner doesn't do it right, mark an **N** in the box.

VERTICAL JUMP SKILL COMPONENTS

TRIALS

Knees and arms

Knees are bent and arms are back to begin skill.

☐ 1 ☐ 2 ☐ 3 ☐ 4 ☐ 5

Feet

Feet are shoulder-width apart.

☐ 1 ☐ 2 ☐ 3 ☐ 4 ☐ 5

Arms

Arms swing forward and up toward the sky.

☐ 1 ☐ 2 ☐ 3 ☐ 4 ☐ 5

Legs

Legs forcefully thrust the body upward.

☐ 1 ☐ 2 ☐ 3 ☐ 4 ☐ 5

Landing

Knees are bent with feet shoulder-width apart.

☐ 1 ☐ 2 ☐ 3 ☐ 4 ☐ 5

Vertical Jump Troubleshooting Chart

IF YOU SEE	THEN TRY THIS
1. Poor body position such as: • knees not bent • arms not back • feet not shoulder-width apart • body upright	• Use a mirror (reflection) or flashlight (shadow) to show the student her body position. The student should have her side to the mirror or wall. • Videotape the student performing the skill. Using a remote to start/stop the action, show the student the tape.
2. Arms not swinging	• Have the student practice swinging the arms and bringing the body upward so the weight shifts to the toes. • Suspend a rope between two game standards. Hang objects (aluminum pie plates, wind chimes, Wiffle balls, etc.) from the rope so the student can touch them if he stands on his toes. The student must swing the arms upward to try to touch the objects while bringing the body weight up onto the toes.
3. Student not forcefully pushing with legs and extending the body upward during flight	• Hang a sheet of paper on the wall. Have a student stand with his side to the wall, holding a piece of chalk in the hand closest to the wall. The student must jump and make a mark on the paper with the chalk. • Suspend a rope between two game standards. Hang objects (aluminum pie plates, wind chimes, Wiffle balls, etc.) from the rope so the student cannot touch them from a standing position. The student must swing the arms upward and jump to try to touch the objects.
4. Poor landing position such as: • legs straight • feet together • arms behind body	• Have the student start on her toes and do a half-squat while keeping the feet shoulder-width apart. • Use a mirror (reflection) or flashlight (shadow) to show the student her body position. The student should have her side to the mirror or wall. • Videotape the student performing the skill. Using a remote to start/stop the action, show the student the tape.

Horizontal Jump

The standing long jump is the most obvious example of a horizontal jump. As with the vertical jump, children enjoy learning the horizontal jump since they can see a result from their movement.

While children generally enjoy jumping, several safety concerns must be addressed. Bending the knees on landing is crucial for student safety. The force of the landing can be further increased when children want to jump *down* from a height. The jumping task should be well defined, and the landing surface should be appropriate. We recommend that all jumping be performed on the same level until mastery of bending the knees is accomplished. When jumping from a height (e.g., off several stacked mats), an appropriate landing surface (e.g., gymnastics crash mat) is essential.

Jumping instruction can begin in kindergarten. However, the NASPE Outcomes Project suggests that a mature pattern for both the vertical and horizontal jump may be expected in the fourth grade (outcome 4-11).

Besides using the movement concepts to reinforce the horizontal jump, we have found the following ideas to be helpful:

- Record how far a child is able to jump.

- Use tumbling mats that are several different colors. Challenge the students to jump to the "red area" or to the second "blue line."

- Make 10 or more learning stations. They should be composed of nonparallel lines that are at least six feet long and positioned six inches apart at the closest point and five feet apart at the widest point (see the diagram on page 15). Students can be challenged to jump across the imaginary river. The children may be further challenged to go to the widest part and jump across the river without getting their feet wet.

Components of the Horizontal Jump

Knees and Arms
—knees are bent and arms are back to begin the jump.

Feet and Body
—feet are shoulder-width apart with a slight forward lean of the body.

Arms
—arms swing forward and out in the direction of travel.

Legs
—legs forcefully thrust the body forward in a stretched position.

Landing
—knees are bent, feet are shoulder-width apart, and arms are in front of the body for balance.

Albemarle County Physical Education Curriculum Revision Committee, 1996, 1-1.

Cue Words

SWING—knees are bent and arms are back to begin jump, feet are shoulder-width apart.

EXPLODE—arms swing forward and up toward the sky, forcefully thrust body upward and forward, landing with knees bent and feet shoulder-width apart.

UP—arms swing forward forcefully and thrust the body up and forward.

OUT—land with arms out in front, knees bent, and feet shoulder-width apart.

Cue Set 1: SWING, EXPLODE

Cue Set 2: SWING, UP, OUT

Partner Skill Check

Skill: **Horizontal Jump**

Jumper's name: _____ Watcher's name: _____

1.

   1   2   3   4   5

Knees and feet

2.

   1   2   3   4   5

Body lean

3.

   1   2   3   4   5

Legs push

4.

   1   2   3   4   5

Landing

Partner Skill Check

Skill: **Horizontal Jump**

Jumper's name: _____ Watcher's name: _____

Watch your partner and mark each component of the skill. Let your partner do the skill 5 times. Each time your partner does it right, mark a **Y** in the box. If your partner doesn't do it right, mark an **N** in the box.

HORIZONTAL JUMP SKILL COMPONENTS

TRIALS

Knees and arms

Knees are bent and arms are back to begin skill.

| 1 | 2 | 3 | 4 | 5 |

Feet and body

Feet are shoulder-width apart with a slight forward lean of the body.

| 1 | 2 | 3 | 4 | 5 |

Arms

Arms swing forward and out in the direction of travel.

| 1 | 2 | 3 | 4 | 5 |

Legs

Legs forcefully thrust the body forward in a stretched position.

| 1 | 2 | 3 | 4 | 5 |

Landing

Knees are bent, feet are shoulder-width apart, and arms are in front for balance.

| 1 | 2 | 3 | 4 | 5 |

Horizontal Jump Troubleshooting Chart

IF YOU SEE	THEN TRY THIS
1. Poor body position such as: • knees not bent • arms not back • feet not shoulder-width apart • body upright	• Use a mirror or flashlight (reflection or shadow) to let the student see his body position. Student should have his side to the mirror or wall. • Videotape the student performing the skill. Using a remote to start/stop the action, show the student the tape.
2. Arms not swinging	• Have the student practice swinging the arms and bringing the body forward so the weight shifts to the toes. • The student works with a partner. Have the partner stand about 18 to 24 inches in front of the student. The partner holds up an object (hoop, picture, pinny, etc.) for the student to touch. The partner should hold the object at a high enough level that the student needs to reach out and up to touch it. The student must swing the arms forward without completing the jump.
3. Student not forcefully pushing with legs and extending the body during flight	• Have the student practice jumping over a hoop. • The student works with a partner. Have the partner stand about three to four feet in front of the student (far enough in front so the partner does not get hit). The partner holds up an object (hoop, picture, pinny, etc.) for the student to touch. The partner should hold the object at a high enough level that the student needs to reach out and up to touch it. The student must swing the arms forward as she jumps and tries to touch, not grab, the object.
4. Poor landing position such as: • legs straight • feet together • arms behind or to side of body	• Have the student do a half-squat keeping the feet shoulder-width apart and arms extended out in front of the body. • Have the student touch his bottom to the chair edge and return to a standing position. Repeat this activity several times.

Gallop

The gallop is a fairly complicated skill with an uneven rhythm. It is a combination of two other locomotor movements, the walk and the leap. Unlike the slide, the gallop moves forward or backward, not to the side. In the gallop the lead leg is propelled forward, while the rear foot quickly closes behind the lead foot. The same foot will take the lead when several gallops are combined.

The gallop is used with dance patterns, but does not have an obvious connection to traditional sport skills. Unfortunately, it is a movement that children rarely observe on the playground. Since very few children will enter elementary school knowing how to gallop, the teacher should be prepared to provide all of the instruction. Because of these conditions and normal development, most children will not master the gallop until the second grade (NASPE outcome 2-18). Of course, some children are ready for this combination and begin successfully imitating the movements of a horse while in kindergarten.

Components of the Gallop

Eyes and Body
—the eyes look in direction of travel, and the body moves in an upright position with a slight forward lean.

Flight
—step forward with the lead foot and the back foot closes. Both feet are temporarily off the ground.

Arms
—arms are bent and swinging forward and back.

Glide
—the body moves with a smooth, rhythmical motion.

Cue Words

GIDDY—the eyes look in the direction of travel, and the body moves in an upright position with a slight forward lean; arms may be bent and in front of the body as the child holds an imaginary pair of reins. The lead foot moves forward.

STEP—the lead foot moves forward.

UP—both feet are temporarily off the ground, and the back foot quickly closes.

Cue Set 1: GIDDY, UP
Cue Set 2: STEP, UP

Partner Skill Check

Skill: **Gallop**

Galloper's name: _____ Watcher's name: _____

1.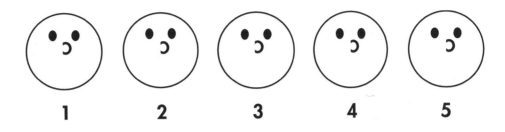

Body lean

2.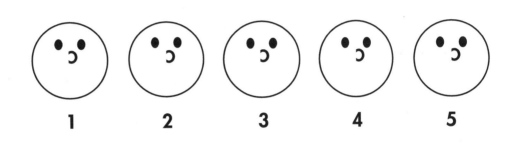

Fly

3.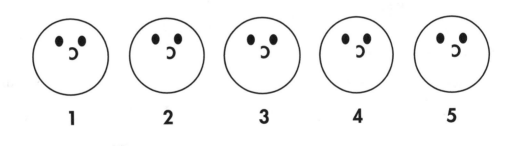

Arms

4.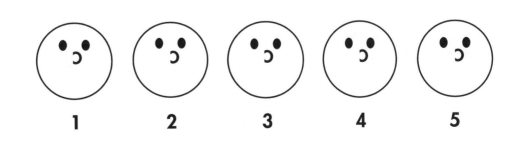

Glide

Partner Skill Check

Skill: **Gallop**

Galloper's name: _____ Watcher's name: _____

Watch your partner and mark each component of the skill. Let your partner do the skill 5 times. Each time your partner does it right, mark a **Y** in the box. If your partner doesn't do it right, mark an **N** in the box.

GALLOP SKILL COMPONENTS

TRIALS

Eyes and body

Eyes look in the direction of travel, and the body moves in an upright position.

☐ 1 ☐ 2 ☐ 3 ☐ 4 ☐ 5

Body

There is a slight forward lean of the body.

☐ 1 ☐ 2 ☐ 3 ☐ 4 ☐ 5

Flight

Step forward with the lead foot and close with the back foot. Both feet are temporarily off the ground.

☐ 1 ☐ 2 ☐ 3 ☐ 4 ☐ 5

Arms

Arms are bent and swing with the body.

☐ 1 ☐ 2 ☐ 3 ☐ 4 ☐ 5

Glide

Body moves with a smooth, rhythmical motion.

☐ 1 ☐ 2 ☐ 3 ☐ 4 ☐ 5

Gallop Troubleshooting Chart

IF YOU SEE	THEN TRY THIS
1. No forward body lean	<ul><li>Use a mirror or flashlight (reflection or shadow) to let the student see her body position. The student should have her side to the mirror or wall.</li><li>Videotape the student performing the skill. Using a remote to start/stop the action, show the student the tape.</li></ul>
2. Feet not coming up off the ground during the flight phase or the back foot passing the front foot	<ul><li>Using floor spots (or carpet squares if outside), have the student gallop over the floor spot. This will encourage the student to take a larger forward stride while galloping.</li><li>Place spots or "landing pads" down on the floor. The student must land on the spot with the lead foot and bring the back foot to the edge of the spot, not touching the spot. Space the spots far enough apart that the student must take a larger forward stride while galloping.</li></ul>
3. Arms kept straight or not swinging with the movement	<ul><li>Have the student stand with his back to the wall about one inch away. The student bends the elbows and swings the arms with light force back toward the wall so that only the elbows touch the wall. The arms will have some limited movement.</li><li>The student works with a partner. The partner stands in front of the student with the hands up at waist level, palms open facing the student. The student swings arms to touch the partner's palms with the fists or hands.</li></ul>
4. Student not galloping with a smooth pattern	<ul><li>Being able to perform any locomotor skill smoothly requires the student to use the components of the skill correctly. To create a smooth, rhythmical motion, you will need to review the components of the skill.</li></ul>

Slide

The slide is the easiest way to move in a sideways direction. When sliding to the right, the right foot takes the lead and there is a brief period of nonsupport as the left leg quickly follows. Children are often motivated to learn the slide because of this uniqueness and the obvious connection between the slide and sports. Children see basketball players using a person-to-person defense, as well as many athletes sliding into the proper position (e.g., baseball/softball shortstops, tennis players returning a serve, etc.).

Once children are successful with the skill of galloping, they are ready to begin learning to slide. The uneven rhythm of the slide and the fact that the child is moving laterally may produce some initial difficulty learning this loco-motor skill. Decreasing the sliding speed and proper instruction in the components should minimize student problems. According to the NASPE Outcomes Project, a mature sliding pattern should occur in the second grade (outcome 2-18).

Components of the Slide

Chin, Eyes, and Body
—the chin is placed over the lead shoulder, the eyes focus in the direction of travel, and the body maintains an upright position

Feet
—feet stay parallel to each other throughout the entire movement as the body moves either to the right or to the left.

Flight
—both feet are temporarily off the ground.

Glide
—the body moves with a smooth, rhythmical motion.

Cue Words

CHIN OVER SHOULDER and CHIN—the chin is placed over the lead shoulder, the eyes focus in the direction of travel, and the body maintains an upright position.

FEET PARALLEL—feet stay parallel to each other throughout the entire movement, even during the flight phase.

MOVE TO THE SIDE—the body moves with a smooth and rhythmical motion, either to the right or to the left.

STEP-TOGETHER—the lead foot moves to the side and the following foot meets the lead foot during the flight phase. This continuous action creates a smooth and rhythmical motion, either to the right or to the left.

Cue Set 1: CHIN OVER SHOULDER, FEET PARALLEL, MOVE TO THE SIDE
Cue Set 2: CHIN, STEP-TOGETHER, STEP-TOGETHER

Partner Skill Check

Skill: **Slide**

Slider's name: _____ Watcher's name: _____

 **1.**

Chin

 **2.**

Feet

 **3.**

Fly

 **4.**

Glide

Partner Skill Check

Skill: **Slide**

Slider's name: _____ Watcher's name: _____

Watch your partner and mark each component of the skill. Let your partner do the skill 5 times. Each time your partner does it right, mark a **Y** in the box. If your partner doesn't do it right, mark an **N** in the box.

SLIDE SKILL COMPONENTS

TRIALS

Chin and eyes

Chin is placed over lead shoulder, eyes look in the direction of travel.

☐ 1 ☐ 2 ☐ 3 ☐ 4 ☐ 5

Body

Body position remains upright.

☐ 1 ☐ 2 ☐ 3 ☐ 4 ☐ 5

Feet

Feet stay parallel to each other.

☐ 1 ☐ 2 ☐ 3 ☐ 4 ☐ 5

Flight

Both feet are temporarily off the ground.

☐ 1 ☐ 2 ☐ 3 ☐ 4 ☐ 5

Glide

Body moves with a smooth, rhythmical motion.

☐ 1 ☐ 2 ☐ 3 ☐ 4 ☐ 5

Slide Troubleshooting Chart

IF YOU SEE	THEN TRY THIS
1. Chin not near the lead shoulder or feet not parallel	• Use a mirror to let the student see her body position. Student should have her side to the mirror or wall. • Videotape the student performing the skill. Using a remote to start/stop the action, show the student the tape.
2. Feet not coming up off the ground during the flight phase	• Standing with his back to the wall, the student slides along the wall using a slow speed. Once he has the idea, he may increase the speed. • Using floor spots (or carpet squares if outside), have the student slide over the spot without touching it.
3. Body turned so the side is not leading the slide	• Standing with her back to the wall, the student slides along the wall using a slow speed. Once she has the idea, she may increase the speed. • Put a rope through a two-foot length of PVC pipe. Suspend the rope and pipe between two game standards. The student holds the pipe in both hands and slides along the length of the rope. Have the student repeat this activity several times.
4. Student not sliding with a smooth pattern	• Being able to perform any locomotor skill smoothly requires the student to use the components of the skill correctly. To create a smooth, rhythmical motion, you will need to review the components of the skill.

Skip

The skip is a rhythmical combination of two other locomotor skills, the walking step and the hop. Once children experience success with the hop, the skill of skipping may be introduced.

Although the skip does not have an obvious connection to other sport skills, many children observe other youngsters performing this skill on the playground and are motivated to learn it. Since the skip is a combination skill (step and hop), a mature skipping pattern may not occur until the second grade (NASPE outcome 2-18). Of course, some children are ready for this combination and begin skipping successfully in kindergarten.

Components of the Skip

Eyes and Body
—the eyes focus in the direction of travel, and the body maintains an upright position.

Step and Hop
—step and hop on the same foot.

Arms
—arms move in opposition.

Flight
—both feet are temporarily off the ground. The nonsupport leg is bent as the hopping leg leaves the ground.

Glide
—the body moves with a smooth, rhythmical motion.

Cue Words

ARMS BENT—arms are bent at a 90 degree angle and swing in opposition to the legs.

STEP-HOP and ONE AND, TWO AND—step forward with the lead leg and immediately hop on that same foot, then step forward with the other foot and immediately hop on that foot. Continue this alternating action, creating a smooth and rhythmical motion.

Cue Set 1: ARMS BENT, STEP-HOP, STEP-HOP

Cue Set 2: ONE AND, TWO AND, ONE AND, TWO AND

Partner Skill Check

Skill: **Skip**

Skipper's name: _____ Watcher's name: _____

1.

Step

1   2   3   4   5

2.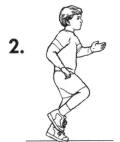

Hop

1   2   3   4   5

3.

Fly

1   2   3   4   5

4.

Glide

1   2   3   4   5

Partner Skill Check

Skipper's name: _____ Watcher's name: _____

Watch your partner and mark each component of the skill. Let your partner do the skill 5 times. Each time your partner does it right, mark a **Y** in the box. If your partner doesn't do it right, mark an **N** in the box.

SKIP SKILL COMPONENTS   TRIALS

Eyes and body

Eyes look in the direction of travel, and the body maintains an upright position.

☐ 1   ☐ 2   ☐ 3   ☐ 4   ☐ 5

Step and hop

Step and hop on the same foot.

☐ 1   ☐ 2   ☐ 3   ☐ 4   ☐ 5

Arms

Arm opposite skipping leg swings forward.

☐ 1   ☐ 2   ☐ 3   ☐ 4   ☐ 5

Flight

Both feet are temporarily off the ground.

☐ 1   ☐ 2   ☐ 3   ☐ 4   ☐ 5

Glide

Body moves with a smooth, rhythmical motion.

☐ 1   ☐ 2   ☐ 3   ☐ 4   ☐ 5

Skip Troubleshooting Chart

IF YOU SEE	THEN TRY THIS
1. No step/hop or student using a gallop pattern	• Use colored floor tape to mark where the feet should be during the movement. Use different color tape for each foot. The same color tape pieces should be approximately five inches apart, and the opposite color tape marks should indicate a stride of about 12 inches. The student must step and hop on the first color and then switch to step and hop on the other color. • Videotape the student performing the skill. Using a remote to start/stop the action, show the student the tape.
2. Arms crossing the midline of the body or not swinging during the skip	• Have the student work with a partner. The partner watches the student skip 30 feet and counts the number of times the arms either cross the midline of the body or do not swing. The object is to score a zero. • Have the student perform a "Step, Hop, Pose." The student does the step and hop and then freezes with the arm opposite the swing leg forward and the arm opposite the hop leg back.
3. The foot not coming up off the ground	• Use several small rubber (nonskid) bugs for the student to hop on and squash. The student skips with one foot squashing a bug on the hop, then skips with the other foot squashing the next bug on the next hop. • Place 10 to 12 ropes in a line parallel to each other and about a foot apart on the floor. The student is perpendicular to the line of ropes. The student must step/hop over each rope. Have the student do this several times to practice the skip.
4. Student not hopping with a smooth pattern	• Being able to perform any locomotor skill smoothly requires the student to use the components of the skill correctly. To create a smooth, rhythmical motion, you will need to review the components of the skill.

Leap

A leap is often described as an exaggerated run. The student takes off on one foot and lands on the other, just like in the run. The flight phase, however, is longer and more obvious. The leap is very difficult to teach in isolation. Students will have to begin their leap with a running approach.

As with the vertical jump, it is helpful to clearly define where the student will begin the approach. Again, children believe that if a 20-foot approach is good, a 1,000-foot approach is better. Carefully marking the starting point for each practice session will eliminate this problem.

Also, besides using the movement concepts to reinforce the leap, we have found the following idea to be helpful. Make 10 or more learning stations. These stations are composed of nonparallel lines that are six inches apart at the closest point and five feet apart at the widest. The lines should be at least six feet long (see the diagram on page 15). Students can be challenged to run and leap across the imaginary river. The children may be further challenged to go to the widest part and leap across the river without getting their feet wet.

By first grade, the student should be able to demonstrate the basic concept of the leap. In kindergarten, children should have developed a mature running pattern (NASPE outcome K-15). This pattern is essential to a leap. The ability to leap and lead with either foot, however, is a fourth grade benchmark (NASPE outcome 4-2).

Components of the Leap

Run
—take several running steps before starting to leap.

Takeoff
—push off the ground with one foot.

Flight
—both feet are temporarily off the ground in a stride position and the arm opposite the lead foot reaches forward.

Landing
—land on the opposite foot from the takeoff foot; knee is bent to absorb force.

Run
—run a few steps after landing.

Cue Words

GO—take several running steps before starting to leap.

PUSH—push off the ground with one foot.

RUN and TAKE OFF ON ONE FOOT—take several running steps before starting to leap. Push off the ground with one foot.

FLY and GET AIRBORNE—both feet are temporarily off the ground, legs are in a stride position, and the arm opposite the lead foot reaches forward.

LAND and LAND ON THE OTHER FOOT—land on the opposite foot from the takeoff foot; knee is bent to absorb force.

RUN AGAIN—run a few steps after landing.

Cue Set 1: GO PUSH, FLY, LAND

Cue Set 2: RUN, FLY, RUN AGAIN

Cue Set 3: TAKE OFF ON ONE FOOT, GET AIRBORNE, LAND ON THE OTHER FOOT

Partner Skill Check

Skill: **Leap**

Leaper's name: _____ Watcher's name: _____

1.

Run

1   2   3   4   5

2.

Takeoff

1   2   3   4   5

3.

Fly

1   2   3   4   5

4.

Land

1   2   3   4   5

Partner Skill Check

Skill: **Leap**

Leaper's name: _____ Watcher's name: _____

Watch your partner and mark each component of the skill. Let your partner do the skill 5 times. Each time your partner does it right, mark a **Y** in the box. If your partner doesn't do it right, mark an **N** in the box.

LEAP SKILL COMPONENTS

TRIALS

Run

Take several running steps before starting to leap.

☐ 1 ☐ 2 ☐ 3 ☐ 4 ☐ 5

Takeoff

Push off the ground with one foot.

☐ 1 ☐ 2 ☐ 3 ☐ 4 ☐ 5

Flight

Both feet are temporarily off the ground.

☐ 1 ☐ 2 ☐ 3 ☐ 4 ☐ 5

Landing

Land on the opposite foot from the take-off foot; knee is bent.

☐ 1 ☐ 2 ☐ 3 ☐ 4 ☐ 5

Run

Run a few steps after the landing.

☐ 1 ☐ 2 ☐ 3 ☐ 4 ☐ 5

Leap Troubleshooting Chart

IF YOU SEE	THEN TRY THIS
1. Student not getting the legs into a good stride position	• Have the student practice walking with very large steps. • Use a mirror or flashlight (reflection or shadow) to let the student see his body position. The student should have his side to the mirror or wall. • Place two ropes parallel in the play area and have the student walk over the ropes. Be sure that the ropes are placed a little wider than the widest stride of the student. This will provide an opportunity for the student to leap over the ropes.
2. Student using two feet to initiate the leap, or not getting enough height on the leap	• Videotape the student performing the skill. Using a remote to start/stop the action, show the student the tape. • Make a hurdle that the student can leap over: using a pool fun noodle, one fun noodle connector, and an 18-inch cone, cut the fun noodle in half and put one half in each end of the connector. Then place the center hole of the connector over the top of the cone. The student will have to push off using one foot to do this activity.
3. Arms not involved in the action	• Find a picture of a hurdler. Show the student the picture and then ask her to try to look like the picture. You can use the fun noodle hurdles described above. • Have the student practice walking with very large giant steps and swinging the stepping leg forward and up. The arm opposite the stepping leg should also swing forward so the arm and leg are parallel.
4. Student landing on both feet	• Have the student run several steps, take a giant step while swinging the opposite arm forward, and begin to run again. Encourage the student to come up off the ground during the giant step. • Set up two ropes parallel to each other and approximately two feet apart. Place a landing spot on the far side of the ropes for the landing foot to touch.

Additional Locomotor Movement Activities

Locomotor Tag

Objective: To practice a variety of locomotor skills within a tag game situation

Equipment: Cones or lines to define the play area

Activity:

1. Specify a locomotor skill to be used in each round.

2. Select two or three students to be "taggers."

3. Taggers try to tag as many players as possible within a set time period (e.g., one to two minutes).

4. When tagged, a player must go to the specified area and demonstrate a movement concept you have chosen. The player could be asked to demonstrate different pathways, different types of force, different levels, etc.

5. Once the player has demonstrated the concept correctly, he returns to the game.

6. Most of the locomotor skills can be used with this game.

Extensions:

1. When a tagger touches a player, the player becomes a tagger and the tagger becomes a player.

2. A player is safe if she can tell the tagger a cue word of the locomotor skill being used before being tagged.

Roadway Signs

Objective: To practice a variety of locomotor skills

Equipment: Easy-to-read signs that list individual locomotor movements and traffic cones

Activity:

1. Write on heavy paper the name of (or show pictures of) the different locomotor movements to be used. The signs should be large enough to read, but small enough to be attached to a traffic cone.

2. Scatter the signs (and cones) throughout the play area.

3. The students move through the area performing the appropriate locomotor movement. When a student comes to a sign, she reads the locomotor movement on the sign and uses that skill until she comes to a new sign.

4. To ensure that all movements are practiced, you may want to put down tape (floor or masking) that the students follow. The "road" should lead the students past each cone.

Extensions:

1. Include movement concepts on the locomotor cards (e.g., run at a slow speed, gallop in a zigzag pathway, etc.).

2. Use different colored floor tape to make a variety of roads. Specify the color road everyone should follow. Students move to the specified color by following the road or until they find an intersection.

Parachute Go Rounds

Objective: To use a variety of locomotor movements while using the parachute

Equipment: Parachute

Activity:

1. Students hold the parachute at waist level with one hand.

2. Students turn a side to the parachute so all are facing in the same direction.

3. You select a locomotor movement they will use when moving in a circle while holding onto the parachute.

4. On "switch," the students turn and change the direction of travel while performing the locomotor skill.

Extensions:

1. Divide the students into groups. When a group is called, those students go under the uplifted parachute using the specified locomotor skill and move to the opposite side.

2. When a group is called, those students go under the uplifted parachute using a specified skill and say the cues out loud, then return to their original location.

On the Move

Objective: To practice a variety of locomotor skills

Equipment: One percussion instrument

Activity:

1. Students stand in their own personal space.

2. Tell the students to begin walking. While the students are walking, tell them what skill will be practiced next. When you strike the instrument once, the students change to that locomotor skill. Then tell the students which skill will come next.

3. You may have a set pattern (e.g., one hit = walking; two hits = running; three hits = galloping, etc.).

Extensions:

1. Once the students have mastered a variety of locomotor skills, you may allow them to select their own locomotor skills to perform each time you strike the instrument.

2. Each student may create his own locomotor routine. The routine should consist of:

   • START = a statue

   • ACTION = three different locomotor movements

   • STOP = a statue

After the student has had time to practice the individual routines, he may perform the routine for another student or the class. The routines may be done in groups of two to four students. You may select the groups, or the students may form their own.

Mover's Licenses

Objective: To demonstrate the ability to perform the locomotor skills

Equipment: Mover's licenses for each student. See Advance Preparation.

Activity:

1. Students may earn their mover's licenses by demonstrating the skills correctly in any of the above activities or combinations of several activities.

2. Or, you may award licenses for demonstrating competencies on a specified number of skills.

Extensions:

1. Students may be given the licenses to keep.

2. Licenses may be posted on the bulletin board by classes. If a student has difficulty maintaining personal space or moving safely, the license may be moved to a section marked "driving school." That student will then practice those skills, so that he may graduate from "driving school" and return to the other activities.

Advance Preparation: Making mover's licenses can be as simple or as complex as you have the time or resources to make them.

- *Less complex:*

Design your mover's license on the computer (a typical license is shown on the next page). Once these are duplicated, each student may write in her own name. If your resources allow, many school secretaries are able to use a school database and print the names of all students on labels. These labels can be placed on the card so they look more official.

- *More complex:*

Every year when individual students' photographs are taken, the photographer returns extra strips or groups of pictures to the school. Traditionally, one of the strips (which has a picture of each student) is cut up, and the individual pictures are attached to each student's permanent school record. Often, more copies are sent to the school than are needed. The classroom teachers or the school secretary will know if there are extra photographs.

You may elect to glue the individual photographs onto the basic license. When the photograph is combined with the student's name (from a label), it looks like a "real license." If time and resources allow, laminating the cards will make them more official and a definite keepsake.

You may be as creative and realistic with your license as resources allow. Height, weight, a signature, and so on, may all be included. We have found this project to be a wonderful public relations tool. When the criteria for earning a license are clearly understood, it is an obvious form of assessment, or a "graduation" of sorts. Many parents are very impressed by this project and often agree to help make the licenses.

Mover's License

This is to certify that

_____

has completed the _____

requirements to be a safe mover in the gymnasium

_____   _____
(date)   (instructor)

Summary

While some locomotor skills (e.g., walk, run) are used daily, others are used in more specific settings (e.g., slide, leap). The challenge for those teaching locomotor skills is to present them in a fun and interesting way in order to keep the students motivated and involved in the lesson. Unfortunately, many teachers are not sure how to do this. By using the movement concept approach (Graham, Holt-Hale, and Parker 1998) and the specific activities outlined in this chapter, we believe your lessons will be exciting and motivating. These lessons are the first step in helping your students to become skillful movers.

Building Skills for Success

Children in the primary grades are very easy to motivate in physical education. For these children, everything physical is fun. Moving, galloping, kicking, throwing, and catching are exciting. Furthermore, making a basket, knocking down a bowling pin, or jumping over a rope are each notable accomplishments for the inexperienced mover.

Unfortunately, young children often become so motivated by *what* they are able to do, that they don't learn *how* to correctly perform a skill. For example, a kindergartner may be able to roll a ball and hit a target even if he steps with the wrong foot. Without correction, this poor motor pattern becomes a habit that is very difficult to correct. When the target or task becomes more difficult, the student will not have the techniques necessary to be successful. The tennis serve will be inefficient, and throwing a ball in from the outfield will be very challenging. The poor habits the child learned in the primary grades will severely impact athletic competencies in adulthood.

Success Starts Here

The college basketball player who is asked to shoot two foul shots with her team trailing the opponents by one point and no time on the clock is under a great deal of pressure. She knows instantly that the first foul shot did not go in the basket. This is the result or the *what happened*. What she really needs to know is *how* to "fix" the shot so that the next one will go in. Due to the years of practice and coaching this athlete has received, she has some knowledge base to work from to improve the next foul shot.

Young children, however, must be provided with such experiences. Unfortunately, once a child discovers that he can hit the target, make a basket, or kick the ball, it is difficult to then go back and have him work on the components of the skill.

It should be obvious that the elementary physical educator should stress the technique or *how to* first. Tying the cues with the components as the child practices is essential. Learning the component parts—whether they include an arm extension, stepping in opposition, or a follow-through—will increase the likelihood of the child developing a skillful movement.

This chapter offers activities that stress the *how to* of performing a skill. We recommend using any or all of these activities with each of the locomotor and manipulative skills. The examples given in each activity are very generic. The only adaptation necessary will be to change the cues and component parts to fit the specific skill being taught.

Suggested Activities for Reinforcing the Components

Statues/Movement

Objective: To evaluate the students' understanding of the skill component

Equipment: Music, tape player (it is helpful to have a remote)

Activity:

1. Students move around the gymnasium in their own personal space while listening to music.

2. When the music stops, the teacher says a cue word.

3. The students freeze in the cue word position.

4. This activity is continued using each component part. For example, with the underhand roll the teacher would say, "Ready," "Arm back," "Step and roll," and "Follow through."

Extensions:

1. Use the same activity listed above without the music.

2. Create your own stop signal—clapping your hands twice and raising them above the head, using a musical instrument, etc.

3. Assign each component a number. Use dice and roll them to select the component that will be demonstrated. You may also use playing cards, other numbered cards, or a spinner number card.

4. Partners may select the component that will be demonstrated.

Sneak Attack

Objective: To check for understanding of the skill components while creating a cooperative environment for the students

Equipment: None

Activity:

1. Call a student by name and say "Sneak attack."

2. Ask the student a question about some part of the skill. For example, when teaching the underhand roll, you might ask, "Where is our hand on the follow-through for the underhand roll?"

3. If the student is able to answer, terrific! If after rephrasing the question and providing sufficient "thinking time," the student is unable to answer, select a student who knows the answer.

4. This student tells the answer to the first student.

5. The first student communicates the answer to you.

6. This activity may be repeated five or more times throughout the class session with different students.

Extensions:

1. Teach this activity to other school personnel. It is a great way to review information in all academic areas.

2. Since you may see your students only once or twice a week, the "sneak attack" may be used to determine how much they remember from your class. It may be used at the start of a class as a review or when you observe the class in another setting, for example, waiting to go to the lunchroom.

Teach the Teacher

Objective: To assess the students' knowledge of how a specific skill is performed. It may also be used as a lesson closure.

Equipment: None

Activity:

1. Select a student to explain how to perform a skill such as the catch.

2. Perform the skill exactly as the student described the skill.

3. The other students determine if you are performing the skill correctly.

4. If you perform the skill incorrectly, the students offer solutions to the problem.

Extensions:

1. Have a different student teach each component.

2. When the classroom teacher arrives to take the children back to their room (or you return the students to their room), have a student teach the classroom teacher how to perform the skill correctly.

Everybody's "It" Tag

Objective: To combine cardiovascular fitness and the acquisition of a specific locomotor or manipulative skill

Equipment: None

Activity:

1. Everybody is "it."

2. Students are scattered within the play area.

3. If tagged, the student moves to a designated practice area. In this area, he demonstrates for you the specified skill by going through each component part slowly and saying the cue words out loud.

Extensions:

1. Have a peer evaluate the components of the skill. You may select a student to go to the designated area as the first "watcher" when the game begins. After the first student is tagged, the watcher observes that student performing the skill while saying the cue words out loud. Then the first watcher returns to the game and the student who was tagged first stays in the area and becomes the new watcher. This rotation continues as long as the game is played.

2. The student moves to the designated area by herself and performs the skill while repeating the cues. The student then returns to the game.

3. Add appropriate equipment to the designated practice areas, for example, softballs, tennis balls, or playground balls.

Orbits

Objective: To demonstrate the proper execution of the skill

Equipment: None

Activity:

1. A rotation (relay) formation is used.

2. By turns, each student runs to the opposite end of the play area and demonstrates one component of a skill. For example, a student may be asked to demonstrate the ready position for the underhand roll.

3. The student returns to his group, tags a group member, and the activity continues.

4. The activity continues until you select another component part to be performed. You may stop the students while running, give them a new component part that needs to be demonstrated, and then the activity may continue. Since you may stop the action and change tasks at any time, the incidence of competition that often occurs in relays is eliminated.

Extensions:

1. Use each of the component parts.

2. Use a variety of locomotor skills to accomplish the task (e.g., skip, slide, gallop, etc.).

3. Have the student demonstrate the component for the next student in line before running (walking, skipping, hopping, etc.) to the other end of the play area and back.

4. Add appropriate equipment. The equipment may be used by each student in line.

Scratch and Match

Objective: To match the component part cards with the cue word cards

Equipment: Make one set of cue word cards and one set of component description cards for each group in the class. Using separate colors for the cue words and the component parts is essential.

Activity:

1. Arrange each group of four to five students in a rotation (relay) formation.

2. On a signal, group members take turns running to the opposite end of the play area to pick up one cue word at a time.

3. Once the group has picked up the cue words, they must place them in the proper order.

4. Then the group members take turns running to the opposite end of the play area to pick up one of the cards with the component parts written on them.

5. The activity is completed when the group members have correctly matched the component parts with the cue words.

Extensions:

1. Use pictures for the defined component parts.

2. Have neighboring groups check each other's answers.

3. Have students pick up a cue word card and its matching component description card, run back to their groups, and then put the two cards in the proper sequence.

Cookie Jar

Objective: To demonstrate components of the specified skill

Equipment: Cookie jar (large container) and laminated cards with the cue words of the skill written on them. You should have several sets of cards so that every student has the opportunity to pick from the "cookie jar."

Activity:

1. One student draws a component card out of the cookie jar.

2. The class demonstrates that component to the teacher.

3. A different student picks the next component card.

Extensions:

1. The student demonstrates the component part to a peer.

2. Place students in groups with a cookie jar (container) for each group.

3. Use different containers and pieces of paper. Die cutting machines are currently available for cutting out shapes for bulletin boards. These dies come in a wide variety of shapes. For example, we have used:

   - A volcano as the container and cut-out dinosaurs for the components
   - Cut-out school buses in September
   - A plastic pumpkin with cut-out ghosts in October
   - A roasting pan with cut-out turkeys in November
   - A gingerbread house with cut-out gingerbread men and women in December
   - Cut-out snowflakes in January
   - A heart tin with cut-out hearts in February
   - Cut-out kites in March
   - Cut-out umbrellas in April
   - Cut-out flowers in May

Jig Saw Puzzle

Objective: To complete a skill component puzzle with a partner

Equipment: One complete puzzle per student pair. To make a skill component jig saw puzzle:

1. On a sheet of paper write or type the cue words and the corresponding descriptions. We recommend that you write the cue word and then list the descriptions under the word. This should help to avoid student confusion.

2. Photocopy the puzzle onto heavyweight paper. You will want to have enough copies to allow the students to work in pairs. You may also want to use different colors of paper for the puzzles.

3. Cut each puzzle into 10 or more pieces. No two puzzles need to be cut the same.

4. Store the puzzle pieces in small plastic bags so different puzzles do not get mixed together.

5. You may want to include the pictures from the picture Partner Skill Check sheets on your puzzle.

6. If you are using a computer to make your puzzle, try using a different font for each component.

Activity:

1. Partners are given one skill component puzzle in a bag.

2. On the start signal, partners will empty the puzzle pieces from the bag and begin to put the puzzle together.

3. Once the students have completed the puzzle, they will take turns demonstrating each component of the skill.

4. This is a great activity if space is an issue.

Extensions:

1. If you have a metal wall, door, or chalkboard that magnets will adhere to, put magnetic tape on the back of the puzzle pieces and have the students put the puzzle together there.

2. Have the students work in small groups of three or four to put the puzzle together.

3. Have the students form groups of three or four. Students take turns running (or any other locomotor skill) to an area where they pick up one piece to their puzzle and bring it back to the group. As the puzzle pieces are brought back, the group begins to put the puzzle together. Students continue to take turns retrieving one puzzle piece at a time until all the pieces have been collected.

Pizza Game

Objective: To have the students build an eight-piece pizza by correctly demonstrating the specific task, such as the overhand throw, underhand roll, catch, kick, etc.

Equipment: One piece of equipment per student pair, e.g., softball, tennis ball, or playground ball. The type of equipment will depend on the skill being practiced.

Activity:

1. Students work with partners while performing the skill. Students take turns as the "thrower" (or roller, or dribbler) and as the "watcher" (or catcher).

2. The thrower earns an imaginary piece of pizza for each successful attempt at the skill. A successful attempt is one in which the thrower demonstrates all of the component parts of the skill.

3. The watcher determines whether the component parts were demonstrated. If the skill is correct, the thrower is awarded the pizza slice. If not, then the watcher must tell the thrower what she needs to correct.

Extensions:

1. Have the pairs keep track of their number of pizza slices. Later the class uses math skills to discover how many total pizza slices were obtained (addition) and/or how many pies were made (addition and division).

2. Have the pairs keep track of their number of correct throws and determine a total for the class. In a follow-up lesson challenge the class to increase the total number of correct throws. You may choose to chart these numbers to motivate the students and reinforce the skill.

Summary

Learning how to perform a skill is necessary for eventual mastery. It involves really thinking about *how* the skill is performed. Successful completion of this cognitive phase is an essential first step toward performing the skill correctly later (Fitts and Posner 1967). When the student understands the components of a skill and can use cue words as a mental checklist for performing the skill, he can begin to correct his own performance. This ability becomes very important when participating in specific sports activities.

The nine activities we described in this chapter are just the beginning. Now that you have tried some of our ideas, you and your students can create appropriate activities of your own. Whether you use ours, create your own, or modify the activities from class to class or year to year, is entirely up to you. Just remember that "thinking" activities are the foundation and should be used when teaching all of the basic locomotor and manipulative skills.

Rolling

One manipulative skill at which young children can experience success quickly is the underhand roll. The obvious connection between the underhand roll and bowling makes this a very motivating activity.

Underhand Roll

A key component of the underhand roll is the step. Since stepping in opposition is essential for mastery of nearly all manipulative skills, the underhand roll may be a logical way to introduce this concept to young children. While the NASPE Outcomes Project does not address the underhand roll, the project suggests that a second grade child should be able to step in opposition while throwing (outcome 2-10).

Children do not have to use a bowling ball to "bowl." Kindergarten children can be successful with balls that are of the appropriate size and weight (e.g., tennis balls, softballs). For older children, many commercially owned bowling alleys have pins, lanes, and plastic balls that may be used by the schools.

Basic Components

Ready Position
—knees bent, facing target, feet shoulder-width apart, eyes on target, object held in dominant hand (palm up) in front of the body.

Arm Back
—swing the rolling arm back at least to waist level.

Step and Roll
—step forward with the opposite foot, swing the rolling arm forward, and release the ball on the ground (low level) while bending at the knees and waist. The front body surface should be facing the target.

Follow Through
—rolling hand continues toward the target in front of the body and finishes above the waist with palm facing upward.

Cue Words

The cue words you select for each phase of the skill will depend on the age of the students you are teaching and your areas of emphasis. We have listed, in usable sets, some of the cue words that we have used to teach the underhand roll. You may use each set individually or mix and match the cue words as needed. We have found that it is beneficial to have the students say the cue words out loud as they practice the skill.

READY—knees bent, facing target, feet shoulder-width apart, eyes on target, object held in dominant hand (palm up) in front of the body.

ARM BACK—swing the rolling arm back at least to waist level.

STEP AND ROLL and STEP AND SWEEP—step forward with the opposite foot, bring the rolling arm forward, and release the ball on the ground (low level) while bending at the knees and waist. The front body surface should be facing the target. (Use the cue "bellybutton" to help reinforce correct body position.)

USE YOUR STEPPING FOOT—step forward with the opposite foot.

SNEAK UP ON THE TARGET—bring the rolling arm forward, and release the ball on the ground (low level) so that there is no bounce.

FOLLOW THROUGH and STATUE OF LIBERTY—rolling hand continues toward the target in front of the body and finishes above the waist with palm facing upward.

SPIDER ON THE SHOULDER—rolling hand continues toward the target in front of the body and finishes above the waist with palm facing upward. Follow-through continues until the fingers of the rolling hand touch the top of the shoulder of the rolling hand.

Cue Set 1: READY, ARM BACK, STEP AND ROLL, FOLLOW THROUGH

Cue Set 2: READY, ARM BACK, STEP AND SWEEP, STATUE OF LIBERTY

Cue Set 3: READY, ARM BACK, STEP AND ROLL, SPIDER ON THE SHOULDER

Cue Set 4: READY, USE YOUR STEPPING FOOT, SNEAK UP ON THE TARGET

Cue Set 5: NO, MAYBE, OKAY, YE-HA

Cues can be more than words and phrases. You may choose to make up a story or scenario that the children can act out as they practice the skill. In this cue set, we are able to teach the four-step bowling approach by pretending that a child is wearing a towel over a swimsuit. The water is cold and the child hesitates to take off the towel and get in the water. Our cues and resulting actions are as follows.

NO (child is holding the towel closed)—knees bent, facing target, feet shoulder-width apart, eyes on target, object held in dominant hand (palm up) in front of the body, nondominant hand on the side of the ball. Take one step with same-side foot.

MAYBE (child begins to open towel)—push the ball out in front of the body with both hands, take one step with the opposite foot.

OKAY (child decides to open towel)—swing the rolling arm back at least to waist level, nondominant arm extends toward the target, take a step with same-side foot.

YE-HA (child throws towel away)—step forward with the opposite foot, bring rolling arm forward, and release the ball on the ground (low level) while bending at the knees and waist. The bellybutton should be facing the target. The rolling hand continues toward the target in front of the body, and finishes above the waist with the palm facing upward.

Suggested Activities for Reinforcing the Components

In the learning process, it is essential that students know how a skill looks, what its component parts are, and how to perform each individual component correctly. In the preceding section, we furnished pictures and descriptions of the underhand roll, divided it into its component parts, and provided possible cue words. Chapter 3 provided nine generic activities that will reinforce these concepts for the underhand roll as well as all locomotor and manipulative skills. In addition to the material found in chapter 3, the following section provides specific activities for reinforcing the components unique to the underhand roll.

Partner Skill Check

Objective: To allow partners to assess each other's progress in learning the skill

Equipment: Partner skill check sheets, pencils, and one ball for each set of partners. If the students cannot read or do not speak English, the picture version of the partner skill check sheet may be useful.

Activity:

1. One partner observes the other student to see if she has the correct form for the *ready* position.

2. If the ready position is correct, then the partner places a *Y* in the first box. If the ready position is not correct, he places an *N* in the first box. Non-readers can put a smiling face if the ready position is correct or a sad face if the ready position is not correct.

3. This evaluation continues until each of the components has been assessed five times.

4. A partner skill check sheet is used for each student.

Extensions:

1. You can use the partner skill check sheet to assess the skill development of each student.

2. You can send partner skill check sheets home with report cards or as individual skills develop.

Success Builders

The success builder activities allow the teacher to address individual needs. If students need additional help on individual component parts, the activities listed will help reinforce correct performance.

Objective: To allow partners to improve areas of deficiency as assessed by the partner skill check.

Equipment: See individual stations. We suggest using an unbreakable mirror and a poster of each component of the underhand roll at each station. The mirror is particularly helpful in these activities because it allows the child to see what he is doing. The easiest way to make the posters would be to photocopy the drawings from this book. Use an opaque projector to enlarge them. Laminating the posters will ensure their use for many years.

Activity:

1. Set up a station for each component in the teaching area. Post a description or a picture of the specific component at the corresponding station.

2. Stations:

Ready

—knees bent, facing target, feet shoulder-width apart, eyes on target, object held in dominant hand (palm up) in front of the body.

Equipment: Component poster, mirror (if available), and partner evaluations

Activity: The student assumes the ready position. The partner checks to see if her position matches the poster. The student refers to the mirror for help. The student then walks around and on a signal from her partner assumes the ready position again. When she has had several successful trials, the partners may return to working on the entire skill.

Partner Skill Check

Skill: **Underhand Roll**

Roller's name: _____   Watcher's name: _____

 **1.**

           1   2   3   4   5

Ready

 **2.** ... ...

1   2   3   4   5

Arm back

 **3.**

1   2   3   4   5

Step and roll

 **4.**

1   2   3   4   5

Follow through

Partner Skill Check

Skill: **Underhand Roll**

Roller's name: _____   Watcher's name: _____

Watch your partner and mark each component of the skill. Let your partner do the skill 5 times. Each time your partner does it right, mark a **Y** in the box. If your partner doesn't do it right, mark an **N** in the box.

START

Ready position

1. Eyes on target
2. Knees bent
3. Feet shoulder-width apart
4. Object in front of body

TRIALS

□ 1　□ 2　□ 3　□ 4　□ 5

ACTION

Arm back

1. Bellybutton faces target

□ 1　□ 2　□ 3　□ 4　□ 5

2. Rolling arm extends back

□ 1　□ 2　□ 3　□ 4　□ 5

Step and roll

3. Step forward on opposite foot

□ 1　□ 2　□ 3　□ 4　□ 5

4. Rolling arm comes forward; ball released on the ground; bellybutton faces the target

□ 1　□ 2　□ 3　□ 4　□ 5

STOP

Follow through

1. Rolling hand continues toward target finishing above the waist

□ 1　□ 2　□ 3　□ 4　□ 5

Arm Back

—bring the rolling arm back at least to waist level.

Equipment: Component poster, mirror (if available), line at waist level on a wall, and partner evaluations

Activity: The student demonstrates a swinging motion with his arm (keeping the arm close to the body) and raising the hand at least as high as the waist during the swing. The partner checks to see if his position matches the poster. To help the partner see the height of the swing, the student should perform the task standing near a wall with a line marked approximately waist high. The student refers to the mirror for help. Once the student can successfully demonstrate to the partner a good arm swing, the partners may return to practicing the entire skill.

Step and Roll

—step forward with the opposite foot, bring the rolling arm forward, and release the ball on the ground (low level) while bending at the knees and waist. The front body surface should be facing the target. (Use cue "bellybutton" to help reinforce correct body position.)

Equipment: Component poster, mirror (if available), whisk broom, jump rope, two chairs, and partner evaluations

Activity: The student steps forward on her opposite foot and sweeps the floor with the rolling hand. The partner checks to see if her position matches the poster. A whisk broom may be added to this activity to facilitate the idea of sweeping the floor. As the student sweeps the floor, she should have the knees bent and the body facing forward in the direction of the sweep. The student refers to the mirror for help. Once the student can successfully demonstrate to her partner a good floor sweep, the partners may return to practicing the entire skill.

To assist students having difficulty with the release point, suspend a jump rope between two chairs and have students practice releasing the ball under the rope. The rope should be low enough that the student must roll the ball on the floor in order for the ball to go under the rope.

Follow Through

—rolling hand continues toward the target in front of the body, and finishes above the waist with palm facing upward.

Equipment: Component poster, mirror (if available), and partner evaluations

Activity: The student starts with the floor sweep described above and finishes by giving he partner an upward "high five" (see figure). The partner checks to see if her position matches the poster. The rolling hand will have to come up to a high level in order for the student to touch her partner's palm. The student refers to the mirror for help. Once the student can successfully give the partner an upward "high five," the partners may return to practicing the entire skill.

Suggested Culminating Activities to Reinforce the Entire Skill

Individual Activities

Bowling Golf

Objective: To improve accuracy with the underhand roll skill

Equipment: At least nine targets of varying sizes placed along the walls of the gymnasium. Three distances from each target should be clearly marked with floor (or masking) tape. A softball for each student and a score sheet will be necessary.

Activity:

1. Each student will begin on a golf "hole" and stand on the piece of tape the greatest distance from the wall.

2. If a student is able to knock down (or hit) the target from the greatest distance on the first roll, she records a "1" for that hole and moves on to the next.

3. If the student is unable to knock down (or hit) the target, then she moves forward to the next closest line and tries again. If successful, she records a "2" for the hole and moves to the next station.

4. If unsuccessful, the student moves to the closest line and tries again. Whether she is successful or not, a "3" is recorded and the student moves to the next station.

Bowling Golf Score Card

Name				
Hole number	Score (circle your score on each hole)			Total
1	1	2	3	
2	1	2	3	
3	1	2	3	
4	1	2	3	
5	1	2	3	
6	1	2	3	
7	1	2	3	
8	1	2	3	
9	1	2	3	
Total				

5. At the end of nine "holes," the score cards are tallied and collected. During a future class, the students may be given another opportunity to obtain a lower score.

Extensions:

1. For younger students, you may not want to keep score.

2. You may adapt the course for the age and/or ability of the students. For example, you may use multiple targets that are close together (like bowling pins) and require that *both* must be hit for a score to be recorded.

3. You may also adapt the course by including a tunnel (folded mat) that the ball must be rolled under. An obstacle could be something that the students would have to roll around by banking the ball off a mat, wall, etc. The adaptations are limited only by the available equipment and your imagination.

4. You may want to shorten the distance that each rolling line is from the wall for the younger children and lengthen it for the older students.

5. You may require that proper form be used or a penalty will be awarded.

6. Integration with mathematics is easy to accomplish in this activity. For example:

   • Students must use addition skills to determine their scores.

   • You may assist the students in using addition and division to determine the class's average score or to determine the average score for a specific hole.

   • The class's average score may be graphed so that the students are able to see the improvement.

7. Students may work in pairs. One may roll, while the other evaluates form and keeps score. Once the target is hit, they change duties and continue. This enables each student to play each "hole" and receive the peer evaluation.

Math Bowling

Objective: To combine practicing the underhand roll and math skills

Equipment: One softball for each student and note cards with numbers

Activity:

1. Tape numbered note cards to each rolling station in the teaching area. The numbers you select will depend on the age of the students and the answers to the math questions you intend to ask.

2. Call out a math problem (for example, "What is 2 + 1?").

3. The students try to roll the ball and hit the appropriate answer.

Extensions:

1. Students may work in pairs to evaluate underhand roll components and check answers.

2. If points are awarded, it is recommended that one point always be given for performing the skill correctly.

3. You may want to lengthen or shorten the distance from the targets depending on the skill level of the children.

4. Students can also use subtraction, multiplication, or division for math problems depending on age and ability.

5. This activity may be used with other content areas. The note cards may contain shapes with the challenge being to hit triangles, squares, etc.

6. The note cards may contain letters. Challenges may include hitting a vowel or a consonant. You may ask, what letter does *physical* begin with? or, what letter does *fun* end with?

7. The students may use flash cards with a partner or a small group.

Color Targets

Objective: To provide students opportunities to improve rolling accuracy by hitting specific targets

Equipment: Construction paper of different colors and sizes (about 8 to 12 targets of each color) taped to the baseboard of the gymnasium or activity area and a ball for each student (softball, tennis ball, etc.)

Activity:

1. Create a "color box" in which samples from each color of construction paper have been placed. You will need more samples than you have students.

2. Select a student to draw a sample color from the color box.

3. The sample color chosen is the color target all students must locate and try to hit with an underhand roll.

4. Students continue to roll toward the targets of the selected color until you give a stop signal.

5. The activity continues until all students have been given an opportunity to draw from the color box.

Extensions:

1. Instead of using different colors, students could select different shapes from the "shape box," letters from the "alphabet box," or words from the "word box."

2. Students can work with partners. The partner chooses the color, shape, letter, or word that will be used for a target. The roller must then try to hit the selected target. Partners take turns selecting targets and rolling.

Create-A-Word

Objective: To create words by hitting letters using the underhand roll

Equipment: One ball (softball or tennis ball) per student, four complete sets of alphabet letters scattered and taped to the baseboard of the gymnasium or activity area. It would be advantageous to have extra copies of vowels and selected consonants (e.g., N, R, S, and T). You will also need paper and markers or a chalkboard and chalk to serve as a "word bank."

Activity:

1. On your start signal, students begin to spell words by hitting letters of the alphabet using an underhand roll.

2. Once a student has created a word, he goes to the "word bank" (paper or chalkboard) and writes the word. It will be helpful to have several word banks so students will not have to wait in line to write their words.

3. A word may be "banked" or written only once.

4. If a student hits a letter that cannot be used to form the word being created, she must hit the letter again to delete it.

Extensions:

1. Students can work with partners. One student rolls the ball to hit letters to spell a word while the partner records the word and evaluates the roll. The roller may not use the letter until the underhand roll is performed properly. When the first partner has spelled a word, the other partner is then given an opportunity to roll.

2. Students working in pairs are given paper and pencil to record the letters they hit and to write down the words they create. Each partner must roll and hit a vowel and two consonants until the pair has six letters to create words. The partners attempt to create six words using one or more of the letters they have hit. Once the partners have created six words and written them down, they will attempt to spell the words by hitting the letters with the ball. Once a word is spelled, it may be checked off the list. If the students are unable to use a letter they have hit, they must hit that letter again to delete it and select another letter.

Partner Activities

Challenges

Objective: To practice the underhand roll in a variety of situations

Equipment: One softball, tennis ball, or playground ball per pair of students and laminated challenge cards. Different types of challenges may require additional equipment.

Activity:

1. Students select a challenge card.

2. Students perform the task described on the card.

3. Possible challenges may include:

   • Roll the ball using hard force (light force, medium force).

   • Roll the ball along a line on the floor.

   • Roll the ball into a cup, cone, net, etc.

   • Roll the ball and hit the target from a specific area on the floor.

Extensions:

1. Place multicolored targets or pictures on a wall (at floor level). Additional targets may be placed against the wall or scattered throughout the play area. These targets could include cones, bowling pins, buckets, or empty two-liter plastic bottles. Have the partner tell the roller which target to hit.

2. Set up game poles or volleyball standards and tie a rope between them. Suspend different objects from the rope (at floor level) and challenge the students to hit them. Possible targets could include hoops, aluminum pie pans, and empty two-liter plastic bottles.

Low Bridge

Objective: To use the underhand roll to move the ball under a low object

Equipment: One softball (or tennis ball) and one folding chair per student pair

Activity:

1. Place a folding chair between two students. The students should be about 10 feet apart, and the chair should be facing one of the students.

2. The students take turns underhand rolling the ball so that it goes under the chair.

3. After each partner has rolled the ball under the chair five times, they may each take one step backward.

Extensions:

1. Turn the chairs so that the sides are toward the partners.

2. Partners may back up only when you give that direction.

3. If a roll is successful (goes under the chair), the roller takes one step backward.

4. If both of the partners roll a ball that goes under the chair, then both may back up. If a subsequent roll does not go under the chair, they must return to the starting point.

Group Activities

Cage Ball Madness

Objective: To perform the underhand roll using a ball to move an object across the play area

Equipment: The object may be a cage ball or any ball larger than the balls being rolled. The balls being rolled may be playground balls or softballs when aiming at a cage ball. When the target is smaller, tennis balls may be used.

Activity:

1. Divide the class into four even groups. Each group stands along one side of a square play area. Students must stay behind their line.

2. Place the cage ball or large ball in the center of the play area.

3. Each group begins the activity with two or more balls.

4. On the start signal, players roll the balls and try to hit the cage ball (large ball in the center) in an effort to move it toward the other group's line.

5. Players continue to roll the balls until the cage ball crosses a group's line. Any ball that stays inside of the area enclosed by the four groups is retrieved by the teacher.

6. Players may only touch the cage ball (large ball) with a rolling ball. They may not touch it with any part of the body.

7. Once the cage ball crosses the designated line, the activity stops and the cage ball is returned to the center of the play area.

8. The activity resumes when each group has the same number of balls to roll. Be sure every player is given a chance to start with a ball.

Extensions:

1. Create two groups rather than four.

2. Students roll a variety of balls at the cage ball in an effort to move the ball across another group's line. This may lead to discussions on which types of balls are better for the task (e.g., playground balls vs. tennis balls).

3. Have groups change positions either before the next round or on a signal during the activity. Be sure that if the students are to change places during the activity, they understand that they may not roll a ball at the cage ball until your signal, and they may not take a ball with them as they change sides.

Switcharoo

Objective: To use an underhand roll to tag the feet of opposing players in an effort to get all players on one side of the play area

Equipment: One to four 6- to 8-inch balls (Nerf balls or light rubber balls). The number will vary based on the skill level of the students.

Activity:

1. Divide the class into two groups and place them on opposite sides of a divided play area.

2. Give each group an equal number of balls to start the activity.

3. On the start signal, players roll the balls and try to hit the feet of the opposing players.

4. If a player is hit, he moves to the other group's side. That player is now a member of the opposing group. When a player changes sides, he may not carry a ball to the opponent's side.

5. When all players are on the same side, the activity is restarted.

Extensions:

1. While the students are performing the activity, watch to see that the underhand roll is being performed correctly. Ask any student having trouble rolling correctly to go to a practice area and work with a partner or designated "teacher assistant."

2. Put up cones or bowling pins across the end lines of the play area. Once all the cones for a group have been knocked over, a new activity is started.

Cone Madness

Objective: To use the underhand roll to hit the opposing group's cones.

Equipment: Cones, bowling pins, or empty two-liter bottles, and eight playground balls

Activity:

1. Divide the class into two groups and place them on opposing sides of a divided play area. Give each group four playground balls.

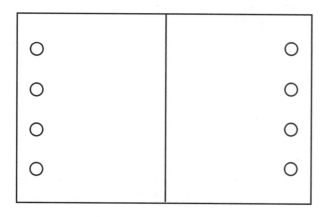

○ = Cone

2. Cones or bowling pins set up on the ends of the play area are used as targets (see figure).

3. Students may not cross the center line.

4. The balls are rolled to knock down the other group's cones. The defenders may use their hands to stop the balls. If any cones are accidentally knocked down, they may not be put back up.

5. When all of a group's cones are down, the activity is restarted.

6. Observe for correct form during the activity. If a student demonstrates incorrect form, he must work on the problem area at one of the practice stations.

Extensions:

1. Use four groups with four sets of cones.
2. Use a variety of balls (volleyballs, tennis balls, softballs, etc.).

Create Your Own Activity

Objective: To allow students to create their own activities to reinforce the underhand roll

Equipment: One piece of paper and pencil per group and a predetermined list of equipment you will allow the students to use in their activities (e.g., bowling pins, cones, jump ropes, softballs, tennis balls, etc.)

Activity:

1. Form groups with two to five students each. You may select the groups or the students may form their own.

2. Students create their own activity using the underhand roll as the basic skill. Students are required to have rules that encourage correct performance of the skill, include all players, and address all safety concerns.

3. The groups write their individual names, the rules of the activity, and the equipment needed on their paper and then show the activity to you.

4. Upon approval of their activity, the students obtain their equipment and begin playing.

5. You must approve all changes to the activities.

Extensions:

1. One group may teach the activity it designed to another group.

2. Groups may teach their activities to the entire class.

Pin Ball

Objective: To use the underhand roll to hit the opposing group's bowling pins

Equipment: Three balls and three plastic bowling pins (indicated by A and B for our purposes here) for each group. Bowling pins need to be color coded for each group (use different colored tape, for example, to mark the cones).

Restraining line

```
         X     A     X
         X     A     X
         X     B     X
         X     A     X
         X     B     X
         X     A     X
         X     B     X
         X           X
```

Activity:

1. Set up a play area with a center line and two restraining lines approximately 12 feet away from the center line.

2. Divide the class into two equal groups and place the groups behind the restraining lines facing each other.

3. Set the six pins up along the center dividing line of the play area, alternating colors (see figure).

4. Give each group three balls.

5. On the start signal, the students roll the balls and try to hit the opposing group's pins. The students may not cross the restraining line.

6. A pin is not down if the ball was rolled from in front of the restraining line.

7. The activity is restarted when all of a group's pins have been knocked down.

Extensions:

1. If a player is hit by a rolled ball, she moves to the other group (similar to Switcharoo) and continues to play.

2. Use empty two-liter bottles, lightweight cones, empty cereal boxes, etc., as the group targets.

Adapted, by permission, from K. Thomas, A. Lee, and J. Thomas, 2000, *Physical education for children: daily lesson plans for elementary school*, 2nd ed. (Champaign, IL: Human Kinetics).

Crazy Dots

Objective: To combine opportunities to practice the underhand roll skill and improve accuracy by rolling the ball over the floor dots on the opposing group's side

Equipment: Six red circles and six blue circles approximately 12 inches wide and one ball (tennis or softball) per student

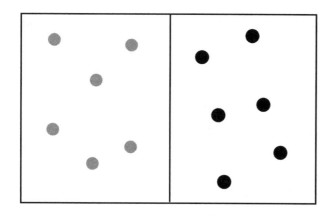

Activity:

1. Divide the play area in half with six color circles randomly placed within each group's area (see figure).

2. Divide the class into two groups.

3. Rolling from his side, each student tries to roll the ball over one of the crazy dots on the opposing group's side.

4. Players may stop a ball from crossing over their crazy dots by using any part of their body.

5. Each time the student rolls a ball across a crazy dot, she gets a point for the group.

6. At the end of five minutes, each group adds up its points.

Extensions:

1. Use more crazy dots.

2. Remove a dot after a ball rolls over it. Start a new activity when all of the dots have been removed from one side.

Athlete's Foot

Objective: To use the underhand roll motion to slide a beanbag under a rope, trying to hit the feet of the opposing players

Equipment: Two volleyball standards, one rope, and one beanbag per student. The rope is suspended between the volleyball standards approximately one foot above floor level.

Activity:

1. Divide the class into two groups with the groups placed on opposite sides of the rope.

2. Give each student a beanbag.

3. On the start signal, players slide their beanbags under the rope and try to hit the feet of the opposing players.

4. If a player is hit, she moves to the other group's side, but may not take the beanbag with her. She is now a member of that group.

5. When all players are on the same side, the activity is restarted.

Extensions:

1. Monitor the skill while the students are playing. Direct any student having trouble with the underhand roll motion to go to the practice area and work with a partner or designated "teacher assistant."

2. Squash the Bug—to work on eye–foot coordination, have the students stop the beanbags by stepping on them.

Adapted, by permission, from J.A. Wessell, PhD, 1974, *Project I CAN* (Northbrook, IL: Hubbard).

Underhand Roll Troubleshooting Chart

IF YOU SEE	THEN TRY THIS
1. Eyes not on the target	• Have the student roll at a target he has designed. • Use color targets on the floor and roll the ball across them (see the Crazy Dot game on page 73). • Use pie plates for targets and place them on the wall at floor level. • Use targets the student must roll through (e.g., cones, chairs, horseshoes).
2. Arm not swinging back	• Have the student swing her arm back to touch a target (pie plate) attached to the wall. The target is placed at the student's waist level in line with the rolling arm. The student will then roll the ball. • With a partner standing behind the roller, the roller swings his arm back and tries to take an object out of the partner's hand. • Put butcher paper on the wall. The student stands sideways with a marker in her rolling hand. As the student moves the rolling hand back, she draws a curvy line on the paper.
3. Hand not near the floor	• Place a toy truck or car on the floor where the hand should follow through and have the student push it forward. You could also try this with a tennis ball. • Have the student use a small whisk broom to sweep the ball forward.
4. Knees not bending to allow the hand to get close to the floor, or one knee touching the floor	• Slide a beanbag across the floor rather than using a ball. • Take a flashlight or projector and shine the light on the student. Have the student watch his shadow as he performs the underhand roll. • Place a six-inch cone approximately one foot in front of the student's dominant leg. Have the student practice the skill without a ball and have him touch his knee to the cone.
5. Ball bouncing when released	• Have a partner check the hand position when the ball is released. • Stretch a rope between two chairs so the rope is approximately 12 inches off the floor. Have the student perform the underhand roll releasing the ball under the rope. *(continued)*

Underhand Roll Troubleshooting Chart *(continued)*

IF YOU SEE	THEN TRY THIS
6. Student not stepping in opposition	• Tie a pinny or necktie around the nondominant foot. • Use spots or footprints on the floor to indicate the proper foot placement.
7. Body not in proper alignment on the follow-through	• Tell the student to point her bellybutton at the target on the follow-through. We call this the "Power of the Bellybutton." This works for many manipulative skills. • See the success builder activities in the text.

Summary

The underhand roll is a skill that children can learn at an early age as long as the equipment is of the appropriate size. Once your students have mastered the basic skill, you can add to the challenge by increasing the distance to the target or decreasing the target's size. Later you could add the four-step approach to complete the transition to the sport of bowling. This will be very motivating for the students!

The skill progression of the underhand roll to the underhand throw to the overhand throw follows a logical sequence: all three skills require the student to step in opposition. As with all physical skills, practice and instruction can greatly enhance the students' mastery of these crucial building blocks.

Underhand Roll Lesson Plan (First Lesson)

Age group: Early primary

Focus: Stepping in opposition

Subfocus: Releasing the ball on the floor

Objectives: To step in opposition 80 percent of the time (**CUE:** "Use your stepping foot"), and release the ball so that there is minimal bouncing four out of five times (**CUES:** "Let the ball sneak up on your target," "The ball has to be quiet—shhhh.")

Materials/Equipment: One ball and one target (piece of construction paper taped to the baseboard) placed for each child

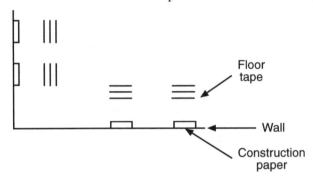

Floor tape

Wall

Construction paper

Advance preparation: A learning station for each child may be helpful. Tape pieces of construction paper to the gymnasium baseboards approximately four feet apart. Use as many pieces of construction paper as you have students. In addition, lines that are parallel to the target (construction paper) may be taped (with floor or masking tape) on the floor at appropriate distances from the wall. This will enable each child to have his own place to practice (see figure).

Organization/Management: Students are in personal space for instruction and warm-up. Later, students will find their own learning stations in the gymnasium for practice.

Warm-up:

Today I would like you to learn the different jobs the arms and legs have. Pretend you are in a parade and you are waving at the crowd. Everyone wave (demonstrate). *Look at your hand that's waving. That is also your rolling hand and it is also your throwing hand.*

Today we will call it our rolling hand. Can you remember that? It's called your . . . . **rolling hand**.

Introduction:

Today we will work on the underhand roll. Everyone stand up. Bring your rolling hand straight back. Excellent.

Take your foot that's on the same side of your body as your rolling hand and step BACK with it. Can you do that? The foot that's left out in front is your stepping foot. Can you say that? It's your. . . ?

Let's do this again. Start with your feet together. Place the foot that's on the same side of your body as your rolling hand back. What do we call the foot that's in front? **(Stepping foot.)**

Some children have a different rolling or throwing hand than other students. That is okay as long as everyone has a stepping foot on a different side of the body than the hand they use for rolling.

Let's stand up straight with our feet together. Can you hold up your rolling hand and step FORWARD with your stepping foot? Now put your feet back together and hang your arms at your sides. Bring back your rolling hand again and use your stepping foot again. (This activity is repeated several times.)

Watch for stepping in opposition. Note: occasionally, a student does not wave with her dominant hand. If there is confusion, place an object on the floor directly in front of the student and ask her to pick it up. Usually she will use her dominant hand. The stepping foot can be taught once hand dominance has been determined.

I am going to put on music. I would like you to move around in general space using any of the locomotor skills we have learned. Who can give me an example of a locomotor skill? (Students provide suggestions.)

Excellent. You will move around and when the music stops, you will freeze, count to three, and then bring your rolling arm back and put your stepping foot forward. Do you understand the directions? (Begin music.)

Repeat this activity for several minutes. Watch to make sure students are stepping in opposition.

Now, when you freeze and put your rolling arm back and your stepping foot forward, I would like you to look at your neighbor and see if he or she is stepping with the proper foot. Again, it doesn't matter if they use a hand for rolling that is different than you use. What is important is that the stepping foot is on a different side than the rolling hand. (Begin music.)

Repeat this activity for several additional minutes. Watch to make sure students are stepping in opposition.

Formation:

FREEZE. Students return to a semicircle formation for instruction.

Now we will practice using our stepping foot to help us roll a ball. This time we will stand up, pull our rolling arm back, step with our stepping foot, and roll an imaginary ball. Everyone stand up and find your personal space. Face me. Pull your rolling hand (your waving arm) toward the back wall. Can you step with your stepping foot and bring your rolling hand down until it touches the floor? To do that you may have to bend somewhere.

Watch me. Where do I bend so that I can touch the floor? **(Knees and waist.)** *Let's try it again. Make sure you touch the floor. Ready position, arm back, and step and roll.*

Watch for release point and stepping in opposition.

This time we need to think about a follow-through. This means we bring our arm up after we let go of the ball. Let's practice the roll again. Remember: ready position, arm back, step and roll, and follow through.

Watch for release point, stepping in opposition, and follow-through.

FREEZE. We are going to have our very own bowling alley today. It will be a special bowling alley, but I'll tell you more about that later.

Look around the gymnasium. There are pieces of construction paper and balls against the wall. Each of you will have one of these places for your own bowling alley today. Can you find your own bowling alley and sit on the tape closest to the wall? GO.

Pick up the ball and stand on your piece of tape facing the construction paper. Face your target, get in the ready position, pull your arm back, step and roll the ball, and follow through. Go get your ball and return to your piece of tape. (Repeat several times.)

Have the children repeat the cues with you. When you think the children can repeat the cues on their own, allow them to practice independently.

Watch for release point and stepping in opposition.

FREEZE. This time our bowling alley will have a secret mission. We need for the balls to sneak up on the target. We don't want the target to hear the balls coming. How could we do that? Release the balls ON the ground.

Pick up a ball and stand on your piece of tape facing the target. Remember, we are going to be sneaky. Face your target, get in the ready position, pull your arm back, step and roll the ball QUIETLY, and follow through. Go get your ball and return to your piece of tape. Keep practicing.

FREEZE. This time I would like you and the person next to you to be partners. One will watch as the other rolls. What do you think you will be looking for? ***(Releasing the ball near the ground and using your stepping foot.)*** *After each roll, tell your partner how he or she is doing.* (After 5 to 10 rolls students exchange duties.)

FREEZE. Time is up. Please return your ball to its place near the wall and line up.

Closure:

Students are lined up to leave.

How can we sneak up on our bowling pins? How do we know which foot to step with? Next time we will practice bowling from farther back AND use real bowling pins.

<blockquote>
c h a p t e r 5
</blockquote>

Throwing

In this chapter, we will discuss both the underhand and the overhand throws. Since both of these skills are necessary in many lifetime activities, their components should be taught at an early age. The NASPE Outcomes Project suggests that a kindergartner should be able to demonstrate the differences between an overhand and an underhand throw (outcome K-11) and that a fourth grader should be able to demonstrate a mature throwing pattern (outcome 4-12).

Underhand Throw

While many individuals may think that the only purpose of the underhand throw is pitching a horseshoe, it is in fact an integral part of many sport skills. The underhand throw is essential to softball pitching, and the underhand toss can also be used to assist a fielder in making an out from a close distance in softball or baseball. In addition, the underhand throwing components are very similar to those of the underhand volleyball serve. With the addition of a racket, the underhand throw is essential to the game of badminton.

Often the purpose of the underhand throw will dictate exactly *how* it is performed. Activities requiring height (e.g., slow-pitch softball pitching and horseshoes) will require that the follow-through be very exaggerated. When the distance to the target is short or if the objective is speed, then the follow-through will be much shorter (e.g., in fast-pitch softball pitching). In this section we will emphasize the skills most relevant to young children—that is, those requiring height.

One factor that greatly affects the initial learning of the underhand throw is the target placement. If a target is placed at a low level, the student may roll rather than throw the ball. If the target is at a high level, the student is also more likely to develop incorrect throwing habits. While students are learning and practicing this skill, a medium-level target is best. Once the student understands how to perform the skill, then we encourage the use of different target heights.

Basic Components

Ready Position
—knees bent, facing target, feet shoulder-width apart, eyes on target, object held in dominant hand (palm up) in front of the body.

Arm Back
—swing the throwing arm back to at least waist level.

Step and Throw
—step forward with the opposite foot, bring the throwing arm forward, and release the ball below the waist. The arm stays straight throughout the entire movement.

Follow Through
—throwing hand continues toward the target in front of the body with palm facing upward.

Cue Words

The cue words you select for each phase of the skill will depend on the age of the students you are teaching and your areas of emphasis. We have listed, in usable sets, some of the cue words we have used to teach the underhand throw. You may use each set individually or mix and match the cue words as needed. We have found that it is beneficial to have the students say the cue words out loud as they practice the skill.

READY—knees bent, facing target, feet shoulder-width apart, eyes on target, object held in dominant hand (palm up) in front of the body.

ARM BACK—bring the throwing arm back at least to waist level.

STEP AND THROW—step forward with the opposite foot, bring the throwing arm forward, and release the ball below the waist. The arm is extended throughout the entire movement.

USE YOUR STEPPING FOOT—step forward with the opposite foot.

LET IT GO—bring the throwing arm forward, and release the ball below the waist. The arm is extended throughout the entire movement. Throwing hand continues toward the target in front of the body and finishes with palm facing upward.

FOLLOW THROUGH and STATUE OF LIBERTY—throwing hand continues toward the target in front of the body and finishes with palm facing upward.

Cue Set 1: READY, ARM BACK, STEP AND THROW, FOLLOW THROUGH

Cue Set 2: ARM BACK, STEP AND THROW

Cue Set 3: READY, ARM BACK, STEP AND THROW, STATUE OF LIBERTY

Cue Set 4: READY, ARM BACK, USE YOUR STEPPING FOOT, LET IT GO

Suggested Activities for Reinforcing the Components

In the learning process, it is essential that students know how a skill looks, what its component parts are, and how to perform each individual component correctly. In the preceding section, we furnished pictures and descriptions of the underhand throw, divided it into its component parts, and provided possible cue words. In addition to the material in chapter 3 that reinforces the concepts for all locomotor and manipulative skills, the following section provides specific activities for reinforcing the components unique to the underhand throw.

Partner Skill Check

Objective: To allow partners to assess each other's progress in learning the underhand throw

Equipment: Partner skill check sheets, pencils, and one ball or beanbag for each set of partners. If the students cannot read or do not speak English, the picture version of the partner skill check sheet may be useful.

Activity:

1. One partner observes the other to see if he has the correct form for the ready position.

2. If the ready position is correct, then the partner places a *Y* in the first box. If the ready position is not correct, he places an *N* in the first box. Nonreaders can put a smiling face if the ready position is correct or a sad face if the ready position is not correct.

3. This evaluation continues until each of the components has been assessed five times.

4. A partner skill check sheet is used for each student.

Extensions:

1. You may use the partner skill check sheet to assess the skill development of each student.

2. You may send partner skill check sheets home with report cards or as individual skills develop.

Partner Skill Check

Skill: **Underhand Throw**

Thrower's name: _____ Watcher's name: _____

1.

        1   2   3   4   5

Ready

2.

        1   2   3   4   5

Arm back

3.

        1   2   3   4   5

Step and throw

4.

        1   2   3   4   5

Follow through

Partner Skill Check

Skill: **Underhand Throw**

Thrower's name: _____ Watcher's name: _____

Watch your partner and mark each component of the skill. Let your partner do the skill 5 times. Each time your partner does it right, mark a **Y** in the box. If your partner doesn't do it right, mark an **N** in the box.

START

Ready position

1. Eyes on target
2. Knees bent
3. Feet shoulder-width apart
4. Object in front of body

TRIALS

1	2	3	4	5
☐	☐	☐	☐	☐

ACTION

Arm back

1. Bellybutton facing target

1	2	3	4	5
☐	☐	☐	☐	☐

2. Throwing arm swings back

1	2	3	4	5
☐	☐	☐	☐	☐

Step and throw

3. Step forward on opposite foot

1	2	3	4	5
☐	☐	☐	☐	☐

4. Throwing arm comes forward; ball released at waist level; arm stays straight

1	2	3	4	5
☐	☐	☐	☐	☐

STOP

Follow through

1. Arm continues toward target

1	2	3	4	5
☐	☐	☐	☐	☐

Success Builders

The success builder activities allow you to address individual needs. If students need additional help on individual component parts, the activities listed will help reinforce correct performance.

Objective: To allow partners to improve areas of deficiency as assessed by the partner skill check.

Equipment: See individual stations. We suggest using an unbreakable mirror and a poster of each component of the underhand throw at each station. The mirror is particularly helpful in these activities because it allows the child to see what she is doing. The easiest way to make the posters would be to photocopy the drawings from this book. Use an opaque projector to enlarge them. Laminating the posters will ensure their use for many years.

Activity:

1. Set up a station for each of the four components in the teaching area. Post a description or a picture of the specific component at the corresponding station.

2. Stations:

Ready

—knees bent, facing target, feet shoulder-width apart, eyes on target, object held in dominant hand (palm up) in front of the body.

Equipment: Component poster, mirror (if available), and partner evaluations

Activity: The student assumes the ready position, and the partner checks to see if her position matches the poster. The student refers to the mirror for help. The student then walks around and on a signal from her partner assumes the ready position again. Once the student can successfully demonstrate to the partner a correct ready position, the partners may return to practicing the entire skill.

Arm Back

—swing the throwing arm back to at least waist level.

Equipment: Mirror, poster, line at waist level on the wall, and partner evaluations

Activity: The student demonstrates a swinging motion with his arm (keeping the arm close to the body) and raising the hand at least as high as the waist during the swing. The partner checks to see if his position matches the poster. To help the partner see the height of the swing, the student should perform the task standing near a wall with a line marked approximately waist high. The student refers to the mirror for help. Once the student can successfully demonstrate to the partner a good arm swing, the partners may return to practicing the entire skill.

Step and Throw

—step forward with the opposite foot, bring the throwing arm forward, and release the ball below the waist. The arm is extended throughout the entire movement.

Equipment: Mirror, poster, footprint outlines or tape (floor or masking), jump rope, two chairs, and partner evaluations

Activity: Place footprints (or floor/masking tape) on the floor. With the partner's help, the student starts from the ready position and steps with the appropriate foot. The partner checks to see if his position matches the poster. The student refers to the mirror for help. The rubber footprints that are currently available from many physical education equipment catalogs may be used very effectively in this station.

To assist students having difficulty with the release point, suspend a jump rope between two chairs. The student practices releasing the ball under the rope. Once the student can successfully demonstrate to the partner a correct arm swing, the partners may return to practicing the entire skill.

Follow Through

—throwing hand continues toward the target in front of the body and finishes with palm facing upward.

Equipment: Mirror, poster, basketball goal, rope with ball attached, and partner evaluations

Activity: Suspend a ball from a basketball goal at the level of the follow-through. The student practices her step and release (without using a ball or beanbag), and must touch the suspended ball on the follow-through. The partner checks to see if her position matches the poster. The student refers to the mirror for help. Once the student can successfully demonstrate to the partner a correct follow-through, the partners may return to practicing the entire skill.

Suggested Culminating Activities to Reinforce the Entire Skill

Individual Activities

Color Targets

Objective: To improve underhand throwing accuracy

Equipment: Construction paper of different colors and sizes (about 8 to 12 targets of each color) taped to the wall of the gymnasium or activity area and a beanbag or ball (yarn ball, tennis ball, etc.) for each student

Activity:

1. Create a "color box" in which samples from each color of construction paper have been placed. You will need more samples than you have students.

2. Select a student to draw a sample color from the color box.

3. The sample color chosen is the color target all students must locate and try to hit with an underhand throw.

4. Students continue to throw toward the targets of the selected color until you give a stop signal.

5. The activity continues until all students have been given an opportunity to draw from the color box.

Extensions:

1. Instead of using different colors, students could select different shapes from the "shape box," letters from the "alphabet box," or words from the "word box."

2. Students can work with partners. The partner chooses the color, shape, letter, or word that will be used for a target. The thrower must then try to hit the selected target. Partners take turns selecting targets and throwing.

Create-A-Word

Objective: To create words by hitting letters using the underhand throw

Equipment: One beanbag or ball (yarn ball or tennis ball) per student and four complete sets of alphabet letters scattered and taped to the wall of the gymnasium or activity area. It would be advantageous to have extra copies of vowels and selected consonants (e.g., N, S, T, R). You will also need paper and markers, or a chalkboard and chalk to serve as a "word bank."

Activity:

1. On your start signal, students begin to spell words by hitting letters of the alphabet using an underhand throw.

2. Once a student has created a word, he goes to the word bank (paper or chalkboard) and writes the word. It will be helpful to have several word banks so students will not have to wait in line to write their words.

3. A word may be "banked" or written only once on the paper or chalkboard.

4. If a student hits a letter that cannot be used to form the word being created, she must hit the letter again to delete it.

Extensions:

1. Students can work with partners. One student collects letters to spell a word while the partner records the word and evaluates the underhand throw. The thrower may not use the letter until the underhand throw is performed properly. When the first partner has spelled a word, the other partner is then given an opportunity to throw.

2. Partners are given paper and pencil to record the letters they hit and to write down the words they create. Each partner must throw and hit a vowel and two consonants until the team has six letters to use to create words. The partners attempt to create six words using one or more of the letters they have hit. Once the partners have created six words and written them down, they attempt to spell the words by hitting the letters with the ball. Once a word is spelled, it may be checked off the list. If the students are unable to use a letter they have hit, they must hit that letter again to delete it and select another letter.

Partner Activities

Challenges

Objective: To practice the underhand throw in a variety of situations

Equipment: One yarn ball, beanbag, or Nerf ball per pair of students and laminated challenge cards. Different types of challenges may require additional equipment.

Activity:

1. Students select a challenge card.

2. Students perform the task described on the card.

3. Possible challenges may include:

   • Throw the ball using medium or light force.

   • Throw the ball releasing at a medium or low level.

   • Throw the ball toward your partner's bellybutton.

   • Throw the ball so that it hits the wall, bounces once, and you are able to catch it.

Extensions:

1. You can place multicolored targets, pictures, or hoops on the wall. Other targets may be cones or buckets that are scattered in the play area. The partner can tell the thrower which target to hit.

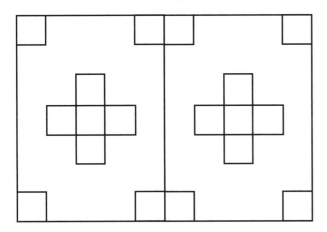

2. Set up game poles or volleyball standards and tie a rope between them. Suspend different objects from the rope and challenge the students to hit them. Possible targets could include hoops, aluminum pie pans, and empty two-liter plastic bottles.

3. To create more permanent targets, you may paint them on the wall of your gymnasium (see figure). Often tumbling mats are attached to the wall for storage. If you paint these targets on the wall behind where tumbling mats are attached, you can cover them when not in use.

4. The pairs keep track of their number of correct throws and keep a total for the class. On a follow-up lesson you can challenge the class to increase the total number of correct throws.

Bag It

Objective: To underhand throw a ball to a partner who will catch it in a plastic grocery bag

Equipment: One yarn ball or beanbag and a plastic grocery bag for each set of partners

Activity:

1. Students stand no closer than 10 feet from a partner. Students take turns being the "thrower" and the "catcher."

2. The thrower tosses the ball underhand to the catcher who tries to catch the ball in the plastic grocery bag.

3. The catch counts if the thrower demonstrates all of the components of the underhand throw and the ball is caught in the bag.

4. Each student has three turns as the thrower and then changes places with his partner to be the catcher.

Extensions:

1. The partners count the number of catches they are able to make in a set time period or the number they are able to catch consecutively.

2. The partners take a step back after each round of successful throws. A round of throws consists of each partner having three throws and three catches.

3. Toy stores sell special Velcro catching surfaces with tennis-ball size balls designed to stick to this surface. Use these items instead of plastic bags. Plastic scoops also make good substitutes for the plastic bags.

Group Activities

Stew Pot

Objective: To demonstrate the proper execution of the underhand throw while throwing a beanbag into a hula hoop

Equipment: Beanbags and hula hoops

Activity:

1. Divide the class into groups of four.

2. Give each group four beanbags (one per person) and one hula hoop.

3. Directions for making the "stew":

   - Have the students make a circle around the pot (a hula hoop lying on the floor) approximately one giant step away from the pot.

   - All stew meat/vegetables (beanbags) must get into the pot for the stew to be cooked.

   - Using correct form, everyone in the group must throw his stew meat/vegetable into the pot. If all of the beanbags make it into the pot, the stew is cooked. If any beanbags miss the target, all of the beanbags are retrieved and the group tries again.

   - After each pot of stew is cooked, the students take one step backward from the pot. Students continue to step back after each pot of stew is cooked.

Extensions:

1. The entire class stands around a large circle. This is the giant stew pot. All of the stew meat/vegetables must get into the pot for the stew to be cooked. The students step back one step after each pot of stew is cooked.

2. Since many beanbags come in colors, assign different colors to the different food groups (green for vegetables, red for meats, yellow for pasta, etc.). Then call out specific foods. The children have to decide what food group it is in and then throw the beanbag. For example, when you call out carrots (a vegetable), the children with green beanbags throw their "carrots" into the stew pot.

Cycle/Recycle

Objective: To improve underhand throwing accuracy while throwing a yarnball between two volleyball nets

Equipment: Two volleyball standards, two volleyball nets, and one yarn ball per student. One net should be placed at regular volleyball height and the other at tennis height (on the same standard).

Activity:

1. Divide the class in half.

2. Place groups on either side of the nets.

3. On the start signal, everyone throws the ball underhand between the nets.

4. Students count the number of balls they were able to throw between nets.

Extensions:

1. The students total the number of accurate throws made by the entire group. These results can be recorded and later charted or graphed to show class improvement.

2. Students who throw the ball between the nets go around the standards and become members of the opposite group.

Reprinted, by permission, from J.A. Wessell, PhD, 1974, *Project I CAN* (Northbrook, IL: Hubbard).

Cage Ball Madness

Objective: To perform the underhand throw using a playground ball to move an object across the play area

Equipment: The object may be a cage ball or any ball larger than the balls being thrown. The balls being thrown may be playground balls or volleyballs when aiming at a cage ball. When the target ball is smaller, tennis balls may be used.

Activity:

1. Divide the class into four even groups. Each group stands along one side of a square play area. Students must stay behind their line.

2. Place the cage ball or large ball in the center of the play area.

3. Each group begins the activity with two or more balls.

4. On the start signal, players throw the balls and try to hit the cage ball (large ball in the center) in an effort to move it toward the other group's line.

5. Players continue to throw the balls until the cage ball crosses a group's line. Any ball that stays inside of the area enclosed by the four groups is retrieved by the teacher.

6. Players may only touch the cage ball (large ball) with a thrown ball. They may not touch it with any part of the body.

7. Once the cage ball crosses the designated line, the activity stops and the cage ball is returned to the center of the play area.

8. The activity resumes when each group has the same number of balls to throw. Be sure every player is given a chance to start with a ball.

Extensions:

1. Create two groups rather than four.

2. Try to throw a variety of balls at the cage ball in an effort to move the ball across another group's line. This may lead to discussions on which balls are better for the task.

3. Have groups change positions either before the next round or on a signal during the activity. Be sure that if the students are to change places during the activity, they understand that they may not throw a ball at the cage ball until your signal, and they may not take a ball with them as they change.

Switcharoo

Objective: To use an underhand throw to tag the feet of opposing players in an effort to get all players on one side of the play area

Equipment: One to four 6- to 8-inch balls (Nerf balls or light rubber balls). The number of balls will vary based on the skill level of the students.

Activity:

1. Divide the class into two groups and place them on opposite sides of a divided play area.

2. Give each group an equal number of balls to start the activity.

3. On the start signal, players throw the balls underhand and try to hit the feet/legs of the opposing players.

4. A player must move to the other group's side when she is hit with a ball or when the ball that she threw is caught in the air by an opposing player before it touches another player or the floor. When a player changes sides, she may not carry a ball to the opponent's side.

5. When all players are on the same side, the activity is restarted.

Extensions:

1. While the students are playing the activity, watch to see that the underhand throw is being performed correctly. Instruct any student having trouble throwing correctly to go to a practice area and work with a partner or designated teacher assistant.

2. Put up cones or bowling pins across the end lines of the play area. Once all the cones for a group have been knocked over, a new activity is started.

Create Your Own Activity

Objective: To allow students to create their own activity to reinforce the underhand throw

Equipment: One piece of paper and pencil per group and a predetermined list of equipment you will allow the students to use in their activities (e.g., bowling pins, cones, ropes, tennis balls, Nerf balls, etc.)

Activity:

1. Form groups with two to five students each. You may select the groups or the students may form their own.

2. Students create their own activity using the underhand throw as the basic skill. Students are required to have rules that encourage correct performance of the skill, include all players, and address all safety concerns.

3. The groups write their individual names, the rules of the activity, and the equipment needed on their paper and then show the activity to you.

4. Upon approval of their activity, the students may obtain their equipment and begin playing.

5. You must approve all changes to the activity.

Extensions:

1. One group may teach the activity it designed to another group.

2. Groups may teach their activities to the entire class.

Pin Ball

Objective: To use the underhand throw to hit the opponent's bowling pins

Equipment: Three balls and three plastic bowling pins (indicated by A and B for our purposes here) for each group. Bowling pins need to be color coded for each team (use different colored tape, for example, to mark the cones).

Restraining line

```
          X    A    X
          X         X
          X    B    X
          X    A    X
          X         X
          X    B    X
          X    A    X
          X         X
          X    B    X
```

Activity:

1. Set up a play area with a center line and two restraining lines approximately 12 feet away from the center line.

2. Divide the class into two equal groups and place the groups behind the restraining lines facing each other.

3. Set the six pins up along the center dividing line of the play area, alternating colors (see figure).

4. Give each group three balls.

5. On the start signal, the students throw the balls and try to hit the opposing group's pins. The students may not cross the restraining line.

6. A pin is not down if the ball was thrown from in front of the restraining line.

7. Restart when all of a group's pins have been knocked down.

Extensions:

1. If a player is hit by a thrown ball, she moves to the other group (similar to Switcharoo) and continues to play.

2. Use empty two-liter bottles, lightweight cones, empty cereal boxes, etc., as the team targets.

Adapted, by permission, from K. Thomas, A. Lee, and J. Thomas, 2000, *Physical education for children: daily lesson plans for elementary school*, 2nd ed. (Champaign, IL: Human Kinetics).

Underhand Throw Troubleshooting Chart

IF YOU SEE	THEN TRY THIS
1. Eyes not on the target	• Have the student throw at a target he has designed. • Use the Color Targets activity as a station (see page 87). • Use pie plates for targets and place them on the wall at medium level. • As an outside activity, have the student throw wet sponges at a target in an effort to soak the target with water.
2. Arm not swinging back	• Have the student swing his arm back to touch a target (pie plate) attached to the wall. The target is placed at the student's waist level in line with the throwing arm. The student then throws the ball. • With a partner standing behind the thrower, the thrower swings his arm back and tries to take an object out of the partner's hand. • Put butcher paper on the wall. Have the student stand sideways with a marker in the throwing hand. As the student moves the throwing hand back, she draws a curvy line on the paper.
3. Student not stepping in opposition	• Tie a pinny or necktie around the nondominant foot. • Use spots or footprints on the floor to indicate the correct foot placement.
4. Body not in proper alignment on the follow-through	• Tell the student to point her bellybutton at the target on the follow-through. We call this the "Power of the Bellybutton." This works for many manipulative skills. • See the success builder activities in the text.

Summary

Children begin throwing at an early age. They may attempt to toss something into the trash can, pitch horseshoes with a grandparent, or throw a ball to a playmate. Regardless of the initial purpose of the child's first attempts at the underhand throw, this skill will become an integral part of many sports. Therefore, instruction must focus on all of the correct mechanics, especially stepping in opposition and proper release of the object.

By mastering the components of the underhand throw, a foundation is established for the successful performance of lifetime sport skills such as badminton, volleyball, and softball. To provide success, we need to offer a variety of opportunities for proper practice and instruction which can greatly enhance the students' mastery of this crucial building block.

Underhand Throw Lesson Plan (Second or Third Lesson)

Age group: Early primary

Focus: Release point for the underhand throw

Subfocus: Accuracy

Objectives: To release the ball below the waist 80 percent of the time (**CUE:** "Let it go below your waist.") and step in opposition as measured by teacher observation (**CUE:** "Use your stepping foot.").

Materials/Equipment: Targets taped to the walls every four feet, beanbags

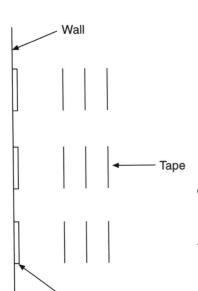

Wall

Tape

Target

Advance preparation: A learning station for each child is helpful. Each learning station is composed of three targets, placed at four foot intervals on the wall (see figure). These targets can be created by making shapes (squares, circles, triangles) with masking tape (see figure on next page); targets may also be hula hoops (use duct tape), laminated copies of drawings, or construction paper. For the purposes of this lesson, the target is made with five adjacent squares. Ideally you will have a set of targets for each student. The targets should be at least two feet above floor level. Place a beanbag or yarn ball at each station and mark three lines for the students to stand behind when practicing. The closest line should be five feet from the wall, the second should be six feet, and the third should be seven feet from the wall.

Organization/Management: Students are in personal space for instruction and warm-up. Later, students will find their own teaching stations in the gymnasium for practice.

Warm-up: Music is playing as students enter the gymnasium. They move in general space to teacher-directed locomotor movements (e.g., slide, gallop, jog, walk, skip, hop, jump). Later, you may suggest ways to perform the locomotor movements. The students may be challenged to move with varying speeds, levels, and amounts of force or to use a specific pathway. For example, they may begin jogging with light force in a curvy pathway at a high level.

Formation: Students find their personal space and sit on the floor facing you.

Introduction:

Today we are going to work on our underhand throw again. We need to really think about accuracy today. But let's review first. Who can tell me the parts of an underhand throw? **(Ready, Arm Back, Step and Throw, Follow Through.)**

Who can show me how we step? That's right, we step with the foot on the OTHER side of our body from the hand we throw with.

Everyone stand up in your personal space. Let's pretend that we have a beanbag in our throwing hand. Let's go through the steps of the underhand throw together: Ready, Arm Back, Step and Throw, Follow Through.

Watch for stepping in opposition.

Excellent. Let's talk about accuracy. When we throw a ball, we want it to go to a target. That target might be a person or a place. One thing that really affects whether the ball gets to our target is where we let go of it, or release it. Watch as I throw my imaginary beanbag. Where do you think the beanbag will go, high or low? (Release the imaginary beanbag at a high level.)

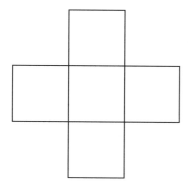

Now where do you think the beanbag will go? (Release the imaginary beanbag at a medium level.) *So if we want the beanbag to go high, we release it high. If we want it to go to a medium level, we release it at that level. Look at the stations that are set up for you. There are five squares at each station.* (See figure.)

Watch as I demonstrate what you will be asked to do. I would like you to stand on the line closest to the target. Say the cues "Ready, Arm Back, Step and Throw, and Follow Through" out loud as you release the beanbag. Your first job will be to use the correct form and perform all of the cues. Later, I will ask you to aim at different targets. When I say go, find a practice space. GO.

Watch for correct form as the students practice the skill and say the cues out loud. After students can successfully perform the skill, provide them with challenges such as the ones listed below.

1. Stand on the closest line and do the following:

   • Hit the middle target five times in a row.

   • Hit the top target.

   • Hit the target on the left.

   • Hit the target on the right.

   • Hit the lower target.

   • Call out which targets the students should hit before they release the beanbags.

2. Stand on the next line back and repeat the sequence.

3. Stand on the line the greatest distance from the target and repeat the sequence.

Watch for release point and stepping in opposition. Remind the students frequently to "Release the beanbag below your waist" and "Use your stepping foot."

FREEZE. Everyone please sit down where you are and listen to my directions. When I say GO, you will find a partner and sit together at one station. Each of you will underhand throw the beanbag five times in a row. Your target will be the one your partner selects. You may select the distance, but he or she will tell you which one to hit. Remember how many times you are successful. After five minutes I'm going to ask you how well you and your partner did.

Oh, one more condition. The skill must be performed correctly. Remember our cues—Ready, Arm Back, Step and Throw, and Follow Through. The throw will only count if you say the cues out loud, step with the correct foot, let go of the beanbag below your waist, AND hit the target. Do you understand these directions? GO.

Circulate and look for stepping in opposition and proper release point.

Closure: As students are lined up to leave, play "teach the teacher:"

1. *Who can tell me how to throw a beanbag underhand correctly?* ***(Ready, Arm Back, Step with the Opposite Foot, Throw, Follow Through.)***

Perform an underhand throw. The students tell you how to correct it. Attempt the skill again and step with the wrong foot. Students correct this. Finally, perform the skill correctly. Repeat the cues "Release the beanbag below your waist" and "Use your stepping foot" often.

2. *How can I change where the beanbag goes?* ***(Where the ball is released will affect where it goes.)***

3. *Tomorrow we will work on accuracy again. Please walk and get in line.*

Overhand Throw

Perhaps no other manipulative skill is as essential to mastering sports as the overhand throw. Not only is the overhand throw needed in nearly every team sport from the baseball pitch to the overhand volleyball serve, but its mastery is also essential in developing proficiency in badminton and tennis. The NASPE Outcomes Project establishes the second grade as the time in which a student should be able to "throw a ball hard demonstrating an overhand technique, a side orientation, and opposition" (outcome 2-10). NASPE also sets the fourth grade as a time when children should be able to demonstrate a mature throwing pattern (outcome 4-12).

Basic Components

Ready Position
—facing target, feet shoulder-width apart, knees bent, eyes on target, object held in front of the body.

T
—body turns as the feet pivot in place and non-dominant side is toward the target. Extend the arms to create a **T** with the object held in the throwing hand, which is extended away from the intended line of travel with the palm facing upward. The nonthrowing hand points toward the target.

Step/Throw/Point
—step with the foot opposite the throwing arm, hip and shoulder rotate toward the target, front body surface faces the target, arm comes through past the head.

Follow Through
—throwing hand continues toward the target and continues down diagonally across the body.

Cue Words

The cue words you select for each phase of the skill will depend on the age of the students you are teaching and your areas of emphasis. We have listed, in usable sets, some of the cue words we have used to teach the overhand throw. You may use each set individually or mix and match the cue words as needed. We have found that it is beneficial to have the students say the cue words out loud as they practice.

READY—facing target, feet shoulder-width apart, knees bent, eyes on target, object held in front of the body.

T and MAKE A T and TURN TO THE T—body turns as the feet pivot in place and nondominant side is toward the target. Extend the arms to create a T with the object held in the dominant hand. The palm is up.

REACH BACK—start with side to the target, reach back with the throwing arm and make a T.

POINT AND LOOK—look and point toward the target.

STEP—step with the opposite foot.

STEP/THROW/POINT and STEP AND THROW—step with the foot opposite the throwing arm, hip and shoulder rotate toward the target, arm comes through past the head.

THROW—step and release the ball.

THROW HARD—hip and shoulder rotate toward the target as the student throws with hard force.

SQUASH THE BUG—the nonstepping foot needs to remain stationary. Students pretend that there is a wasp (or other undesirable insect) under their foot. When they release the ball, they leave that foot still and their pivot will "squash the bug."

FOLLOW THROUGH and HUG THYSELF—the throwing arm continues toward the target and comes down diagonally across the body, almost as if the student is hugging herself.

Cue Set 1: READY, T, STEP/THROW/POINT, FOLLOW THROUGH

Cue Set 2: MAKE A T, POINT AND LOOK, STEP AND THROW, SQUASH THE BUG

Cue Set 3: TURN TO THE T, STEP AND THROW, HUG THYSELF

Cue Set 4: REACH BACK, THROW

Cue Set 5: REACH BACK, STEP, THROW HARD

Suggested Activities for Reinforcing the Components

In the learning process, it is essential that students know how a skill looks, what its component parts are, and how to perform each individual component correctly. In the preceding section, we furnished pictures and descriptions of the overhand throw, divided it into its component parts, and provided possible cue words. In addition to the material in chapter 3 that reinforces the concepts for all locomotor and manipulative skills, the following section provides specific activities for reinforcing the components unique to the overhand throw.

Partner Skill Check

Objective: To allow partners to assess their own skill progress with the overhand throw and learn to evaluate the skills of others

Equipment: Partner skill check sheets, pencils, and one ball for each set of partners. If the students cannot read or do not speak English, the picture version of the partner skill check sheet may be useful.

Activity:

1. One partner observes the other to see if he has the correct form for the ready position.

2. If the ready position is correct, then the partner places a *Y* in the first box. If the ready position is not correct, he places an *N* in the first box. Nonreaders can put a smiling face if the ready position is correct or a sad face if the ready position is not correct.

3. This evaluation continues until each of the components has been assessed five times.

4. A partner skill check sheet is used for each student.

Extensions:

1. You can use the partner skill check sheet to assess the skill development of each student.

2. You can send partner skill check sheets home with report cards or as individual skills develop.

Success Builders

The success builder activities allow you to address individual needs. If students need additional help on individual component parts, the activities listed below will help reinforce correct performance.

Objective: To allow partners to improve areas of deficiency as assessed by the partner skill check.

Equipment: See individual stations. We suggest using an unbreakable mirror and a poster of each component of the overhand throw at each station. The mirror is particularly helpful in these activities because it allows the child to see what she is doing. The easiest way to make the posters would be to photocopy the drawings from this book. Use an opaque projector to enlarge them. Laminating the posters will ensure their use for many years.

Activity:

1. Set up a station for each component in the teaching area. Post a description or a picture of the specific component at the corresponding station.

2. Stations:

Partner Skill Check

Skill: **Overhand Throw**

Thrower's name: _____ Watcher's name: _____

1.

  1   2   3   4   5

Ready

2.

  1   2   3   4   5

T

3.

  1   2   3   4   5

Step/throw/point

4.

  1   2   3   4   5

Follow through

Partner Skill Check

Skill: **Overhand Throw**

Thrower's name: _____ Watcher's name:_____

Watch your partner and mark each component of the skill. Let your partner do the skill 5 times. Each time your partner does it right, mark a **Y** in the box. If your partner doesn't do it right, mark an **N** in the box.

START

Ready position

1. Eyes on target
2. Knees bent
3. Feet shoulder-width apart
4. Object in front of body

TRIALS

1	2	3	4	5
☐	☐	☐	☐	☐

ACTION

T

1. Side to target

1	2	3	4	5
☐	☐	☐	☐	☐

2. Throwing arm extended back, other arm pointing at target

1	2	3	4	5
☐	☐	☐	☐	☐

Step/throw/point

3. Step forward on opposite foot

1	2	3	4	5
☐	☐	☐	☐	☐

4. Hip and shoulder turn to target; hand points in direction of throw

1	2	3	4	5
☐	☐	☐	☐	☐

STOP

Follow through

1. Arm continues across body after the release; bellybutton points toward target

1	2	3	4	5
☐	☐	☐	☐	☐

Ready

—facing target, feet shoulder-width apart, knees bent, eyes on target, object held in front of the body

Equipment: Component poster, mirror (if available), and partner evaluations

Activity: The student assumes the ready position. The partner checks to see if her position matches the poster. The student refers to the mirror for help. The student then walks around and on a signal from her partner assumes the ready position again. When she has had several successful trials, the partners may return to working on the entire skill.

—body turns as the feet pivot in place and nondominant side is toward the target. Arms are extended in the shape of a T with the object held in the throwing hand. The throwing hand is extended away from the intended line of travel with the palm facing upward. The nonthrowing hand points toward the target.

Equipment: Component poster, mirror (if available), and partner evaluations

Activity: The student assumes the T position. The partner checks to see if his position matches the poster. The student refers to the mirror for help. The student then assumes the ready position facing a set target. On a signal from his partner, the student assumes the T position. When he has had several successful trials, the partners may return to working on the entire skill.

Step/Throw/Point

—step with the foot opposite to the throwing arm, hip and shoulder rotate toward the target. The front body surface should be facing the target (use the cue "bellybutton" to help reinforce correct body position), and the arm comes through past the head.

Step

Equipment: Component poster, mirror (if available), rubber footprints (currently available from catalogs) or tape (floor or masking), and partner evaluations

Activity: *Power Stride*—footprints (or tape) are placed on the floor. With the partner's help, the student starts from the ready position, makes a T, and steps with the appropriate foot. The partner checks to see if her position matches the poster. The student refers to the mirror for help. When she has had several successful trials, the partners may return to working on the entire skill.

Throw and Point

Equipment: Component poster, mirror (if available), partner evaluations, 15- to 20-foot length of cotton or nylon rope, two game standards, one-inch diameter PVC pipe cut to length of four inches with ends filed or taped. (If equipment availability is limited, see extension 1 below.)

Activity: *Rocket Launcher*—Place the game standards 10 to 12 feet apart. Thread the rope through the PVC pipe and then tie the rope between the game standards so it is approximately eye level to the students. Students work in pairs or groups of four with partners standing at opposite game standards. Students are told to stay clear of the rope while their partners are throwing. One partner starts in the **T** position with the "rocket" (PVC pipe) in her throwing hand. The thrower uses step/throw to propel the rocket down the rope to the opposite standard. The partner at the opposite game standard retrieves the rocket and performs the step/throw, sending the rocket back toward the partner.

Extensions:

1. If you have limited space and/or no game standards, stretch the rope between two chairs. Have the students sit with their nonthrowing side toward their partner and throw the rocket. Students should finish the throw with both hands touching the floor in the direction of the throw.

2. Tie a towel, rag, etc., around the rope at the ends near the game standards to prevent the rocket from hitting the game standards.

Release Point

Equipment: Component poster, mirror (if available), jump ropes, two volleyball poles, and partner evaluations

Activity: *Let 'er Rip*—Stretch the jump ropes between two volleyball poles leaving approximately 12 inches between the ropes. The top rope should be at about shoulder height to the thrower. Have the student practice releasing the ball between the ropes. The partner checks to see if the thrower's position matches the poster. The thrower refers to the mirror for help.

Follow Through

—throwing hand continues toward the target and continues down diagonally across the body.

Equipment: Component poster, mirror (if available), and partner evaluations

Activity: Have the student get into the step-throw position facing a set target. The student practices his step and release (without a ball or beanbag). The partner checks to see if his position matches the poster. The student refers to the mirror for help. When he has had several successful trials, the partners may return to working on the entire skill.

Suggested Culminating Activities to Reinforce the Entire Skill
Individual Activities

Color Targets

Objective: To improve overhand throwing accuracy by hitting a specified target.

Equipment: Construction paper of different colors and sizes (about 8 to 12 targets of each color) taped to the wall of the gymnasium or activity area and a beanbag or ball for each student (yarn ball, tennis ball, etc.)

Activity:

1. Create a "color box" in which samples from each color of construction paper have been placed. You will need more samples than you have students.

2. Select a student to draw a sample color from the color box.

3. The sample color chosen is the color target all students must locate and try to hit with an overhand throw.

4. Students continue to throw toward the targets of the selected color until a stop signal is given.

5. The activity continues until all students have had an opportunity to draw from the color box.

Extensions:

1. Instead of using different colors, students could select different shapes from the "shape box," letters from the "alphabet box," or words from the "word box."

2. Students work with partners. The partner chooses the color, shape, letter, or word that will be used for a target. The thrower must then try to hit the selected target. Partners take turns selecting targets and throwing.

Create-A-Word

Objective: To create words by using the overhand throw to hit letters

Equipment: One beanbag or ball (tennis ball or yarn ball) per student, four complete sets of alphabet letters scattered and taped to the walls of the gym or activity space. It would be advantageous to have extra copies of vowels and selected consonants, e.g., N, R, S, T. You will also need paper and markers or a chalkboard and chalk to serve as a "word bank."

Activity:

1. On your start signal, students begin to spell words by hitting letters of the alphabet using an overhand throw.

2. Once a student has created a word, he goes to the word bank (paper or chalkboard) and writes the word. It will be helpful to have several word banks so students will not have to wait to record their word.

3. A word may be "banked" or written only once on the paper or chalkboard.

4. If a student hits a letter that cannot be used to form the word being created, he must hit the letter again to delete it.

Extensions:

1. Working in pairs, one student hits letters to spell a word while the other records the word and evaluates the throw. The thrower may not use the letter until the overhand throw is performed properly. When the first partner has spelled a word, the other partner is given an opportunity to throw.

2. Partners are given paper and pencil to record the letters they hit and to write down the words they create. Each partner must throw and hit a vowel and two consonants. The pair now has six letters to use to create words. The partners attempt to create six words using one or more of the letters they have hit. Once the partners have created six words and written them down, they will attempt to spell the words by hitting the letters with the ball. Once a word is spelled, it may be checked off the list. If the students are unable to use a letter they have hit, they must hit that letter again to delete it and select another letter.

Partner Activities

Challenges

Objective: To practice the overhand throw in a variety of situations

Equipment: One yarn ball, beanbag, or Nerf ball per pair of students and laminated challenge cards. Different types of challenges may require additional equipment.

Activity:

1. Students select a challenge card.

2. Students perform the task described on the card.

3. Possible challenges may include:

   • Throw the ball using medium or heavy force.

   • Throw the ball, releasing at a medium level (high level).

   • Throw the ball toward your partner's bellybutton.

   • Throw the ball so that it hits the wall, bounces once, and you are able to catch it.

Extensions:

1. Place multicolored targets, hoops, cones, or buckets on a wall or in the play area and have the partner tell the thrower which target to hit.

2. Set up game poles or volleyball standards and tie a rope between them. Suspend different objects from the rope and challenge the students to hit them. Possible targets include hoops, aluminum pie pans, and empty two-liter plastic bottles.

3. To create more permanent targets, you may paint them on the wall of your gymnasium. If you paint these targets on the wall behind where tumbling mats are often attached for storage, you can cover them when not in use.

4. Partners keep track of their number of correct throws and keep a total for the class. In a follow-up lesson, challenge the class to increase the total number of correct throws.

Wall Ball

Objective: To improve the overhand throw and the catch while working with a partner

Equipment: One ball (playground or volleyball) per student pair

Activity:

1. Partners stand at least 15 feet from the wall.

2. One partner throws the ball overhand against the wall. The throw must be at least 10 feet high.

3. The other partner has to catch the ball after it comes off the wall but before it hits the ground.

4. When the partner has caught the ball, he overhand throws the ball back to the wall from the place it was caught.

5. Partners count how many successful catches they have in a row.

Extensions:

1. Allow the ball to bounce once before it is caught.

2. Place a target on the wall and challenge the partners to hit it.

Group Activities

Cage Ball Madness

Objective: To perform the overhand throw using a ball to move an object across the play area

Equipment: The object may be a cage ball or any ball larger than the balls being thrown. The balls being thrown may be playground balls or volleyballs when aiming at a cage ball. When the target is smaller, tennis balls may be used.

Activity:

1. Divide the class into four even groups. Each group stands along one side of a square play area. Students must stay behind their line.

2. Place the cage ball or large ball in the center of the play area.

3. Each group begins the activity with two or more balls.

4. On the start signal, players throw the balls and try to hit the cage ball (large ball in the center) in an effort to move it toward the other group's line.

5. Players continue to throw the balls until the cage ball crosses a group's line. Any ball that stays inside of the area enclosed by the four groups is retrieved by the teacher.

6. Players may only touch the cage ball (large ball) with a thrown ball. They may not touch it with any part of the body.

7. Once the cage ball crosses the designated line, the activity stops and the cage ball is returned to the center of the play area.

8. The activity resumes when each group has the same number of balls to throw. Be sure every player is given a chance to start with a ball.

Extensions:

1. Create two groups rather than four.

2. Try to throw a variety of balls at the cage ball in an effort to move the ball across another group's line. This may lead to discussions on which balls are better for the task (e.g., playground balls versus tennis balls).

3. Have groups change positions either before the next round or on a signal during the activity. Be sure that if the students are to change places during the activity they understand that they may not throw a ball at the cage ball until your start signal, and they may not take a ball with them as they change sides.

Switcharoo

Objective: To use an overhand throw to tag the feet of opposing players in an effort to get all players on one side of the play area

Equipment: One to four 6- to 8-inch balls (Nerf balls, yarn balls, or light rubber balls). The number of balls will vary based on the skill level of the students.

Activity:

1. Divide the class into two groups and place them on opposite sides of a divided play area.

2. Give each group an equal number of balls to start the activity.

3. On the start signal, players throw the balls and try to hit the feet/legs of the opposing players.

4. A player must move to the other group's side either when she is hit with a ball or when the ball she threw is caught in the air by an opposing player before it touches another player or the floor. When a player changes sides, she may not carry a ball to the opponent's side.

5. When all players are on the same side, the activity is restarted.

Extensions:

1. While the students are playing, watch that the overhand throw is being performed correctly. Instruct any student having trouble throwing correctly to go to a practice area and work with a partner or designated teacher assistant.

2. Put up cones or bowling pins across the end lines of the play area. Once all of the cones for a group have been knocked over, a new activity is started.

Create Your Own Activity

Objective: To allow students to create their own activity to reinforce the overhand throw

Equipment: One piece of paper and pencil per group and a predetermined list of equipment you will allow the students to use in their activities (e.g., bowling pins, cones, jump rope, softballs, tennis balls, etc.)

Activity:

1. Form groups with two to five students each. You may select the groups or the students may form their own.

2. The groups create their own activity using the overhand throw as the basic skill. Students are required to have rules that encourage correct performance of the skill, include all players, and address all safety concerns.

3. The groups write their individual names, the rules of the activity, and the equipment needed on their paper and then show the activity to you.

4. Upon approval of their activity, the students may obtain their equipment and then begin playing.

5. You must approve all changes to the activity.

Extensions:

1. One group may teach the activity it designed to another group.

2. Groups may teach their activities to the entire class.

Pin Ball

Objective: To use the overhand throw to hit the opposing group's bowling pins

Equipment: Three balls and three plastic bowling pins (indicated by A and B for our purposes here) for each group. Bowling pins need to be color coded for each group (use different colored tape, for example, to mark the cones).

Activity:

1. Set up a play area with a center line and two restraining lines approximately 12 feet from the center line.

2. Divide the class into two equal groups and place the groups behind the restraining lines facing each other.

3. Set the six pins up along the center line of the play area, alternating colors (see figure).

4. Give each group three balls.

5. On the start signal, the students throw the balls and try to hit the opposing group's pins. The students may not cross the restraining line.

6. A pin is not down if the ball was thrown from in front of the restraining line.

7. The activity is restarted when all of a group's pins have been knocked down.

Extensions:

1. If a player is hit by a thrown ball, she moves to the other group (similar to Switcharoo) and continues to play.

2. Use empty two-liter bottles, lightweight cones, empty cereal boxes, etc., as targets.

Adapted, by permission, from K. Thomas, A. Lee, and J. Thomas, 2000, *Physical education for children: daily lesson plans for elementary school*, 2nd ed. (Champaign, IL: Human Kinetics).

Cycle/Recycle

Objective: To improve overhand throwing accuracy while throwing a yarn ball over a volleyball net.

Equipment: Two game standards, one volleyball net, and one yarn ball per student. The net is placed at regular volleyball height.

Activity:

1. Divide the class in half.

2. Place the groups on either side of the net.

3. On the start signal, everyone throws the ball overhand over the net.

4. Have the students count the number of successful throws they were able to make over the net.

Extensions:

1. Have the students total the number of throws the entire group made. These results can be recorded and later charted or graphed to show class improvement.

2. Each time a student throws the ball over the net, he goes around the standards and becomes a member of the other group.

Reprinted, by permission, from J.A. Wessell, PhD, 1974, *Project I CAN* (Northbrook, IL: Hubbard).

Summary

Although children begin throwing at an early age, a mature throwing pattern will not emerge without proper instruction. The overhand throw is probably the manipulative skill most crucial to later sport skill development. The baseball or softball player who steps with the wrong foot and has trouble getting the ball in from the outfield probably began as the kindergartner who practiced stepping with the wrong foot and never learned to get the arm back when throwing. The habits that are practiced in the younger grades become the permanent motor patterns as students get older.

Since many aspects of the overhand throw transfer to important sport skills (such as the tennis and volleyball serves), this skill should be introduced in the early grades and practiced often. Proper instruction that begins at this time will provide success and, hopefully, continued participation throughout the student's lifetime. To provide the maximum practice, children may practice throwing to a wall. Throwing to a partner should begin as soon as the students have learned to catch. The next chapter will detail methods for teaching proper catching skills.

Overhand Throw Troubleshooting Chart

IF YOU SEE	THEN TRY THIS
1. Eyes not on the target	• Have the student throw at a target he has designed. • Use the Color Targets activity as a station (see page 105). • Place a two-liter bottle on top of a cone and have the student try to knock it off. • As an outside activity, have the student throw wet sponges at a target to soak the target with water. • Use aluminum pie plates for targets.
2. Not enough arm extension	• Encourage the student to use harder force when throwing the object. • Have the student touch a wall located behind her while forming the T position and then throw the object.
3. Hand of the throwing arm not going past the ear	• Ask the student to picture herself listening to music on a small radio and then throwing the radio past her ear to her partner. • Have the student use the Rocket Launcher activity in the Step/Throw/Point station (see page 104). • Hang a yarn ball from a basketball goal so the ball is at ear height. Put the student in the T position (side orientation) and have her hit the ball with an open palm.
4. Student not stepping in opposition	• Tie a pinny or necktie around the nondominant foot. • Use floor spots or footprints on the floor to indicate the proper foot placement.
5. Limited hip and shoulder rotation	• Have the student check the position of his bellybutton after the throw. The bellybutton should be pointing in the direction of the target. • Use rubber tubing or Dynabands and have a partner hold the tubing to add resistance while the student goes through the rotation motion.
6. Student not continuing the follow-through	• Use extension 1 of the Rocket Launcher activity (see page 104) to stress the complete follow-through. • Place a small cone in front of and to the nonthrowing side of the student's body. The cone should be far enough away so the student can step and extend the arm on the throw. The student throws the ball and then touches the top of the cone on the follow-through.

Overhand Throw Lesson Plan (Second Lesson)

Age group: Primary

Focus: Overhand throw

Subfocus: Arm extension, force production

Objectives: To extend the arm to promote force 80 percent of the time (**CUE:** "Reach back," "Throw hard") and step in opposition 80 percent of the time as measured by teacher and peer observation (**CUE:** "Use your stepping foot").

Materials/Equipment: One yarn ball for each child

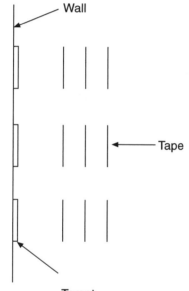

Wall

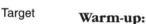

Tape

Target

Advance preparation: Each child should have her own learning station for this lesson. The learning stations should be spaced around the gymnasium and have three targets taped to the wall. The targets should be at least two feet above the floor level, but may vary in height. Be sure that targets are at the appropriate height for the overhand throw and not the underhand throw or underhand roll. Targets may be hula hoops (use duct tape), laminated copies of drawings, laminated pieces of construction paper, or you might decide just to use the tape to make targets (e.g., triangles, squares, rectangles, etc.). Place a yarn ball at each station and mark lines for the students to stand behind when practicing. These lines should be at least five feet from the wall and then at appropriate increments thereafter (see figure).

Organization/Management: Students will be in personal space for instruction and warm-up. Later, students will find their own learning stations in the gymnasium for practice.

Warm-up:

Today, we are going to use our arms a lot to work on our throwing. When I put on the music, I would like you to begin moving in general space with a locomotor skill of your choice. Who can name a locomotor skill? (Repeat the question several times until skip, slide, gallop, run, and walk are all mentioned.)

When the music stops, I would like you to FREEZE and perform an arm stretching exercise. Just in case you can't think of one, who can show me an arm warm- up exercise? (Call on several children. Begin music.)

Watch to make sure students are performing the locomotor skills correctly, that they are using a variety of skills, and that the arm stretching exercises are sufficient for the day's activity.

Formation:

Students find their own personal space and sit down.

Introduction:

Today we will continue working on throwing overhand. The overhand throw is used in many games. It can be used to throw to people or to targets. Since we will concentrate on throwing hard today, we will practice with targets. Why do you think we will throw at the wall today and not partners? ***(We are throwing hard and don't want to hurt anyone.)***

*Who can tell me which foot you step with on the overhand throw? **(The "stepping foot.")** Now who can tell me the components of the overhand throw?* ***(READY, MAKE A T, STEP/ THROW/ POINT, and FOLLOW THROUGH.)*** *Everyone stand up in your personal space and let's practice those steps. Remember to step with the stepping foot.*

Students practice the overhand throw as you repeat the cues out loud. Watch specifically for stepping in opposition.

FREEZE. Please sit down. Let's brainstorm how to throw hard. Watch me as I pretend to throw. Could the ready position help me throw harder? Could the T make me throw harder? Yes. Because if I stretch my arm out, I can generate more force when I throw. Think about a tiny baseball bat—only a foot long (use a ruler to demonstrate). Can I hit a ball farther with a bat this size, or a longer bat? Yes, the longer bat would be better. So if a longer bat is better for hitting, a longer arm is better for throwing. When we throw, we must reach back and then when we step/throw/point, we will have more force.

Again, why will we throw at the wall today and not at partners? ***(We are throwing hard and don't want to hurt anyone.)*** *Should we ever try to throw at a person as hard as we can?* ***NO.***

When I say GO, you will find a learning station, pick up the yarn ball, stand on the middle line, and work on extending your arm and throwing hard. GO.

Watch students to ensure that they have full arm extension and are stepping in opposition. Repeat the cues "Reach back," "Throw hard," and "Use your stepping foot" often.

Formation:

After five minutes, tell the students to FREEZE and sit down at their stations.

You are doing very well extending your arms. We need to work on our accuracy too. There are three shapes or targets in front of you. You must call out which one you will hit before the ball leaves your hand. Count how many times you are successful. You may stand on any of the three lines. GO.

Watch the students to ensure that they have full arm extension and are stepping in opposition. Repeat the cues "Reach back," "Throw hard," and "Use your stepping foot" often.

FREEZE. How many of you were successful 10 or more times? 20 or more times? Excellent. When I say GO, I would like you to find a partner and sit together at one station. GO. Partners, you will challenge your partner to hit a specific target, but he or she may choose the distance. After five throws, you will change jobs. Partners, you must also make sure that the skills are being done correctly, specifically making a T and stepping with the stepping foot. GO.

Watch the students to ensure that they have full arm extension and are stepping in opposition. Repeat the cues "Reach back," "Throw hard," and "Use your stepping foot" often.

Formation:

After five minutes, stop the class and have them sit down at their stations.

This time, you and your partner (if you both agree) may change the challenge. You may now tell your partner not only which target to hit, but which line to stand on. If you both don't agree to do this change, that's fine, just keep practicing. GO.

Closure:

As students are lined up to leave, ask the following questions:

1. *What are some of the safety concerns we have with throwing hard?* ***(Use a target on the wall and not a partner.)***

2. *What is one thing we can do to throw harder?* ***(Extend the arm.)***

3. *Which foot should I step with if I am right handed?* ***(The left foot.)***

4. *Which foot should I step with if I am left handed?* ***(The right foot.)***

chapter 6

Catching

One of the manipulative skills most neglected in the elementary grades is catching. Many injuries occur to children who are put into game situations involving this skill. Unfortunately, well-meaning coaches often stress how to throw without ever teaching *how* to catch what is thrown. Because the fear of catching can become overpowering, it is essential that this skill be introduced early and with appropriate safety considerations, that is, using equipment that is both soft and easily caught by small hands.

Objects may be caught above the waist (with the thumbs together) or below the waist (with the little, or pinkie, fingers together). Teachers should emphasize catching the ball with "10 fingers" in an effort to stop students from trapping the ball against their body.

The NASPE Outcomes Project suggests that a kindergartner should be able to catch a ball before it bounces twice (outcome K-10), a second grader should be able to catch a gently thrown ball with properly positioned hands (outcome 2-11), and a fourth grader should exhibit a mature catching pattern (outcome 4-12). Regardless of age, appropriate safety precautions should be used. For example, yarn balls, Nerf balls, or beanbags should be used when children are learning the mechanics of the catch. In addition, instruction should be included to teach students to use the proper amount of force when throwing and to throw the ball to a partner only when he is watching and ready.

Basic Components

Ready Position
—face the target, feet shoulder-width apart, knees bent, eyes on approaching object, elbows bent near sides, hands held in front of body.

Step and Reach—as the ball is released, step toward the thrower and extend the arms and hands to meet the ball. To catch throws above the waist, hands are held in front of the body (elbows bent near sides) with thumbs together. To catch throws below the waist, hands are held in front of the body (elbows bent near sides) with little (pinkie) fingers together. (The following rhyme may help your students with catching: "If the ball is high, reach to the sky. If the ball is low, reach to your toes.")

Fingers Only
—use only fingers and thumbs to catch the object. The ball should not be trapped against the body.

Give
—absorb the force of the object by bringing the arms back toward the body.

Cue Words

The cue words you select for each phase of the skill will depend on the age of the students you are teaching and your areas of emphasis. We have listed, in usable sets, some of the cue words we have used to teach catching. You may use each set individually or mix and match the cue words as needed. We have found that it is beneficial to have the students say the cue words out loud as they practice.

Catch above the waist:

W and READY—feet apart, knees bent, elbows near sides, thumbs up with the hands in front of the chest, and eyes on the approaching object. The tops of the thumb nails are touching. The index finger forms the outside of the **W**. The rest of the fingers are curved toward each other, leaving an opening large enough to catch the object.

REACH OUT and REACH—step forward with one foot and extend the arms toward the object.

CATCH and USE YOUR FINGERS—catch the object with the fingers ONLY (no trapping it against the body).

ABSORB THE FORCE and PULL—pull the arms back toward the body.

Cue Set 1: W, REACH OUT, CATCH, ABSORB THE FORCE
Cue Set 2: READY, REACH, USE YOUR FINGERS, PULL

Catch below the waist:

V and READY—feet apart, knees bent, elbows near sides, pinkies down with the hands below the waist, and eyes on the approaching object. The tops of the pinkies are touching forming a **V**. The rest of the fingers are curved toward each other, leaving an opening large enough to catch the object.

REACH DOWN and REACH—step forward with one foot and extend the arms downward toward the object.

CATCH and GRAB—catch the object with the fingers ONLY (no trapping it against the body).

ABSORB THE FORCE and PULL—pull the arms back toward the body.

Cue Set 1: V, REACH DOWN, CATCH, ABSORB THE FORCE
Cue Set 2: READY, REACH, GRAB, PULL

Suggested Activities for Reinforcing the Components

In the learning process, it is essential that students know how a skill is supposed to look, what its component parts are, and how to perform each individual component correctly. In the preceding section, we furnished pictures and descriptions of the catch, divided it into its component parts, and provided possible cue words. In addition to the material in chapter 3 that reinforces the concepts for all locomotor and manipulative skills, the following section provides specific activities for reinforcing the components unique to the catch.

Show Off

Objective: To provide opportunities for students to demonstrate the components of the catch

Equipment: One cone and one ball per student, music, tape player. Cones should be of varying heights.

Activity:

1. Scatter cones around the gymnasium. Place a ball on top of each cone. Use different sizes of cones and balls.

2. Students move around the gymnasium in their own personal space while listening to the music.

3. When the music stops, the students move to the closest cone.

4. When you say the cue word "W," the students freeze in the **W** position. When you say "Reach out," the students reach to the ball, taking it off the cone. When you say "Catch" the students remove the ball from the cone. When you say "Absorb the force" the students remove the ball from the cone and pull it toward the body. (Cues may be given in any order.)

5. When the music starts, the students replace the ball on the top of the cones and begin moving.

6. The next time the music stops, the students must go to a different size cone.

7. Continue this activity using each component part.

Extensions:

1. Use the same activity without the music.

2. Create your own stop signal—clapping your hands twice and raising your arms above your head, using a musical instrument, etc.

3. Students have partners and on the signal both go to the same cone. One student takes the ball off the cone and becomes the "holder." The holder tells the catcher which component to demonstrate and then tosses the ball to the catcher. The ball can be held at different levels to practice the catch both above and below the waist. If the component part to be demonstrated is the reach, the catcher stands close enough to be able to take the ball out of the holder's hands.

Towel Catchers

Objective: To reinforce the concept of absorbing the force of the object being caught by using a towel

Equipment: A towel for each set of partners and an object to be caught (e.g., beach ball, balloon, beanbag, playground ball, etc.)

Activity:

1. Students form groups of four (two sets of partners).

2. Partners hold a towel stretched between them so it can be used to catch an object (ball).

3. On your signal, one set of partners throws the ball to the other set of partners who try to catch it in the towel before it touches the floor.

4. The ball can be thrown either with the hands or with the towel.

Extensions:

1. Using two or three beach balls, perform the action as a whole group activity with the students scattered throughout the play area.

2. Put up a volleyball net and divide the students into two even groups. Using two or three beach balls, have the students throw and catch the balls over the net using only the towels.

Partner Skill Check

Objective: To allow partners to assess each other's progress while learning to catch correctly

Equipment: Partner skill check sheets, pencils, and one ball for each set of partners. If the students cannot read or do not speak English, the picture version of the partner skill check sheet may be useful.

Activity:

1. One partner observes the other to see if she has the correct form for the **W** position.

2. If the **W** position is correct, then the partner places a *Y* in the first box. If the **W** position is not correct, she places an *N* in the first box. Nonreaders can put a smiling face if the **W** position is correct or a sad face if the **W** position is not correct.

3. This evaluation continues until each of the components has been assessed five times.

4. A partner skill check sheet is used for each student.

Extensions:

1. You can use the partner skill check sheet to assess the skill development of each student.

2. You can send partner skill check sheets home with report cards or as individual skills develop.

Partner Skill Check   Skill: **Catch—Above the Waist**

Catcher's name: _____ Watcher's name: _____

1.

      1   2   3   4   5

Ready

2.

      1   2   3   4   5

Step and reach

3.

      1   2   3   4   5

**Fingers only—
thumbs touch**

4.

      1   2   3   4   5

Give

Partner Skill Check   Skill: **Catch—Below the Waist**

Catcher's name: _____   Watcher's name: _____

1.   1   2   3   4   5

Ready

2.   1   2   3   4   5

Step and reach

3.   1   2   3   4   5

**Fingers only—
pinkies touch**

4.   1   2   3   4   5

Give

Partner Skill Check

Skill: **Catch**

Catcher's name: _____   Watcher's name:_____

Watch your partner and mark each component of the skill. Let your partner do the skill 5 times. Each time your partner does it right, mark a **Y** in the box. If your partner doesn't do it right, mark an **N** in the box.

START   **TRIALS**

Ready position

   1. Eyes on target
   2. Knees bent
   3. Feet shoulder-width apart
   4. Object in front of body

   ☐ 1   ☐ 2   ☐ 3   ☐ 4   ☐ 5

ACTION

Step and reach

   1. Step toward the thrower

   ☐ 1   ☐ 2   ☐ 3   ☐ 4   ☐ 5

   2. Arms extend to meet the ball

   ☐ 1   ☐ 2   ☐ 3   ☐ 4   ☐ 5

Fingers only

   3. Use W or V finger position

   ☐ 1   ☐ 2   ☐ 3   ☐ 4   ☐ 5

   4. Ball not trapped against body

   ☐ 1   ☐ 2   ☐ 3   ☐ 4   ☐ 5

STOP

Give

   1. Absorb the force of the object by bringing the arms back to the body

   ☐ 1   ☐ 2   ☐ 3   ☐ 4   ☐ 5

Success Builders

The success builder activities allow the teacher to address individual needs. If students need additional help on individual component parts, the activities listed below will help reinforce correct performance.

Objective: To allow partners to improve areas of deficiency as assessed by the partner skill check. It also allows the teacher to address individual needs.

Equipment: See individual stations. We suggest using an unbreakable mirror and a poster of each component of the catch at each station. The mirror is particularly helpful in these activities because it allows the child to see what she is doing. The easiest way to make the posters would be to photocopy the drawings from this book. Use an opaque projector to enlarge them. Laminating the posters will ensure their use for many years.

Activity:

1. Set up a station for each of the four components in the teaching area with a description or a picture of the specific component posted at the corresponding station.

2. Stations:

Ready

—facing target, feet shoulder-width apart, knees bent, eyes on approaching object, hands held in front of body (elbows near sides and bent) with thumbs together. To catch throws below the waist, hands are held in front of the body (elbows near sides and bent) with little (pinkie) fingers together.

Equipment: Component poster, mirror (if available), and partner evaluations

Activity: The student assumes the ready position. The partner checks to see if her position matches the poster. The student refers to the mirror for help. The student then walks around and on a signal from her partner assumes the ready position again. Once the student can successfully demonstrate to the partner a good ready position, the partners may return to practicing the entire skill.

Step and Reach

—as the ball is released, step toward the thrower and extend the arms and hands to meet the ball.

Equipment: Component poster, mirror (if available), 28-inch cone or adjustable batting tee, tennis ball, and partner evaluations

Activity: Place a tennis ball on top of a cone or tee. Have the student stand behind the cone. There should be enough room to allow the student to step and fully extend his arms to pick the ball off the cone/tee. To begin, the student assumes the ready position. On a signal from his partner, the student steps forward toward the cone, extends his arms toward the ball, and removes the ball from the cone/tee. The student refers to the mirror for help. Once the student can successfully demonstrate to the partner a good step and reach, the partners may return to practicing the entire skill.

Fingers Only

—use only fingers and thumbs to catch the object. The ball should not be trapped against the body.

Equipment: Component poster, mirror (if available), balloon or beach ball, and partner evaluations

Activity: Have the partner toss the balloon or beach ball up into the air. The catcher must move to the balloon/ball and grasp it with his fingers. Partners should do this several times making sure that the catcher is using the fingers and not the palm or chest when catching. The student refers to the mirror for help. Once the student can successfully demonstrate the ability to catch the balloon/ball using the fingers, the partners may return to practicing the entire skill.

Give

—absorb the force of the object by bringing the arms back toward the body.

Equipment: Component poster, mirror (if available), different size balls (tennis ball, Nerf ball, playground ball), and partner evaluations

Activity: The student bounces the ball on the floor and catches the ball as it comes back down. Stress the idea of giving with the ball as if catching an egg. Once the student can successfully "give" with the ball, have him bounce the ball off the wall and give with the catch. To enhance the practice, have the student use different size balls along with different amounts of force. The student refers to the mirror for help. Once the student can successfully demonstrate the ability to give while catching the ball, the partners may return to practicing the entire skill.

Suggested Culminating Activities to Reinforce the Entire Skill

Individual Activities

Party Time

Objective: To provide all students the opportunity to practice the catch by themselves

Equipment: Nine-inch balloon or small beach ball for each student

Activity:

1. Create different movement challenges for the students to try with the balloon or ball. All catches should be made using the fingers and thumbs of both hands. Emphasize the catch skill components while the students are performing these activities.

2. Challenges can include:
   - Catch the balloon at a high level (medium, low).
   - Throw the balloon forward and run to get under it to catch it.
   - Toss/hit the balloon to a high level and clap before catching it (or spin, sit then stand up, hit the bottom of the foot with the hand, twiddle the thumbs, slap the knees, etc.)
   - Bounce the balloon off a body part and catch it.
3. Student-generated challenges can also be used to practice the catch.

Extensions:

1. Try all of the above challenges using a beach ball, soft rubber ball, rubber chicken, or water balloon if outside.
2. Have students count the number of correct catches they are able to make in a set number of throws or a specified amount of time.
3. Have students use a playground ball and bounce it off the floor before catching it.
4. Put a six-inch ball inside a stocking and have the students bounce the ball onto the floor and catch it with two hands as it bounces up. They should try catching the stocking instead of the ball.

Hanging Around

Objective: To practice catching a ball as it swings toward you

Equipment: Rope, two game standards, old stockings or plastic grocery bags, and one six-inch ball or playground ball per student. Suspend a rope about six to seven feet off of the floor between two game standards. Attach to the rope the old stockings with six-inch balls placed in the toe, or plastic grocery bags with playground balls inside. You will need one ball per student (see figure).

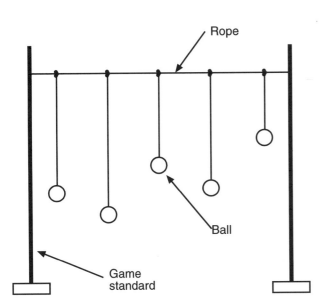

Rope

Ball

Game standard

Activity: This activity can be done with an entire class or as a station with a smaller group of students.

1. Have the student push the ball away from her so the ball swings away but does not go over the top of the rope.
2. The student catches the ball as it swings back.
3. The ball can be suspended at shoulder or waist height. This can provide practice for both an above-the-waist and below-the-waist catch.

Extensions:

1. Using the six-inch balls inside the stockings, have the student bounce the suspended ball onto the floor and catch it as it bounces back. For this activity the ball must be suspended at waist level.
2. Students are paired and stand on opposite sides of the rope, swinging the ball back and forth to each other. See the Swing Catch activity on page 126.

Partner Activities

Challenges

Objective: To practice the catch in a variety of situations

Equipment: One Nerf ball, soft rubber ball, or playground ball per pair of students and laminated challenge cards

Activity:

1. Students draw a challenge card.

2. Students perform the task described on the card.

3. Possible challenges could include:

   - Bounce the ball to your partner so he can catch it.

   - Throw the ball up in the air for your partner to catch.

   - Toss or bounce the ball to one side or the other of your partner so she must move before catching the ball.

   - Throw the ball to your partner at different levels.

Extensions:

1. Have the pairs keep track of their number of correct catches and keep a total for the class. In a follow-up lesson challenge the class to increase the total number of correct catches.

2. Place multicolored targets on a wall or in the play area and have the partner tell the catcher which target to hit. The ball must hit the target, then bounce on the floor to be caught.

3. Set up game poles or volleyball standards and tie a rope between them. Suspend hula hoops from the rope and challenge the students to throw the ball through the hoops allowing their partners to catch the ball on the other side. Every time the ball is caught, the partners earn one point.

Swing Catch

Objective: To practice catching a ball as it swings toward you

Equipment: Three volleyball standards, two ropes, and one stocking with a tennis ball inside per pair of students

Activity:

1. Tie the stocking with the tennis ball inside to the bottom of the net (or rope).

2. Partners stand on opposite sides of the rope.

3. One partner pushes the ball away so that it swings toward the catcher but does not go over the top of the rope.

4. The other partner catches the ball

5. The activity continues with partners alternating pushing and catching the ball.

Extensions:

1. Release the ball using different amounts of force.

2. Use different size balls in the stockings.

3. Have the pairs keep track of their number of correct catches and keep a total for the class. In a follow-up lesson challenge the class to increase the total number of correct catches.

Surprise Catch

Objective: To practice catching the ball at a variety of levels

Equipment: Game standards, volleyball net, one soft rubber ball or softball-size yarn ball for each set of partners

Activity:

1. Set up the volleyball net with the top of the net approximately six feet off the floor.

2. Have the partners throw the ball over or under the net to each other. (Some nets have very large spaces between the net threads. If this is the case, children may be challenged to throw THROUGH the nets.)

3. The partner on the other side of the net must try to catch the ball using the correct form (above-the-waist or below-the-waist catch).

4. Have the partners keep track of their number of correct catches.

Extensions:

1. To increase the challenge, students will make a "net" with two 28-inch or larger cones and a rope by taping (use duct tape) the rope across the top of the cones and spreading the cones apart. The ball is tossed either over or under the "net" to the partner. The partner must try to catch the ball using the correct form.

2. Place sheets (or a parachute) over a volleyball net so partners cannot see the toss coming over or under the net. Partners must tell each other before they throw the ball. (Yarn balls or Nerf balls must be used.)

3. Stand a folding mat (4-, 5-, or 6-feet wide) on its side to create a wall. Have the partners toss the ball over the mat.

4. Have partners keep track of their number of correct catches and keep a total for the class. In a follow-up lesson challenge the class to increase the total number of correct catches.

Partner Pass

Objective: To improve students' catching skills while working with a partner

Equipment: Two playground balls per pair of students

Activity:

1. Partners pass a ball back and forth using a chest pass (see chapter 7).

2. After the chest pass can be successfully performed, the students begin using a bounce pass to pass the ball back and forth.

3. After the students are able to both bounce and chest pass successfully, they each select the type of pass they will perform. Player A may use *only* the chest pass, while Player B may use *only* the bounce pass.

4. On the start signal (a three-part signal is best, e.g., ready, set, go), Player A chest passes the ball to Player B at the same time that Player B bounce passes the ball to Player A.

5. Repeat several times using the start signal each time the passes are attempted.

Extensions:

1. Have the partners exchange passes so that the bounce passer now practices the chest pass and the previous chest passer performs the bounce pass.

2. Have the students try the activity without using any verbal communication.

3. Give the students balls of different sizes to pass to each other.

Three Ball Juggle

Objective: To control three balls bouncing alternately between partners

Equipment: Three playground balls

Activity:

1. Students work in pairs.

2. Player A starts with two playground balls (ball 1 and ball 3), and Player B starts with one playground ball (ball 2).

3. Player A starts the juggle by using one bounce to get ball 1 to Player B. Player B must use one bounce to get ball 2 to Player A before catching ball 1, bounced from Player A.

4. Once the juggle has been started, each partner will have only one ball at a time in their hands (see figure).

Extensions:

1. Once the partners have mastered the three ball juggle, have them try four or five playground balls.

2. Have partners try playing with three or more balls of different sizes.

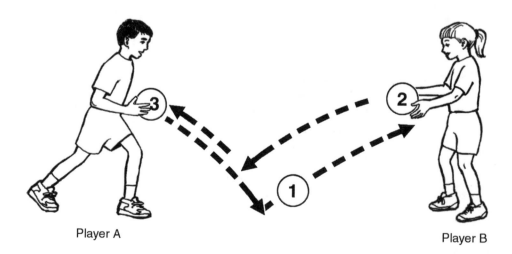

Player A   Player B

Wall Ball

Objective: To improve catching and throwing skills while working with a partner

Equipment: One ball (playground or volleyball) per student pair

Activity:

1. Partners stand at least 15 feet from the wall.

2. One partner throws the ball against the wall at least 10 feet high.

3. The other partner has to catch the ball after it comes off the wall but before it hits the ground.

4. When the partner has caught the ball, she must throw the ball back to the wall from the place where it was caught.

5. Partners count how many successful catches they have in a row.

Extensions:

1. Allow the ball to bounce once before it is caught.

2. Place a target on the wall and challenge the partners to hit it.

Group Activities

Volcano

Objective: To catch the balls on the outside of the circle of mats before they hit the ground

Equipment: Four folding mats and one yarn or Nerf ball per student

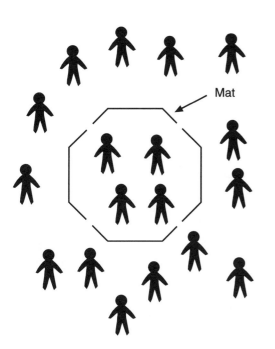

Mat

Activity:

1. Stand the folding mats on their sides to form the "volcano" (circle).

2. Place four students inside the volcano.

3. Place the other students outside the volcano (see figure).

4. On the signal, all outside students throw their lava rocks (balls) into the volcano.

5. The students inside the volcano throw the lava rocks out.

6. The students on the outside of the volcano count how many lava rocks they catch with their hands.

Extensions:

1. Use balloons or beach balls for the lava rocks.

2. Designate a "special" ball that when caught enables that person to switch places with a player inside the volcano (this is done on a rotating basis).

Cycle/Recycle

Objective: To catch a thrown ball before it hits the floor

Equipment: Two volleyball standards, one volleyball net, and one yarn ball per student

Activity:

1. Divide the class in half.
2. Place the groups on either side of the net.
3. On the start signal, everyone throws their yarn balls over the net.
4. Students must catch the balls with their hands only.
5. Students count the number of balls they caught.

Extensions:

1. Students can throw their balls through or under the net to be caught on the other side.
2. Every time a student catches the ball with hands only, that student plus the student that threw the ball switch sides by going around the net to the other side.
3. Every time a student catches the ball with hands only, that student goes around the standards and becomes a member of the other group.

Adapted, by permission, from J.A. Wessell, PhD, 1974, *Project I CAN* (Northbrook, IL: Hubbard).

Catchball

Objective: To catch the ball at a variety of levels

Equipment: Sixteen 6-inch Nerf balls (10 are needed for the activity and 6 are required in the practice area) and six Frisbees

Activity:

1. Divide the class into two groups and place the groups on either half of the play area.
2. Give each group five balls to start the activity.
3. On the signal, players begin to throw or bounce the balls to the other group.
4. Students are expected to catch the ball using only their hands.
5. If the ball is dropped or not caught with the hands, the student must go to the practice area.

Practice area:

- Each group has three balls placed behind or near the side to create a practice area. Spread the balls apart and place each ball in a Frisbee so it will not roll.
- To practice, the student picks up a ball, throws it against a wall, and catches it on the rebound.
- The ball must be caught three consecutive times with the hands only before the student may return to the activity.

Extensions:

1. While students are playing, observe their skill performance. Instruct any student having trouble catching correctly to go to the practice area and work with you. The practice area is a common area for both groups.

2. Any student who has not caught a ball within a 30-second time period must go to the practice area (for a predetermined amount of time).

Switcharoo

Objective: To catch a thrown ball in an effort to get the entire group on the same side of the play area

Equipment: One to four Nerf balls (eight inches in diameter). The number will vary based on the skill level of the students.

Activity:

1. Divide the class into two groups and place them on opposite sides of a divided play area.

2. Give each group an equal number of balls to start the activity.

3. On the start signal, players roll (or throw) the balls and try to hit the feet/legs of the opposing players.

4. If a player is hit, she moves to the other group's side. That player is now a member of that group. When a player changes sides, she may not carry a ball to the opponent's side.

5. When all players are on the same side, the activity is restarted.

Extensions:

1. While the students are playing, ensure that the catch is being performed correctly. Instruct any student having trouble catching correctly to go to a practice area and work with a partner or designated teacher assistant.

2. Put up cones or bowling pins across the end lines of the play area. Once all the cones for a group have been knocked over, a new activity is started.

Star Pass

Objective: To improve catching proficiency while working in a group

Equipment: One less ball than the number of students in a group

Activity:

1. Students form a circle of five or more members with one student holding a playground ball.

2. The player with the ball must toss it to another player that is not standing beside him while saying that player's name.

3. The player receiving the ball must toss it to another player that is not standing beside him while saying that player's name.

4. This rotation continues until the ball gets back to the first player to toss the ball.

5. Once the rotation is successfully completed twice, first player adds another ball.

6. After two more successfully completed rotations, first player adds another ball. This continues until the number of balls equals one less than the number of players.

Triangle Pass

Objective: To improve catching proficiency while working in a group

Equipment: Two playground balls per group of three students

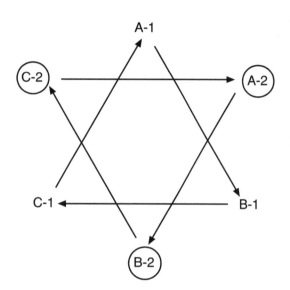

Activity:

1. Students form a triangle with Players A and B holding playground balls.

2. Player A bounce passes to Player B as Player B bounce passes to Player C.

3. Students continue the passing rotation.

Extensions:

1. Students may use a chest pass instead of a bounce pass.

2. It is possible to employ two overlapping triangles. It is important that the players within each triangle work ONLY with their group. Group 1 players bounce pass the balls ONLY to other members of Group 1. Group 2 players chest pass the balls ONLY to members of Group 2 (see figure).

Create Your Own Activity

Objective: To allow students to create their own catching activities

Equipment: One piece of paper and pencil per group and a predetermined list of equipment you will allow the students to use in their activities (e.g., cones, jump ropes, Nerf balls, beach balls, yarn balls, softballs, tennis balls, etc.)

Activity:

1. Form groups with two to five students in each. You may select the groups or the students may form their own.

2. Students create their own activity using the catch as the basic skill. Students are required to have rules that promote correct performance of the skill, include all players, and address all safety concerns.

3. The groups write their individual names, the rules of the activity, and the equipment needed on their paper and then show the activity to you.

4. Upon approval of the activity, the students are allowed to check out the necessary equipment and begin playing.

5. You must approve all changes to the activity.

Extensions:

1. One group may teach the activity it designed to another group.

2. Selected groups may teach their activities to the entire class.

Catch Troubleshooting Chart

IF YOU SEE	THEN TRY THIS
1. Eyes not on the target	• Have the student's partner hold a ball while moving it through different levels at different speeds. The student tracks the ball with her eyes. • The student hits a balloon up with her hands and tracks the movement of the balloon with her eyes. • Use the Color Targets activity from chapter 5 (see page 105) as a station.
2. Body not in line with the oncoming object	• The partner tosses balloon, beach ball, or Nerf ball into the air toward his partner. The receiving partner allows the object to hit his chest. Hands are out to the side—no catching. • The receiver moves in the direction the partner points. The partner then adds the object.
3. Student not extending arms toward the ball	• Partners stand about arm's-length apart. The throwing partner extends her arms and holds the ball out. The receiving partner steps and extends her arms to take the ball. • Use a balloon or beach ball to provide more time for the receiver to reach out and catch the object.
4. Hands not in the catching position	• The throwing partner holds a ball and moves it to different levels. The catching partner must move his hands in response to the ball position. (The ball is not thrown.) • The throwing partner tosses the beach ball at different levels. Watch for hand positions.
5. Student not giving with the ball	• Elephant catch—As the receiving partner catches the ball, she pretends the ball is heavy like an elephant and absorbs the force. • Water balloon toss (outside)—Have the student toss a water balloon to her partner and the partner try to catch the balloon so it does not break. Stress the need to GIVE with the balloon.
6. Student trapping the ball against the body	• Skunk ball—The student tosses the ball to his partner. If the ball hits the arms and/or chest as it is caught, the catcher has been sprayed by a skunk (stinker). Ask the class if there are any stinkers. • Detective—Have the student put baby powder on his hands before catching the ball. The receiving partner tries to catch the ball so he leaves only his fingerprints on the ball.

Summary

The skill of catching is essential for most games and sports. A catch cannot occur without a thrown object, which is why the catch should be taught simultaneously with the throw. Since these skills are so essential to later games and sports play, they should be introduced in kindergarten, incorporated into the activities you teach, and reviewed often. With proper instruction and appropriate equipment, children can master throwing and catching by the fourth grade.

The catching skills learned in this chapter will greatly assist your students with the next section, passing. Again, proper instruction, appropriate use of force when passing, and safe equipment will enhance student learning of these important skills.

Catch Lesson Plan (First Lesson)

Age group: Early primary

Focus: Catching

Subfocus: Reaching forward to catch the ball

Objectives: To step and reach forward to catch a balloon (and later a playground ball) on four out of five attempts (**CUE:** "Reach"), and to catch a balloon (and later a playground ball) with fingers and thumbs only on four out of five attempts (**CUE:** "Use your fingers").

Materials/Equipment: One balloon, one playground ball, and one beanbag for each child

Organization/Management: Students are in personal space for warm-up, instruction, and practice. Review movement concepts during warm-up.

Warm-up:

Today we're going to warm up with music again. When the music starts, I would like you to move in general space. When the music stops, you will freeze in your own personal space. What are some of the safety ideas we need to remember when moving in general space? **(Watch where you're going. Keep space between each person.)** (Begin music.)

Watch for students moving safely.

Stop the music and remind the children about moving safely again. Restart the music and add variations to the movement.

Can you walk at a high level? A medium level? A low level? Can you move in a zigzag pathway? A curvy pathway? A straight pathway? Can you move with heavy force? Light force? Can you find a way to move where you are going sideways? Backwards? Can you move at a slow speed? A medium speed? A fast speed? Can you move at a low level and a medium speed?

Observe children for problem areas with each of the movement concepts and provide instruction and corrections as needed.

Formation:

Students find personal space in the gymnasium and face you.

Introduction:

Today we are going to work on catching. To catch properly, we need to really reach to catch the ball. Stand up in your personal space. Show me how you reach forward. Now reach high. Reach to one side. Reach to the other side. Pretend you are reaching to catch a butterfly (or a firefly). Notice that you are stepping when you catch and you are reaching your arms out. This is very important if you want to be a good catcher.

I will give each of you a balloon. You will sit in your space with the balloon in your lap while I finish passing out the balloons. When I say GO, I would like you to stand up in your personal space, hit the balloon into the air, and catch it. Remember to keep your personal space. GO.

Focus on students staying in their own personal space.

FREEZE. Please sit down and place the balloons in your lap. When you were catching your balloon, did you have to reach to catch it? **(Yes.)** *This time, just before you catch your balloon, I want you to say the word "reach." GO.*

Watch students reaching (and saying "reach") as they catch. Be sure to also monitor proper use of personal space.

FREEZE. Please sit down and place the balloon in your lap. I watched each of you very carefully when you were catching. I saw all of you reaching. That's terrific. What part of your body did you use to catch the balloon? (Students usually respond, **"hands!"**). *Not just your hands. You really catch with... your FINGERS. Excellent. When we use our fingers and thumbs to catch, we have 10 chances to catch or 10 things working to help us catch. It is much better to use your fingers and thumbs than just your arms. When you use only your arms, you have only two chances to catch—10 is much better.*

This time, when I say GO, I'd like you to hit the balloon into the air and say the word "reach" as you reach and the word "fingers" when you catch it. Raise your hand if you think you can do that. Great. GO.

Watch students reaching (and saying "reach") and using fingers (and saying "fingers") as they catch. Be sure to also monitor proper use of personal space.

FREEZE. Please sit down and place the balloon in your lap. You did a wonderful job keeping your personal space, reaching for the balloon, and using just your fingers to catch. Balloons are pretty easy to catch. Why? **(They move slowly.)** *That's right. Raise your hand if you are ready to try something a little harder. I knew you were.*

Students return balloons to the storage bin and select a playground ball. When this is accomplished, each child finds a personal space on the floor.

When we catch a ball, we use the same skills as we use with a balloon. What were the two things we concentrated on with the balloons? **(Reaching and using our fingers.)** *That's right. When I say "GO," I would like you to stand up in your personal space, drop the ball, and catch it (demonstrate several times). Make sure you reach and use your fingers. It might help if you say those words out loud. GO.*

Observe students for reaching and using fingers.

FREEZE. Sit on the floor with the ball in your lap. This time, when I walk around the gymnasium, I will be looking for good reachers and good finger users. If you are reaching and using your fingers, I will let you go to the wall and bounce your ball against the wall. This will give you a little different way to catch. But be careful to use those 10 fingers to catch with and not your arms. GO.

Invite students who are performing the skill correctly to bounce the ball against the wall. Again, monitor students closely to make sure they are NOT catching in their outstretched arms but are actually using their fingers and thumbs.

After several minutes of successful practice, children exchange playground balls for beanbags. Each student finds his personal space and balances the beanbag on his head.

This time we will combine tossing with catching. When I say GO, I would like you to toss the beanbag at a medium level (demonstrate this) and catch it by reaching and using your fingers. If I see you tossing at a medium level, reaching, and using your fingers, I may ask you to try a high level. But right now, everyone will toss at a medium level. If you understand, clap once. GO.

Observe students for proper toss, reaching, and use of fingers to catch beanbags. Invite students who are performing well to try tossing the beanbags at a higher level.

At the end of practice, children return beanbags to the storage bin and line up for their teacher.

Closure:

Students are lined up to leave.

Girls and boys, who can tell me some things I must remember when catching? **(Reach and use your fingers.)** *Good.*

Watch me catch and use just my arms (demonstrate). What's wrong with that? That's right, I only have two chances to catch rather than ten. Excellent! You did very well and we will continue catching next time.

chapter 7

Passing

A wide variety of sports require accurate passes to successfully play the game. These sports range from football, water polo, and team handball, which use the one-handed pass, to basketball and soccer, which use the two-handed overhead pass.

In this chapter, we will focus on the bounce pass and the chest pass found in basketball. While these are distinct skills, they are very similar. The unique features of each of these skills will be addressed in individual descriptions, components, cues, a few very specific activities, partner skill check sheets, and success builder activities.

All of the culminating activities, however, are easily adapted for either the chest pass or the bounce pass. Moreover, all of the activities described in this chapter will pertain to passing in general, but specific adaptations will be included if needed.

Bounce Pass

While we often think of the bounce pass strictly in the sport of basketball, variations of this skill are found on any playground. While children quickly grasp the concept of bouncing a ball to a partner, they often push the ball *down* rather than *away*. Connecting the movement concepts of near and far with the bounce pass will assist in its mastery. While the NASPE Outcomes Project does not address this skill, it has been our experience that children should be able to perform the bounce pass by the second grade. Therefore, instruction in this essential manipulative skill should begin early in the primary grades.

Basic Components

Ready Position
—facing target, feet shoulder-width apart, knees bent, eyes on target, ball held with thumbs together and fingers on the sides of the ball. Hold the ball close to the body at chest level.

Step and Push
—step forward with one foot while extending arms FORWARD and DOWNWARD and releasing the ball so that it bounces closer to the target than to the passer.

Follow Through
—after the ball is released, hands are turned so that palms are facing away from each other with the thumbs pointing downward. There is a wrist snap with this action.

Cue Words

The cue words you select for each phase of the skill will depend on the age of the students you are teaching and your areas of emphasis. We have listed, in usable sets, some of the cue words we have used to teach the bounce pass. You may use each set individually or mix and match the cue words as needed. We have found that it is beneficial to have the students say the cue words out loud as they practice the skill.

READY—facing target, feet shoulder-width apart, knees bent, eyes on target, ball held with thumbs together and fingers on the side of the ball. Hold the ball close to the body at chest level.

STEP AND PUSH—step forward with one foot while extending the arms and releasing the ball toward the target.

PUSH—hold the ball near the body at chest level with the thumbs together and fingers on the side of the ball. Push the ball from the chest.

FOLLOW THROUGH and THUMBS DOWN—after ball is released, hands are turned so that palms are facing away from each other with the thumbs pointing downward. There is a wrist snap with this action.

AWAY—step forward with one foot while extending arms and releasing the ball toward the target. After the ball is released, hands are turned so that palms are facing away from each other with the thumbs pointing downward. There is a wrist snap with this action.

Cue Set 1: READY, STEP AND PUSH, FOLLOW THROUGH

Cue Set 2: READY, STEP AND PUSH, THUMBS DOWN

Cue Set 3: PUSH, AWAY

Suggested Activities for Reinforcing the Components of the Bounce Pass

In the learning process, it is essential that students know how a skill looks, what its component parts are, and how to perform each individual component correctly. In the preceding section, we furnished pictures and descriptions of the bounce pass, divided it into its component parts, and provided possible cue words. In addition to the material in chapter 3 that reinforces the concepts for all locomotor and manipulative skills, the following section provides specific activities for reinforcing the components unique to the bounce pass.

Partner Skill Check

Objective: To allow partners to assess each other's progress learning the skill

Equipment: Partner skill check sheets, pencils, and one ball for each set of partners. If the students cannot read or do not speak English, the picture version of the partner skill check sheet may be useful.

Activity:

1. One partner observes the other to see if she has the correct form for the ready position.

2. If the ready position is correct, then the partner places a *Y* in the first box. If the ready position is not correct, she places an *N* in the first box. Non-readers can put a smiling face if the ready position is correct or a sad face if the ready position is not correct.

3. This evaluation continues until each of the components has been assessed five times.

4. A partner skill check sheet is used for each student.

Extensions:

1. You may use the partner skill check sheet to assess the skill development of each student.

2. You may send partner skill check sheets home with report cards or as individual skills develop.

Partner Skill Check

Skill: **Bounce Pass**

Passer's name: _____   Watcher's name: _____

1.

1   2   3   4   5

Ready

2.

1   2   3   4   5

Step

3.

1   2   3   4   5

Push

4.

1   2   3   4   5

Thumbs down

Partner Skill Check

Skill: **Bounce Pass**

Passer's name: _____   Watcher's name: _____

Watch your partner and mark each component of the skill. Let your partner do the skill 5 times. Each time your partner does it right, mark a **Y** in the box. If your partner doesn't do it right, mark an **N** in the box.

START

TRIALS

Ready position

1. Eyes facing target
2. Knees bent
3. Feet shoulder-width apart
4. Object held in front of body

1	2	3	4	5

ACTION

Step

1. Step forward with one foot

1	2	3	4	5

2. Bellybutton facing target

1	2	3	4	5

Push

3. Arms extended

1	2	3	4	5

4. Push the ball out and downward

1	2	3	4	5

STOP

Follow through

1. Thumbs point down

1	2	3	4	5

© A.Y. Colvin, N.J. Markos, and P.J. Walker, 2000, *Teaching the Nuts and Bolts of Physical Education* (Champaign, IL: Human Kinetics).

Success Builders

The success builder activities allow you to address individual needs. If students need additional help on individual component parts, the activities listed below will help reinforce correct performance.

Objective: To improve areas of deficiency as assessed by the partner skill check

Equipment: See individual stations. We suggest using an unbreakable mirror and a poster of each component of the bounce pass at each station. The mirror is particularly helpful in these activities because it allows the child to see what she is doing. The easiest way to make the posters would be to photocopy the drawings from this book. Use an opaque projector to enlarge them. Laminating the posters will ensure their use for many years.

Activity:

1. Set up a station for each of the three components in the teaching area with a description or a picture of the specific component posted at the corresponding station.

2. Stations:

Ready

—facing target, feet shoulder-width apart, knees bent, eyes on target, ball held with thumbs together and fingers on the side of the ball. Hold the ball at chest level.

Equipment: Component poster, mirror (if available), and partner evaluations

Activity: The student assumes the ready position. The partner checks to see if her position matches the poster. The student refers to the mirror for help. The student then walks around and on a signal from her partner assumes the ready position again. Once the student can successfully demonstrate proper position for holding the ball (with thumbs behind the ball and at chest level), the partners may return to practicing the entire skill.

Step and Push

—step forward with one foot while extending arms *forward* and *downward* and releasing the ball so that it bounces closer to the target than to the passer.

Equipment: Mirror, poster, tape (floor or masking) or circle target on the floor, partner evaluations, and rope suspended between two chairs

Activity 1: The student demonstrates a step forward and push toward a target on the floor. The student should push his arms and hands toward the marked target. The partner checks to see if his position matches the poster. The student refers to the mirror for help. Once the student can successfully demonstrate to the partner a good step/push, the partners may return to practicing the entire skill.

Activity 2: The student attempts to bounce pass the ball to her partner by passing it under the rope.

Activity 3: The student attempts to see how far apart he can stand from his partner and still bounce pass the ball under the rope and have his partner catch it before it bounces more than once.

Follow Through

—after ball is released, hands are turned so that palms are facing away from each other with the thumbs pointing downward. There is a wrist snap with this action.

Equipment: Mirror, poster, opaque projector (or some means of shining light onto the student), and partner evaluations

Activity: The student demonstrates the follow-through in front of the mirror or light. The partner looks for the wrist snap as the student demonstrates this component. The partner checks to see if her position matches the poster. The student refers to the mirror for help. Once the student can successfully demonstrate to the partner a good follow-through, the partners may return to practicing the entire skill.

Suggested Culminating Activities to Reinforce the Entire Bounce Pass Skill

Partner Activities

Not On My Side

Objective: To develop the bounce pass while trying to push an object across a partner's line

Equipment: One ball (playground ball, lightweight rubber ball, etc.), one dome cone (half sphere cone-type equipment) or other object that will slide when hit with a ball, and a line between the two partners (court markings, masking tape, etc.)

Activity:

1. Partners stand on either side of the dividing line with the center of the dome cone placed on the line.

2. Each partner performs a bounce pass trying to hit the dome cone and push it across the line onto the partner's side. The object may only be moved with a bounce pass.

3. If one of the partners uses any other pass to move the dome cone, it is returned to the starting position and the activity is restarted.

4. The activity continues until the dome cone has been pushed totally across the dividing line.

5. Once one of the partners has pushed the dome cone across the dividing line, a new activity is started.

Extensions:

1. Use empty cereal boxes, paper plates, flat playground balls, hula hoops, etc., instead of dome cones.

2. Increase the challenge by using a hula hoop and require that the student specify where on the hoop the ball should hit (e.g., outside edge of the hoop, inside edge of the hoop, etc.).

Three-Ball Juggle

Objective: To control three balls bouncing alternately between partners

Equipment: Three playground balls

Activity:

1. Students find partners.

2. Player A starts with two playground balls (ball 1 and ball 3). Player B starts with one playground ball (ball 2).

3. Player A starts the juggle by using one bounce to get ball 1 to Player B. Player B must use one bounce to get ball 2 to Player A before catching ball 1, bounced from Player A.

4. Once the juggle has been started, each partner will have only one ball at a time in their hands (see figure).

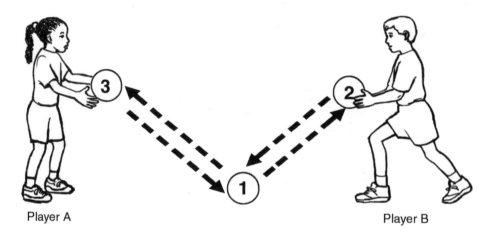

Player A   Player B

Extensions:

1. Once the partners have mastered the three-ball juggle, have them try with four or five playground balls.

2. Have partners try to "juggle" three or more balls of different sizes.

Group Activities

It's Yours, Not Mine!

Objective: To use the bounce pass to push all objects onto the opponent's side

Equipment: 8 to 10 playground balls or light rubber balls and 12 to 15 objects (hoops, dome cones, empty boxes, etc.) that can slide on the floor when hit by a ball

Activity:

1. Set up a play area with a center line and two restraining lines approximately 8 feet away from the center line.

2. Divide the class into two equal groups and place the groups behind the restraining lines facing each other.

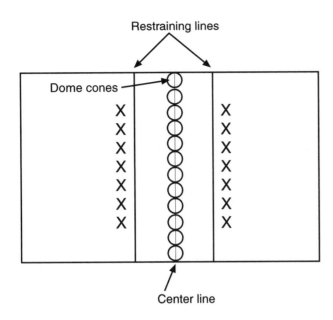

Restraining lines

Dome cones

X   X
X   X
X   X
X   X
X   X
X   X
X   X

Center line

3. Set the target objects up along the center dividing line (see figure).

4. Give each group four to five balls.

5. On the start signal, the students bounce pass the balls and try to hit the targets in the middle of the play area. The students may not cross the restraining line when they bounce pass the ball.

6. Players try to hit the targets and slide them past the opposing group's restraining line.

7. The activity is restarted when all of the targets have been pushed into one group's play area.

Extensions:

1. Use empty two-liter bottles, lightweight cones, empty cereal boxes, etc., as targets.

2. Set a time limit for the activity and count the number of targets that are hit and moved during the specified time.

Switcharoo

Objective: To use a bounce pass to tag the feet of opposing players in an effort to get all players on one side of the play area

Equipment: One to four 6- to 8-inch balls (light rubber balls work best). The number of balls will vary based on the skill level of the students.

Activity:

1. Divide the class into two groups and place them on opposite sides of a divided play area.

2. Give each group an equal number of balls to start the activity.

3. On the start signal, players pass the balls and try to hit the feet/legs of the opposing players.

4. A player must move to the other group's side when she is hit with a ball. When a player changes sides, she may not carry a ball to the opponent's side.

5. When all players are on the same side, the activity is restarted.

Extensions:

1. While the students are playing the activity, ensure that the bounce pass is being performed correctly. Instruct any student experiencing difficulty in passing correctly to go to a practice area and work with a partner or designated teacher assistant.

2. Put up cones or bowling pins within 10 feet of the center line. Once all the cones for a group have been knocked over, a new activity is started.

Cage Ball Madness

Objective: To perform a bounce pass using a playground ball to move an object across the play area

Equipment: The object may be a cage ball or any ball larger than the balls being passed. The balls being passed may be playground balls, basketballs, or volleyballs when aiming at a cage ball.

Activity:

1. Divide the class into four even groups. Each group stands along one side of a square play area. Students must stay behind their line.

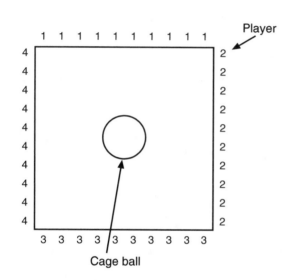

Player

Cage ball

2. Place the cage ball or large ball in the center of the play area (see figure).

3. Each group begins the activity with two or more balls.

4. On the start signal, players pass the ball and try to hit the cage ball (large ball in the center) in an effort to move it toward the other group's line.

5. Players continue to pass the ball until the cage ball crosses a group's line. Any ball (used for passing) that stays inside of the area enclosed by the four groups' lines is retrieved by the teacher.

6. Players may only touch the cage ball (large ball) with a passed ball. They may not touch it with any part of the body.

7. Once the cage ball crosses the designated line, the activity stops and the cage ball is returned to the center of the play area.

8. The activity resumes when each group has the same number of balls to pass. Be sure every player is given a chance to start with a ball.

Extensions:

1. Create two groups rather than four.

2. Try to pass a variety of balls at the cage ball in an effort to move the ball across another group's line. This may lead to discussions on which balls are better for the task (e.g., basketballs versus Nerf balls).

3. Have groups change positions either before the next round or on a signal during the activity. Be sure that if the students are to change places during the activity they understand that they may not pass a ball at the cage ball until your signal, and they may not take a ball with them as they change.

Pin Ball

Objective: To use the bounce pass to hit the opposing group's bowling pins

Equipment: Three balls and three plastic bowling pins (indicated by A and B for our purposes here) for each group. Bowling pins need to be color coded for each group (use different color tape, for example, to mark the pins).

Activity:

Restraining line

```
        |   A   |
    X   |   A>  |   X
    X   |   B>  |   X
    X   |   A>  |   X
    X   |   A>  |   X
    X   |   B>  |   X
    X   |   A>  |   X
    X   |   B   |   X
    X   |       |   X
```

1. Set up the play area with a center line and two restraining lines approximately eight feet away from the center line.

2. Divide the class into two equal groups and place the groups behind the restraining lines facing each other.

3. Set the six pins up along the center dividing line of the play area, alternating colors (see figure).

4. Give each group three balls.

5. On the start signal, the students bounce pass the balls and try to hit the opposing group's pins. The students may not cross the restraining line.

6. A pin is not considered "down" if the ball was passed from in front of the restraining line.

7. The activity is restarted when all of a group's pins have been knocked down.

Extensions:

1. If a player is hit by a passed ball, she moves to the other group (similar to Switcharoo) and continues to play.

2. Use empty two-liter bottles, lightweight cones, empty cereal boxes, etc., as targets.

Adapted, by permission, from K. Thomas, A. Lee, and J. Thomas, 2000, *Physical education for children: daily lesson plans for elementary school*, 2nd ed. (Champaign, IL: Human Kinetics).

Additional activities to work on the bounce pass can be found in the "suggested culminating activities to reinforce bounce and chest passing skills" section, which follows the chest pass section.

Bounce Pass Troubleshooting Chart

IF YOU SEE	THEN TRY THIS
1. Eyes not on the target	• Have the student pass to a target he has designed. • Use the Color Targets activity on page 154 as a station. • Place a two-liter bottle on top of a cone and have the student try to knock it off. • Use aluminum pie plates for targets.
2. Incorrect hand position on the ball	• Draw the hand positions on the ball. • Have the student put her hands in baby powder and then place them on a ball.
3. Student not stepping when passing the ball	• Have the student step on a mat or a rug as she passes the ball. • Have the student stand near a line (a rope or tape on the floor can be used). She must step over the line while passing the ball.
4. Arms not fully extended on the pass	• Have the student practice reaching out and grabbing an object placed an arm's length away from the body. • Place a suspended aluminum pie plate in front of the student and have him try to hit the pie plate with his outstretched hands.
5. Body not in proper alignment on the follow-through	• Tell the student to point her bellybutton at the target on the follow-through. We call this the power of the bellybutton. This works for many manipulative skills. • See the Success Builders activities in the text.
6. Ball not bouncing in the proper spot (hitting the ground too close or too far away from the target)	• Place a target (piece of tape or hula hoop) on the floor between the partners for them to hit. • Have the partners pass the ball under a table.

Chest Pass

Although it may appear in other sports (team handball, speedball, etc.), the chest pass is usually considered to be specific to the game of basketball. We suggest teaching the chest pass after teaching the bounce pass. The additional strength required for the chest pass makes it more challenging for young children (since the ball must be pushed out, not down). In addition, a bounce pass is easier to catch than a chest pass and will be easier to practice.

Children should use a ball that they can hold properly. A playground ball is the appropriate size for young children. If the ball is too large or too heavy, the children will get "under the ball" and throw it in an arc rather than straight.

While the NASPE Outcomes Project does not address the chest pass, we have found that students can usually master this skill in the third grade. It should be introduced when children have achieved a competent level in catching to be successful, and should be introduced early in the primary curriculum if possible.

Basic Components

Ready Position
—facing target, feet shoulder-width apart, knees bent, eyes on target, ball held with thumbs together and fingers on the sides of the ball. Hold the ball close to the body at chest level.

Step and Push
—step forward with one foot while extending arms and releasing ball toward the target.

Follow Through
—after ball is released, hands are turned so that palms are facing away from each other with the thumbs pointing downward. There is a wrist snap with this action.

Cue Words

The cue words you select for each phase of the skill will depend on the age of the students you are teaching and your areas of emphasis. We have listed, in usable sets, some of the cue words we have used to teach the chest pass. You may use each set individually or mix and match the cue words as needed. We have found that it is beneficial to have the students say the words out loud as they practice the skill.

READY—facing target, feet shoulder-width apart, knees bent, eyes on target, ball held with thumbs together and fingers on the side of the ball. Hold the ball close to the body at chest level.

PUSH—hold the ball near the body at chest level with the thumbs together and fingers on the side of the ball. Push the ball from the chest.

STEP AND PUSH—step forward with one foot while extending the arms and releasing the ball toward the target.

AWAY—step forward with one foot while extending arms and releasing the ball toward the target. After the ball is released, hands are turned so that palms are facing away from each other with the thumbs pointing downward. There is a wrist snap with this action.

FOLLOW THROUGH and THUMBS DOWN—after the ball is released, hands are turned so that palms are facing away from each other with the thumbs pointing downward. There is a wrist snap with this action.

Cue Set 1: READY, STEP AND PUSH, FOLLOW THROUGH

Cue Set 2: READY, STEP AND PUSH, THUMBS DOWN

Cue Set 3: READY, AWAY

Cue Set 4: PUSH, AWAY

Suggested Activities for Reinforcing the Components of the Chest Pass

In the learning process, it is essential that students know how a skill looks, what its component parts are, and how to perform each individual component correctly. In the preceding section, we furnished pictures and descriptions of the chest pass, divided it into its component parts, and provided possible cue words. Chapter 3 provides nine generic activities that will reinforce these concepts for the chest pass as well as all locomotor and manipulative skills. In addition to the material found in chapter 3, the following section provides specific activities for reinforcing the components unique to the chest pass.

Partner Skill Check

Objective: To allow partners to assess each other's progress learning the skill

Equipment: Partner skill check sheets, pencils, and one ball for each set of partners. If the students cannot read or do not speak English, the picture version of the partner skill check sheet may be useful.

Activity:

1. One partner observes the other to see if he has the correct form for the ready position.

2. If the ready position is correct, then the partner places a *Y* in the first box. If the ready position is not correct, he places an *N* in the first box. Non-readers can put a smiling face if the ready position is correct or a sad face if the ready position is not correct.

Partner Skill Check

Skill: **Chest Pass**

Passer's name: _____ Watcher's name: _____

1.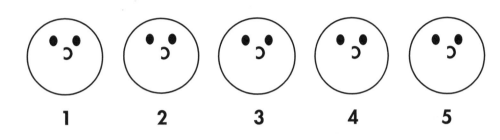

1   2   3   4   5

Ready

2.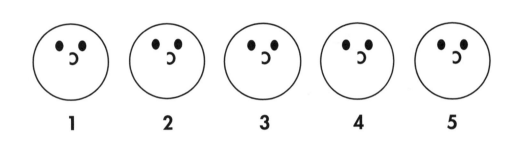

1   2   3   4   5

Step

3.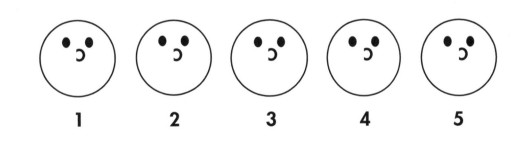

1   2   3   4   5

Push

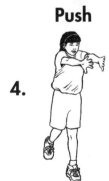

4.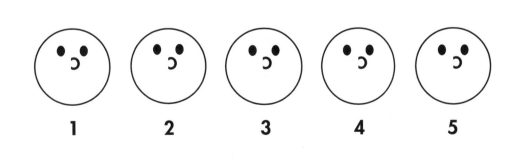

1   2   3   4   5

Thumbs down

Partner Skill Check

Skill: **Chest Pass**

Passer's name: _____ Watcher's name: _____

Watch your partner and mark each component of the skill. Let your partner do the skill 5 times. Each time your partner does it right, mark a **Y** in the box. If your partner doesn't do it right, mark an **N** in the box.

START

TRIALS

Ready position

1. Eyes facing target
2. Knees bent
3. Feet shoulder-width apart
4. Object held in front of body

☐ 1 ☐ 2 ☐ 3 ☐ 4 ☐ 5

ACTION

Step

1. Step forward with one foot

☐ 1 ☐ 2 ☐ 3 ☐ 4 ☐ 5

2. Bellybutton facing target

☐ 1 ☐ 2 ☐ 3 ☐ 4 ☐ 5

Push

3. Arms extended

☐ 1 ☐ 2 ☐ 3 ☐ 4 ☐ 5

4. Push the ball out

☐ 1 ☐ 2 ☐ 3 ☐ 4 ☐ 5

STOP

Follow through

1. Thumbs point down

☐ 1 ☐ 2 ☐ 3 ☐ 4 ☐ 5

3. This evaluation continues until each of the components has been assessed five times.

4. A partner skill check sheet is used for each student.

Extensions:

1. You can use the partner skill check sheet to assess the skill development of each student.

2. You can send partner skill check sheets home with report cards or as individual skills develop.

Success Builders

The success builder activities allow you to monitor student progress and address individual needs. If students need additional help on individual component parts, the activities listed below will help reinforce correct performance.

Objective: To improve areas of deficiency as assessed by the partner skill check

Equipment: See individual stations. We suggest using an unbreakable mirror and a poster of each component of the chest pass at each station. The mirror is particularly helpful in these activities because it allows the child to see what she is doing. The easiest way to make the posters would be to photocopy the drawings from this book. Use an opaque projector to enlarge them. Laminating the posters will ensure their use for many years.

Activity:

1. Set up a station for each of the three components in the teaching area with a description or a picture of the specific component posted at the corresponding station.

2. Stations:

Ready

—knees bent, facing target, feet shoulder-width apart, eyes on target, ball held with thumbs together and fingers on the side of the ball. Hold the ball at chest level.

Equipment: Component poster, mirror (if available), and partner evaluations

Activity: The student assumes the ready position. The partner checks to see if his position matches the poster. The student refers to the mirror for help. The student then walks around and on a signal from his partner assumes the ready position again. Once the student can successfully demonstrate to the partner a good ready position, the partners may return to practicing the entire skill.

Step and Push

—step forward with one foot while extending the arms and releasing the ball toward the target.

Equipment: Mirror, poster, tape (floor or masking) or circle target on the floor, and partner evaluations

Activity 1: The student demonstrates a step forward and push toward a target on the wall. The student should push her arms and hands toward the marked target. The partner checks to see if her position matches the poster. The student refers to the mirror for help. Once the student can successfully demonstrate to the partner a good step/push, the partners may return to practicing the entire skill.

Activity 2: Place several targets on the wall. The partner selects the target to be hit. The student steps and pushes the ball toward the appropriate target. Once the student can successfully demonstrate to the partner a good step/ push, the partners may return to practicing the entire skill.

Follow Through

—after ball is released, hands are turned so that palms are facing away from each other with the thumbs pointing downward. There is a wrist snap with this action.

Equipment: Mirror, poster, opaque projector (or some means of shining light onto the student), and partner evaluations

Activity: The student demonstrates the follow-through in front of the mirror or light. The partner looks for the wrist snap as the student demonstrates this component. The partner checks to see if her position matches the poster. The student refers to the mirror for help. Once the student can successfully demonstrate to the partner a good follow-through, the partners may return to practicing the entire skill.

Suggested Culminating Activities to Reinforce Bounce and Chest Passing Skills

Individual Activities

Color Targets

Objective: To improve passing accuracy by hitting a specific target

Equipment: Construction paper of different colors and sizes (about 8 to 12 targets of each color) taped to the floor of the gymnasium or activity area with a wall or obstacle behind the target and a ball for each student (playground ball, Nerf ball, etc.)

Activity:

1. Create a "color box" in which samples from each color of construction paper have been placed. You will need more samples than you have students.

2. Select a student to draw a sample color from the color box.

3. The sample color chosen is the color target all students must locate and try to hit with a bounce pass.

4. Students continue to pass toward the targets of the selected color until you give a stop signal.

5. The activity continues until all students have had an opportunity to draw from the color box.

Chest Pass Adaptation: Targets should be placed on the wall. Proper distance from the wall will be dictated by student ability and safety.

Extensions:

1. Instead of using different colors, students could select different shapes from the "shape box," letters from the "alphabet box," or words from the "word box."

2. Students work with partners. The partner chooses the color, shape, letter, or word that will be used for a target. The passer must then try to hit the selected target. Partners take turns selecting targets and passing. Targets may be spread throughout the activity area, and the partner may catch the pass.

3. Targets may be placed on the wall so that the student has to stand at an appropriate distance and bounce pass the ball to the floor and then to the target or chest pass the ball directly to the target.

4. Targets may be placed on the floor and wall so that the student has to stand at an appropriate distance and bounce pass the ball to the floor target and then to the wall target.

Create-A-Word

Objective: To create words by hitting letters using the pass

Equipment: One ball (Nerf ball or playground ball) per student and four complete sets of letters scattered and taped to the wall of the gymnasium or activity area. It would be advantageous to have extra copies of vowels and selected consonants (e.g., N, R, S, T). You will also need paper and markers or a chalkboard and chalk to serve as a "word bank."

Activity:

1. On your start signal, students begin to spell words by hitting letters using a pass.

2. Once a student has created a word, she goes to the word bank (paper or chalkboard) and writes the word. It will be helpful to have several word banks so students will not have to wait in line to write their words.

3. A word may be "banked" or written only once on the paper or chalkboard.

4. If a student hits a letter that cannot be used to form the word being created, she must hit the letter again to delete it.

Extensions:

1. Students work with partners. One student hits letters to spell a word while the other partner records the word and evaluates the pass. The passer may not use the letter until the pass is properly performed. When the first partner has spelled a word, the other partner is then given a turn.

2. Students work with partners. Partners are given paper and pencil to record the letters they hit and to write down the words they create. Each partner must pass and hit a vowel and two consonants until the pair has six letters to use to create words. The partners attempt to create six words using one or more of the letters they have hit. Once the partners have created six

words and written them down, they attempt to spell the words by hitting the letters with the ball. Once a word is spelled, it may be checked off the list. If the students are unable to use a letter they have hit, they must hit that letter again to delete it and select another letter.

Partner Activities

Hot Potato

Objective: To improve chest passing accuracy while passing the ball through a hoop

Equipment: One hula hoop suspended from either a basketball backboard or rim, game standards, and one ball for each set of partners

Activity:

1. Partners stand on opposite sides of the suspended hoop.

2. On your signal the partners use the chest pass to get the ball through the hoop.

3. Partners count the number of times the ball goes through the hoop during the time limit.

4. Students may only count the passes that go through the hoop and are performed correctly.

Extensions:

1. Try the activity without a time limit. This will slow the skill down to allow lesser skilled students to have some success.

2. Use two nets instead of suspended hoops. Place one at tennis height and the other at volleyball height and chest pass between the nets.

Back It Up

Objective: To develop passing skills while trying to increase the distance between partners

Equipment: One ball (playground ball, lightweight rubber ball, etc.) for each set of partners

Activity:

1. Students face each other and pass the ball back and forth once.

2. If the ball is passed and caught without difficulty, the students take one step backward and chest pass the ball back and forth again.

3. After each successful pass and catch, the partners each take a step backward.

4. This continues until either the distance between the two cannot be covered or the skill is no longer being performed correctly. When this occurs, the two return to the starting point and begin again.

Extensions:

1. Introduce the idea of measurement and have the partners place a cone (or other object) to show the farthest distance they were able to attain. They may use a tape measure to determine the exact distance. This measure-

ment can be recorded and compared to class totals, later results, or even graphed and displayed on the bulletin board.

2. If the ball is passed and caught without difficulty, the student who threw the ball takes one step backward. After each successful pass and catch, the partner who threw the ball takes a step backward. This continues until the distance between the two cannot be covered by one pass or until the pass is not caught successfully. When this occurs, the two return to the starting point and begin again.

From *Complete elementary physical education guide* by Rosalie Bryant and Eloise McLean Oliver. Copyright © 1975. Reprinted with permission of Prentice Hall Direct.

Challenges

Objective: To practice the pass in a variety of situations

Equipment: One playground ball, light rubber ball or basketball per pair of students and laminated challenge cards. Different types of challenges may require additional equipment.

Activity:

1. Students select a challenge card.

2. Students perform the task described on the card.

3. Possible challenges may include:

   • Pass the ball using hard force (light force, medium force).

   • Pass the ball toward your partner's chest.

   • Pass the ball so that it hits the wall, bounces once, and the student or his partner is able to catch it.

   • Pass the ball and hit a target (chest high) on the wall.

   • Pass the ball through a hoop held chest high by your partner or through a suspended hoop.

Extensions:

1. Place multicolored targets, hoops, cones, or buckets in the play area or on the wall (chest high) and have the partner tell the passer which target to hit.

2. Set up game poles or volleyball standards and tie a rope between them. Supend different objects from the rope and challenge the students to hit them. Possible targets include hoops, aluminum pie pans, and empty two-liter plastic bottles.

3. To create more permanent targets, you may paint them on the wall of your gymnasium. Often, tumbling mats are attached to the walls for storage. If you paint these targets on the wall behind where tumbling mats are attached, you can cover them when not in use.

4. Have the pairs keep track of their number of correct passes, and keep a total for the class. In a follow-up lesson challenge the class to increase the total number of correct passes.

Slide and Pass

Objective: To improve passing accuracy while moving

Equipment: One ball (playground ball, volleyball, or basketball) per pair of students

Activity:

1. Student partners face each other and pass the ball back and forth.

2. After the second pass, each partner slides once (in the same direction), stops, and passes again.

3. This activity is repeated for the entire length of the gymnasium.

Extensions:

1. Students pass and slide without stopping.

2. Students face each other, dribble the ball twice, and then pass to their partners. After the second pass, each partner slides once (in the same direction), stops, dribbles, and passes again. This activity is repeated for the entire length of the gymnasium.

Net Pass

Objective: To improve passing accuracy by passing a ball through a target

Equipment: Three volleyball standards, two volleyball nets, one hula hoop per pair, rope and string, and one playground ball for each pair. The nets should be placed at the regular volleyball height. Tie the hoops to the bottom of the nets.

Activity:

1. Partners stand on opposite sides of the hoop.

2. Partners must pass the ball to each other so it goes through the hoop.

3. Partners must let the ball bounce before catching it.

4. Students count the number of balls they were able to pass through the hoops.

Extensions:

1. Students total the number of passes the entire group made. These results can be recorded and later charted or graphed.

2. Each time a student passes the ball through the hoop, she takes one step back. This continues until the student can no longer pass the ball through the hoop. The student then starts over.

Group Activities

Cycle/Recycle

Objective: To practice passing accuracy in a movement setting

Equipment: Two volleyball standards, one volleyball net, and one playground ball per student. The net should be placed at regular volleyball height.

Activity:

1. Divide the class in half.

2. Place the groups on either side of the net.

3. On the start signal, everyone uses a bounce pass to pass the ball under the net.

4. Students count the number of balls they were able to pass under (or between) the net(s).

Adaptations for Chest Pass: Place a second net between the standards at tennis net height. Students chest pass the ball between the two nets.

Extensions:

1. Students total the number of passes the entire group made. These results can be recorded and later charted or graphed to show class improvement.

2. Each time a student passes the ball under (or between) the net(s), he goes around the standards and becomes a member of the other group.

Adapted, by permission, from J. A. Wessell, PhD, 1974, *Project I CAN* (Northbrook, IL: Hubbard).

Create Your Own Activity

Objective: To allow students to create their own activities to reinforce passing skills

Equipment: One piece of paper and pencil per group and a predetermined list of equipment you will allow the students to use in their activities (e.g., bowling pins, cones, ropes, playground balls, light rubber balls, etc.)

Activity:

1. Form groups with two to five students each. You may select the groups or the students may form their own.

2. Students create their own activity using the pass (either bounce or chest) as the basic skill. Students are required to have rules that encourage correct performance of the skill, include all players, and address all safety concerns.

3. The groups write their individual names, the rules of the activity, and the equipment needed on their paper, and then show the activity to you.

4. Upon approval of their activity, the students obtain their equipment and begin playing.

5. You must approve all changes to the activity.

Extensions:

1. Groups may teach their activities to other groups.

2. Groups may teach their activities to the entire class.

Triangle Pass

Objective: To improve passing proficiency while working with a group

Equipment: Two playground balls per group of three students

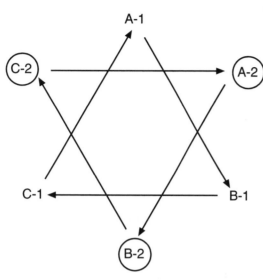

Activity:

1. Students form a triangle. Players A and B each have a playground ball.

2. Player A bounce passes her ball to Player B as he bounce passes his ball to Player C.

3. When this is accomplished, Player B bounce passes the ball to Player C as soon as Player C has passed her ball to Player A.

Extensions:

1. Chest passes may be used.

2. It is possible to employ two overlapping triangles. It is important that the players within each triangle work only with their group. Group 1 players bounce pass the balls only to other members of their group. Group 2 players chest pass the balls only to members of that group (see figure).

Star Pass

Objective: To improve passing proficiency while working with a group

Equipment: Four playground balls per group of five (or higher using odd numbers)

Activity:

1. Students form a circle with one player holding a playground ball.

2. The player with the ball bounce passes it to another player that is not standing beside her while saying that player's name.

3. The player receiving the ball passes it to another player that is not standing beside him while saying that player's name.

4. This rotation continues until the ball gets back to the first player to pass the ball.

5. Once the rotation is successfully completed twice, the first player adds another ball.

6. After two more successfully completed rotations, the first player adds another ball. This continues until the number of balls equals one less than the number of players.

Extensions:

1. Chest passes may be used.

2. A combination of bounce and chest passes may be used.

Chest Pass Troubleshooting Chart

IF YOU SEE	THEN TRY THIS
1. Eyes not on the target	• Have the student pass to a target she has designed. • Use the Color Targets activity as a station (see page 154). • Place a two-liter bottle on top of a cone and have the student try to knock it off. • Use aluminum pie plates for targets.
2. Incorrect hand position on the ball	• Draw the hand positions on the ball. • Have the student put his hands in baby powder and then place them on a ball.
3. Student not stepping when passing the ball	• Have the student step on a mat or rug as she passes the ball. • Have the student stand near a line (rope or tape on the floor can be used). She must step over the line while passing the ball.
4. Arms not fully extended on the pass	• Have the student practice reaching out and grabbing an object placed an arm's length away from the body. • Place a suspended aluminum pie plate in front of the student and have him try to hit the pie plate with his outstretched arms.
5. Body not in proper alignment on the follow-through	• Tell the student to point her bellybutton at the target on the follow-through. We call this the power of the bellybutton. This works for many manipulative skills. • See the Success Builders activities in the text.
6. Ball hitting the target at too high or too low a level.	• Suspend two ropes between two game standards. Place the ropes at least waist- and neck-high so that the ball can be passed correctly through them and reach the target. • Have the student practice passing the ball to a target on the wall.

Summary

Basketball has become one of the biggest sports in our country. There are professional teams for both women and men that provide *all* students—girls and boys—with potential role models. Often students will play basketball during recess, at home, in youth leagues, or at camps and try to move the ball like one of the professional players. Without proper instruction this becomes a frustrating task.

One of the most efficient ways to move the ball down the court is by means of the pass. Learning to properly and accurately pass a ball to a partner or teammate becomes very important to the student's overall success in the game. Students and recreational players can use the bounce pass and the chest pass effectively once they understand how and when to execute a pass. Maintaining the proper body position, stepping with the pass, and pushing the ball out are components that students must understand before they will experience repeated success with these skills.

Teachers are usually the first individuals who the student will come in contact with that are able to provide instruction by using specific components and cues for a skill. This is an opportunity we should take seriously. As we help our students become skillful movers they may, in turn, become more interested in participating in physical activities outside of the physical education classroom setting.

Bounce Pass and Chest Pass Lesson Plan (First Lesson)

Age group: Early primary

Focus: Pushing the ball away from the passer

Subfocus: Movement concepts of force and direction (Down and Away)

Objectives: To push the ball away in the bounce pass so that the ball bounces closer to the receiver than to the passer four out of five times as measured by peer observation. (**CUE:** "Push away.")

Materials/Equipment: One playground ball, one hula hoop, and one target for each child. One dome cone (or other object that can be pushed across the floor) is needed for each pair of children.

Advance preparation: Place targets around the gymnasium. These targets may be hoops, construction paper, etc. Each student will need his own target. The targets should be no higher than three feet above the floor. Place floor tape (or masking tape) on the floor about 8 to 10 feet in front of the target.

Organization/Management: Students are in personal space for instruction and warm-up. Later, students will find their own learning stations in the gymnasium for practice.

Introduction/Warm-up:

Today we are going to learn some directions and practice using them. The words are UP and DOWN, and AWAY and NEAR. When I start the music, we will move around the gymnasium in general space using a locomotor skill that I call out. When the music stops, I will ask you to march in place and make your arms go UP or DOWN or have them NEAR or AWAY from your body. Do you understand these directions?

Begin music and call out jog, skip, gallop, walk, slide. Add directions of UP or DOWN or NEAR or FAR when music stops. Watch for correct performance of locomotor skills and correct use of directions.

FREEZE. Now I want you to pretend that you have a ball in your hand. Show me how you would make it go DOWN. Go UP. Go AWAY. Stay NEAR. Excellent. Now, we are going to use our locomotor movements again and when the music stops, you will freeze and make your imaginary ball go in the direction I call out. Do you understand these directions? (Begin music.)

Watch for correct performance of locomotor skills and correct use of directions.

FREEZE. Please find a personal space and sit down. This time we will practice using these directions with a real ball. We are going to learn the bounce pass. To do this skill, we stand up, hold the ball at our chest, and PUSH it away from us. It is important that it go AWAY from us. Watch as I bounce pass the ball near the wall. (Demonstrate passing the ball to the floor area near a wall.)

Notice that I can bounce the ball off the floor and have it hit the target. To do that I have to PUSH the ball AWAY from me. To keep my balance, it helps to put one foot in front when I pass the ball. It really doesn't matter which foot is in front as long as one is. And this is for what? **(Balance.)** *Great.*

Look around the gymnasium. There are pieces of construction paper and balls against the wall. Each of you will have one of these places for your own use to work on the bounce pass. Can you find your own target and sit on the tape in front of it? GO.

Pick up the ball and stand on your piece of tape facing the construction paper. Face your target, get in the ready position, PUSH the ball away from you and try to hit the target. Go get your ball and return to your piece of tape. (Repeat several times.)

The children repeat the cues with you. When they can repeat the cues ("push away") on their own, they are allowed to practice independently.

Watch for students pushing the ball away.

FREEZE. If you are able to hit your target three times in a row, you may take ONE giant step backwards. Whenever you are able to bounce pass the ball and hit the targets three times in a row, you may take another step back. Do you understand these directions? GO.

Watch for students pushing the ball away. Repeat "push away" frequently.

FREEZE. Everyone sit down where they are. If you are able to perform the bounce pass easily, you may try this next challenge. (Demonstrate as you explain.) *You will place a hula hoop one step away from the wall. You will have to bounce the ball so that it hits the floor inside the hula hoop and then bounces up to hit your target on the wall. Do you understand these directions? If you think you are ready to try this, raise your hand.* (Dismiss children in small groups to obtain hula hoops.) *Everyone return to your targets. GO.*

Watch for students pushing the ball away. Repeat "push away" frequently.

FREEZE. Everyone find a partner and sit down. You are doing very well pushing the ball away. Are you ready for something really challenging? You and your partner will need only one ball for the two of you and one dome cone. One of you can bring the hoop and put it on the pile and then pick up a dome cone. The other one can return ONE of the balls you have. (Dismiss children by groups to obtain/return equipment.) *Excellent.*

Now watch (student) and I perform this skill. We have a dome cone between us. We will take TWO steps back from the dome cone. I want to PUSH the ball AWAY so that it hits the dome cone and PUSHES it closer to (student). (Student) will try to bounce pass the dome cone back toward me. When I say GO, you and your partner will find a space in the gymnasium, place your dome cone on the floor, and take two steps back from the dome cone. You may then try to PUSH the dome cone away from each other using the bounce pass. Do you understand these directions? GO.

Watch for the students pushing the ball away. (Contact with the dome cone is of secondary concern.) Repeat the cue "push away" frequently.

FREEZE. Time is up. Please return your equipment to where it belongs and line up for your teacher.

Closure:

Students are lined up to leave.

*Do you think it is more important to pass the ball down or away for the bounce pass? **(Away.)** We spent a lot of time pushing the ball away. If (student) is my partner and I bounce pass to (student), does the ball hit the ground closer to her or me to have a good pass? **(Student.)***

Next time we will practice passing the ball to a moving target.

Dribbling

The manipulative skill of dribbling—used in both soccer and basketball—is designed for controlling *and* moving objects. The basketball and soccer dribbles, however, are two very distinct actions. While one skill involves the hands (basketball dribble) and the other involves the feet (soccer dribble), they will be combined in this chapter because they share the unique combination of movement and manipulation. The NASPE Outcomes Project suggests that fourth graders should be able to "hand dribble and foot dribble a ball and maintain control while traveling within a group" (outcome 4-5).

Basketball Dribble

Young children begin bouncing balls soon after they discover that balls can bounce. The obvious connection between the bounce and the basketball dribble is very motivating for young children. Unfortunately, their enthusiasm for the skill often takes precedence over learning correct technique.

While children gravitate toward using a "real basketball" for dribbling, their small hands are not large enough to correctly dribble a regulation-size basketball. We suggest using playground balls or smaller (junior or intermediate) basketballs when practicing. The regulation-size basketball may be appropriate in middle school, when the children's skill and hand size increase.

One of the most challenging aspects of the dribble is the transition from the closed skill of standing in one location and dribbling a ball to the very open skill of dribbling a ball in a game situation. Children often have difficulty controlling the ball and being able to feel where it is. By having students perform many repetitions and slowly increasing the challenge of the skill, you can help them master these components smoothly. While total mastery of the basketball dribble may take many years, children should begin instruction in the primary grades.

Basic Components

Ready Position
—knees bent, feet shoulder-width apart, eyes looking forward, object held in both hands in front of the body.

Push
—one hand contacts the ball at waist level or below and pushes it downward using the finger pads only. (Make sure students are using the pads of all four fingers and the thumb. If they are told to use their fingertips to dribble, the fingertips become so rigid at ball contact that the children are unable to develop a feel for the ball.) The wrist flexes and the elbow extends downward as the ball is pushed down.

Eyes Forward
—as the ball is contacted, the head is up and the eyes are focused forward.

Keep Ball in Front of Body
—the ball should be bounced diagonally in front of the body and away from the feet.

Cue Words

The cue words you select for each phase of the skill will depend on the age of the students you are teaching and your areas of emphasis. We have listed, in usable sets, some of the cue words we have used to teach the basketball dribble. You may use each set individually or mix and match the cue words as needed. It is beneficial to have the students say the words out loud as they practice the skill.

READY—knees bent, feet shoulder-width apart, eyes looking forward, object held in both hands in front of the body.

WAVE GOODBYE—one hand contacts the ball at waist level or below and pushes the ball downward using only the pads of the fingers. The wrist flexes and the elbow extends downward as the ball is pushed down.

HELLO—the wrist and elbow flex upward to waist level as the ball rebounds off the floor.

USE YOUR TICKLE FINGERS—children are asked which part of their hands they use to tickle someone. Those same parts of the hands (or tickle fingers) are used to dribble. Make sure the students are using the pads of all four fingers and the thumb. One hand contacts the ball at waist level or below and pushes the ball downward using only the pads of the fingers. The wrist flexes and the elbow extends downward as the ball is pushed down.

PUSH—at contact the ball is pushed toward the floor as the arm extends.

Cue Set 1: READY, WAVE GOODBYE, HELLO

Cue Set 2: USE YOUR TICKLE FINGERS, PUSH

Suggested Activities for Reinforcing the Components

In the learning process, it is essential that students know how a skill is supposed to look, what its component parts are, and how to perform each individual component correctly. In the preceding section, we furnished pictures and descriptions of the basketball dribble, divided it into its component parts, and provided possible cue words. Since the basketball dribble is a movement skill, it may be difficult to isolate its components completely. You may find it necessary to combine several components when using the activities found in chapter 3 that reinforce the concepts for all locomotor and manipulative skills. In addition to the material in chapter 3, the following section provides specific activities for reinforcing the components unique to the basketball dribble.

Partner Skill Check

Objective: To allow partners to assess each other's progress learning the skill

Equipment: Partner skill check sheets, pencils, and one ball for each set of partners. If the students cannot read or do not speak English, the picture version of the partner skill check sheet may be useful.

Activity:

1. One partner observes the other to see if he has the correct form for the ready position.

2. If the ready position is correct, then the partner places a *Y* in the first box. If the ready position is not correct, he places an *N* in the first box. Nonreaders can put a smiling face if the ready position is correct or a sad face if the ready position is not correct.

3. This evaluation continues until each of the components has been assessed five times.

4. A partner skill check sheet is used for each student.

Extensions:

1. You may use the partner skill check sheet to assess the skill development of each student.

2. You may send partner skill check sheets home with report cards or as individual skills develop.

Partner Skill Check   Skill: **Basketball Dribble**

Dribbler's name: _____ Watcher's name: _____

 **1.**

1   2   3   4   5

Ready

 **2.**

1   2   3   4   5

Push

 **3.**

1   2   3   4   5

Eyes forward

 **4.**

1   2   3   4   5

**Move ball in
front of body**

Partner Skill Check   Skill: **Basketball Dribble**

Dribbler's name: _____ Watcher's name: _____

Watch your partner and mark each component of the skill. Let your partner do the skill 5 times. Each time your partner does it right, mark a **Y** in the box. If your partner doesn't do it right, mark an **N** in the box.

START

Ready position

1. Eyes forward
2. Knees bent
3. Feet shoulder-width apart
4. Object held in front of body

TRIALS

1	2	3	4	5
☐	☐	☐	☐	☐

ACTION

Push

1. Contact ball about waist level

1	2	3	4	5
☐	☐	☐	☐	☐

2. Use fingertips only as arm extends downward

1	2	3	4	5
☐	☐	☐	☐	☐

Eyes forward

3. Head up

1	2	3	4	5
☐	☐	☐	☐	☐

4. Eyes look forward

1	2	3	4	5
☐	☐	☐	☐	☐

Keep the ball in front of the body

5. Bounce ball in front of body and away from feet

1	2	3	4	5
☐	☐	☐	☐	☐

Success Builders

The success builder activities allow you to address individual needs. If students need additional help on individual component parts, the activities listed below will help reinforce correct performance.

Objective: To allow partners to improve areas of deficiency as assessed by the partner skill check

Equipment: See individual stations. We suggest using an unbreakable mirror and a poster of each component of the basketball dribble at each station. The mirror is particularly helpful in these activities because it allows the child to see what she is doing. The easiest way to make the posters would be to photocopy the drawings from this book. Use an opaque projector to enlarge them. Laminating the posters will ensure their use for many years.

Activity:

1. Set up a station for each of the four components in the teaching area with a description or a picture of the specific component posted at the corresponding station.

2. Stations:

Ready

—knees bent, feet shoulder-width apart, eyes looking forward, object held in both hands in front of the body.

Equipment: Component poster, mirror (if available), a ball, and partner evaluations

Activity: The student assumes the ready position. The partner checks to see if her position matches the poster. The student refers to the mirror for help. The student then dribbles the ball and on a signal from her partner assumes the ready position again. Once the student can successfully demonstrate the ready position to the partner, partners may return to practicing the entire skill.

Push

—one hand contacts the ball around waist level or below and pushes the ball down using the finger pads only. The wrist flexes and the elbow extends downward as the ball is pushed down.

Equipment: Component poster, mirror (if available), a ball, and partner evaluations

Activity 1: The student demonstrates the push motion with his hand without the ball. The fingers are slightly bent to show that the ball would contact the finger pads and not the palm. The partner checks to see if the student's position matches the poster. The student refers to the mirror for help. If the push is correct, the student is allowed to use a ball. Once the student can successfully demonstrate a good push (with proper use of the finger pads) to the partner, the partners may return to practicing the entire skill.

Activity 2: The student demonstrates the push motion while sitting or kneeling. Often, decreasing the distance of the ball from the floor can increase the student's control of the dribble. Once the student can successfully demonstrate a good push (with proper use of the finger pads) to the partner, the partners may return to practicing the entire skill.

Activity 3: With the partner's help, the student starts from the ready position and pushes her hand down without the ball. The partner checks to see if her position matches the poster. The student refers to the mirror for help. If the wrist flexion and elbow extension are correct, the student is allowed to use a ball. Once the student can successfully demonstrate good wrist flexion and elbow extension to the partner, the partners may return to practicing the entire skill.

Eyes Forward

—as the ball is contacted, the head is up and the eyes are focused forward.

Equipment: Component poster, balls, and partner evaluations

Activity 1: The student dribbles the ball while the partner watches. The watching partner raises one, two, three, four, five, or no fingers. The dribbling partner has to keep his head up and be able to tell the partner how many fingers were raised.

Activity 2: Partners each have a ball and face each other. One student (the leader) performs various movements while the other student mirrors the movements without looking at the ball or losing control.

Keep Ball in Front of Body

—the ball should be bounced diagonally in front of the body and away from the feet.

Equipment: Component poster, mirror (if available), a ball, and partner evaluations

Activity 1: The student kneels on the knee on the same side as the dominant hand. The other leg is bent at the knee with the foot on the floor. The student practices dribbling the ball. Since one knee is bent, it will be easier to keep the ball bouncing in front of the body.

Activity 2: The student assumes a stride position with the leg opposite the dribbling hand forward. The student should practice from this position, then progress to moving at a slow speed while keeping the ball in front of the body and away from the feet.

Suggested Culminating Activities to Reinforce the Entire Skill
Individual Activities

Color Targets

Objective: To improve the basketball dribble by dribbling on specific targets

Equipment: Laminated construction paper of different colors and sizes (about 8 to 12 targets of each color) taped to the floor of the gymnasium or activity area and a ball for each student (basketball, playground ball, etc.)

Activity:

1. Create a "color box" in which samples from each color of construction paper have been placed. You will need more samples than you have students.

2. Select a student to draw a sample color from the color box.

3. The sample color chosen is the color target all students must locate and dribble toward.

4. Students continue to dribble standing in front of the targets of the selected color until you give a stop signal.

5. The activity continues until all students have been given an opportunity to draw from the color box.

Extensions:

1. Instead of using different colors, students could select different shapes from the "shape box," letters from the "alphabet box," or words from the "word box."

2. Students work with partners. One partner chooses the color, shape, letter, or word that will be used for a target. The other must dribble to the selected target. Partners take turns selecting targets and dribbling.

Create-A-Word

Objective: To create words by contacting the letters using the basketball dribble

Equipment: One ball (basketball, playground ball, etc.) per student and four complete sets of laminated alphabet letters scattered and *securely taped* to the floor of the gymnasium or activity area. It would be advantageous to have extra copies of vowels and selected consonants (e.g., N, R, S, T). You will also need paper and markers or a chalkboard and chalk to serve as a "word bank."

Activity:

1. On your start signal, students begin to spell words by dribbling on different letters of the alphabet.

2. The ball must bounce on the letter three times in a row in order for that letter to be used. Students must dribble the ball continuously. If the dribble stops, the last letter collected does not count.

3. Students should continue to dribble the ball on the floor while moving to the next letter.

4. Once a student has created a word, he goes to the word bank (paper or chalkboard) and writes the word. It will be helpful to have several word banks so students will not have to wait in line to write their words.

5. A word may be "banked" or written only once on the paper or chalkboard.

6. If a student dribbles on a letter that cannot be used to form the word being created, she must dribble on the letter three times to delete it.

Extensions:

1. Students work with partners. One student contacts letters to spell a word while the partner records the word and evaluates the basketball dribble. If the dribbler has not performed the skill correctly, he must make the correction before the letter can be used. When the first partner has spelled a word, the other partner is then given an opportunity to dribble.

2. Students work with partners. Partners are given paper and pencil to record the letters they contact and to write down the words they create. Each partner must dribble and hit a vowel and two consonants. The pair now has six letters to use to create words. The partners attempt to create six words using one or more of the letters they have contacted. Once the partners have created six words and written them down, they attempt to spell the words by dribbling the ball three times on each letter. Once a word is spelled, it may be checked off the list. If the students are unable to use a letter they have contacted, they must dribble on that letter three times to delete it and select another letter.

Musical Hoops

Objective: To improve control of the dribble while moving

Equipment: One ball per student, music and tape player, stop watch, and 15+ hula hoops scattered around the gymnasium

Activity:

1. As the music is played, students dribble around the gymnasium avoiding the hula hoops.

2. When the music stops, students must dribble while finding the *first available* hoop, place one foot in it, and continue to dribble.

3. Time the class to determine how long it takes for everyone to find a hoop.

Extensions:

1. You may use a variety of colors of hoops and require that students go to a specific color when the music stops.

2. You may require the students to use their dominant hand while dribbling to the hoop and their nondominant hand when they have one foot in the hoop.

Cross the Line

Objective: To improve dribbling skill using either hand

Equipment: One ball per student

Activity:

1. Each student begins moving in general space while dribbling a ball.

2. When the student crosses a line marked on the gymnasium floor (basketball, volleyball, or badminton court lines), she must change hands and dribble with the other hand.

3. The student continues to move and change hands each time she crosses a line.

Extensions:

1. Use music. When the music stops, students must stop and maintain control of the ball. If a student has trouble, she retrieves the ball and continues.

2. Use music that varies in tempo and challenge the students to move with the beat of the music.

3. Challenge the students to move the ball at different levels and at different speeds and still change hands when crossing the lines, all the while maintaining control.

To the Beat

Objective: To improve students' ability to control the ball while changing directions and/or dribbling with either hand

Equipment: One ball per student and music

Activity:

1. Students stand in their personal space and face a leader.

2. Everyone has a ball. When the music begins, the leader performs actions while dribbling in place and the students mirror the actions.

Extensions:

1. Add movements to the activity. If the leader moves backward, the students move forward. If the leader moves to the right, the students move to the left.

2. Select a line dance that the students know and see if they can dribble the ball while performing the steps.

It's Crowded

Objective: To improve students' ability to keep their eyes looking forward while dribbling

Equipment: One ball per student

Activity:

1. Each student dribbles a ball in general space.

2. Begin to decrease the size of the space in which the students may dribble until their movement is limited.

3. Slowly increase the size of the play area.

Extensions:

1. As the space decreases, ask the students to place their bodies at a different level while continuing to dribble.

2. Students begin from a standing position and slowly lower their bodies to the floor while maintaining the dribble. Once students are sitting down, they dribble the ball around the basement (their body) before returning to a standing position.

Double Trouble Dribble

Objective: To improve dribbling coordination by dribbling two balls at the same time

Equipment: Two balls of the same size per student

Activity:

1. Students kneel on both knees and hold a ball in each hand.

2. Students attempt to dribble both balls at the same time. (*Hint:* The task is easier if the balls are pushed down at the same time and allowed to rebound at the same time.)

Extensions:

1. After the student can control the double trouble dribble, he may stand up and attempt to maintain control.

2. The student who can accomplish the first extension may be challenged to move slowly around the gymnasium while maintaining control of two balls.

3. The following may be performed with partners with each pair using a total of two balls:

   • Partners kneel and face each other. Partner A double trouble dribbles the balls five times and then Partner B takes over. The two balls never stop bouncing. After Partner B is successful, Partner A dribbles.

   • Once the students can complete the activity, they may be challenged to stand up and face each other and repeat the same drill.

   • One partner may stand still, while the partner double trouble dribbles around her. Then they change positions.

Partner Activities

Challenges

Objective: To practice the basketball dribble in a variety of settings

Equipment: One ball per pair of students and laminated challenge cards

Activity:

1. Students select a challenge card.

2. Students perform the task described on the card.

3. Possible challenges may include:

   • Dribble the ball using hard force (light force, medium force).

   • Dribble the ball while changing levels with your body.

   • Dribble the ball at different levels (high, medium, low).

   • Dribble the ball walking toward your partner and then dribble backward to the starting spot.

   • Dribble the ball around your body, keeping your feet stationary.

   • Dribble with the hand you write with. Dribble with the other hand.

- Dribble in a straight pathway, a curvy pathway, a zigzag pathway.
- Dribble two balls at the same time.

Extensions:

1. Place multicolored targets on a floor and have the partner tell the dribbler which target to dribble on.

2. Use hula hoops, ropes, or carpet squares to create a maze for the dribbler to dribble around.

3. Set up game poles or volleyball standards with a volleyball net or rope between them. The dribbler must dribble under the net/rope. Adjust the net/rope so that it is about two feet off the ground at the low end and five feet off the ground at the high end.

Follow the Leader

Objective: To improve the basketball dribbling skill while following the actions of a partner.

Equipment: One ball (basketball, playground ball) per student

Activity:

1. Everyone has a partner.

2. One partner is the leader and the other is the follower.

3. The leader walks around dribbling his ball while the follower mirrors his movements.

4. After a short period of time the leader becomes the follower and the follower becomes the leader.

Extensions:

1. The leader moves at different speeds (fast, medium, or slow).

2. The leader uses different locomotor movements while dribbling.

3. Make larger groups; for example, groups of four, six, or eight.

Group Activities

Create Your Own Activity

Objective: To allow students to create their own activity to reinforce the basketball dribble

Equipment: One piece of paper and pencil per group and a predetermined list of equipment you will allow students to use in their activities (e.g., bowling pins, cones, ropes, hula hoops, basketballs, Nerf balls, etc.)

Activity:

1. Form groups with two to five students each. You may select the groups or the students may form their own.

2. Students create their own activity using the basketball dribble as the basic skill. Students are required to have rules that encourage correct performance of the skill, include all players, and address all safety concerns.

3. The groups write their individual names, the rules of the activity, and the equipment needed on their paper and then show the activity to the teacher.

4. Upon approval of their activity, the students may collect the necessary equipment and begin playing the activity.

5. You must approve all changes to the activity.

Extensions:

1. Groups may teach their activities to other groups.

2. Groups may teach their activities to the entire class.

Rip and Roar

Objective: To dribble the ball while avoiding being tagged

Equipment: One ball and one pinny (or necktie, or flagbelt and flag) for each student dribbler. The two taggers do not need pinnies.

Activity:

1. Select two taggers.

2. Give everyone else a "tail" (pinny). The tails are placed in the back of the students' pants.

3. The taggers start in the center of the gymnasium or play area. Everyone else is scattered throughout the area.

4. The taggers count to five while the other students dribble around. After counting to five, the taggers run around trying to pull the tails of the other students.

5. If a student's tail is pulled or her dribble is out of control, she must go to a designated area and dribble five times while saying the cue words out loud. The student may then return to the activity.

Extensions:

1. Give the taggers a ball to dribble.

2. Set a time limit for each group of taggers and rotate after that time has expired.

Mine Field

Objective: To practice the basketball dribble while avoiding obstacles

Equipment: One ball (basketball, playground ball) per student and approximately 20 traffic cones or other objects (e.g., two-liter bottles, dome cones, jump ropes, etc.)

Activity:

1. Scatter the cones throughout the gymnasium or play area.

2. Students take the ball they are using to their own personal space.

3. On the start signal, students begin to dribble around the mines.

4. If a student hits a mine with his ball, he must go to the designated practice area.

5. The student in the designated area must dribble five times while saying the cue words out loud.

6. The student may then return to the activity.

Extensions:

1. Play dribble tag. Choose a student or several students to be taggers. Once a student is tagged, he goes to a designated practice area and has a peer evaluate the components of the basketball dribble. You may select a student to go to the designated area as the first "watcher" when the game begins. When the tagged student finishes demonstrating the basketball dribble, the first watcher returns to the game and the student who was tagged stays in the area and becomes the new watcher. After he watches the next tagged student perform the skill, the watcher returns to the game. This rotation continues as long as the activity is played.

2. If several students are waiting, they may double-up and be watched by the same person. Every effort should be made to minimize waiting time.

Hoop Ball

Objective: To improve students' ability to keep the ball away from an opponent while keeping their eyes forward

Equipment: Hula hoops and balls (enough of each so that half of the students have a hula hoop and the other half have a ball)

Activity:

1. Scatter the hula hoops within the play area and have half of the students stand inside their own hoop

2. The other half of the students dribble through the play area and try to avoid the hoops.

3. The students within the hoops try to touch a ball as students dribble past.

4. If a ball is touched, the two students trade places.

Extensions:

1. Hoops may be more spread out for lower skilled students. As children improve, hoops may be moved closer together.

2. Students within the hoops may be permitted to step one foot out of the hoop and reach to touch a ball.

Summary

Children are motivated at an early age to imitate the dribbling patterns of basketball players—and they are often allowed to continue practicing their self-taught dribble without receiving proper instruction. Correcting improper dribbling techniques can take a great deal of effort. To minimize this situation, instruction in proper dribbling techniques should begin in kindergarten and continue through the primary grades. Avoid the "slapping" that usually occurs with young dribblers by stressing the use of the finger pads and the smooth pushing motion—and your students will succeed on the courts!

Basketball Dribble Troubleshooting Chart

IF YOU SEE	THEN TRY THIS
1. Ball bouncing lower and lower	• Review the concept of force with the student. • Hold the ball on the bottom while the student pushes on the top of the ball. You control the bounce of the ball. • Have the student work with a partner. The student pushes the partner's hand down while the partner offers slight resistance.
2. Student using part of the hand besides the fingers	• Have the student practice "spider pushups" (fingertips of each hand push against each other so the palms of each hand touch and then move away). Fingertips stay in contact at all times. • Put baby powder or chalk on the ball. The student dribbles trying to get the powder on his fingertips only. • Hold the ball on the bottom as the student pushes with the fingertips on the top of the ball. You control the movement of the ball while watching the student's fingers.
3. Student keeping the wrist straight or locked	• Have the student practice waving goodbye to an ant. • Hold the ball on the bottom as the student pushes with the fingertips on the top of the ball. You control the movement of the ball while watching the student's wrist. • Place a piece of paper on a wall extending from knee to chest level. Have the student face the paper with a marker in her hand. The student marks the paper using an up/down movement of the wrist.
4. Arm not fully extended while pushing the ball down	• Have the student practice the arm motion without the ball. • Place a piece of paper on a wall extending from knee to chest level. Have the student face the paper with a marker in her hand. The student marks the paper using an up/down movement of the wrist and arm.
5. Student watching the ball instead of looking forward	• Have the students work in pairs. One partner dribbles a ball while following the locomotor movements of the other partner. The leading partner should start walking and then increase the speed as the dribbler becomes more proficient. • Have the student dribble a ball while you hold up a picture or a number of fingers for a couple of seconds. The student must be able to tell you what he saw.
6. Ball bouncing off the student's feet	• Have the student stand on a specific spot on the floor. Place a dribble spot next to the student and have the student dribble the ball on the spot. • Put a hula hoop on the floor and have the student dribble the ball inside the hoop. • Have the student try to dribble while on her knees.

Basketball Dribble Lesson Plan (Second Lesson)

Age group: Second grade

Focus: Keeping the head up when dribbling

Subfocus: Keeping eyes focused forward, not down, during the dribble

Objective: To keep the head up (not watch the ball) on four out of five dribbling attempts as measured by teacher observation (**CUE:** "Eyes Forward").

Materials/Equipment: One playground ball for each child

Organization/Management: Students are in personal space for warm-up, instruction, and practice.

Warm-Up:

*Today we're going to warm up with music again. When the music starts, I would like you to jog in general space. When the music stops you will FREEZE in your own personal space. What are some of the safety ideas we need to remember when moving in general space?(**Watch where you're going. Keep space between each person.**)* (Begin music.)

Watch for students moving safely. Stop the music and remind children about moving safely.

This time, I'm going to make it more challenging for you to move. You may use only the locomotor movement of the skip, AND you must stay on this half of the gymnasium. (Select two students to demonstrate the skip.) Do you understand what you are to do? GO.

Watch for students moving safely and performing the skip correctly. Stop the children several times to change the locomotor movement and to decrease the size of the space they may move in.

Formation:

After the FREEZE command, tell the students to find a personal space in the gymnasium and face you.

Introduction:

*When we did our warm-ups today, I kept making the space smaller. How did this smaller space affect your movement? (**Had to move slower and really look where we were going.**) That's right. Today we are going to work on the basketball dribble again. It is also a skill that requires you to start slowly and also to really look where you are going.*

*First, we need to review what we learned about the dribble last time. Who can tell me the parts of the dribble? (**Ready, Push, Eyes Forward, and Keep the Ball in Front.**) That's right.*

*Which part of our hand do we dribble with?(**Finger pads.**)* (Avoid using the term "fingertips," as students will literally push with their fingertips. Encourage the use of the finger pads.)

When I call your birth month (the month you were born) you will get a ball and then return to your space. Make sure you select a ball you can dribble easily; it should NOT be too big for you.

Dismiss students by month of the year to obtain balls for dribbling.

We are going to play "Follow the Leader." Using your fingers pads to push the ball, keep your eyes on me. I want you to do everything I do. If your ball should get away from you, go get it and return to your spot.

Have the students mirror your movements. Your movements may include:

- On both knees: (1) dribble the ball with the dominant hand, then the nondominant hand, (2) dribble the ball from the right hand to the left hand forming a **V** shape in front of the body

- With left foot on the floor and kneeling on right knee: (1) dribble the ball with the right hand, (2) dribble the ball forward a few inches and back

- With right foot on the floor and kneeling on left knee: (1) dribble the ball with the left hand, (2) dribble the ball forward a few inches and back

- Standing in a straddle position: dribble the ball from the right hand to the left hand forming a **V** shape in front of the body

- Stride position (left foot forward): dribble the ball with the right hand and raise a certain number of fingers

Watch for correct form. If the students have difficulty with the "Follow the Leader" activity, review the skill.

FREEZE and sit down in your space. Dribbling is not very difficult when you stay in one place. Moving around makes it hard. Just like with the warm-up we did today, you have to really watch where you're going. It's hard to watch where you're going and watch the ball at the same time, so you'll have to really "feel" for the ball so you know where it is.

When the music starts, I would like you to stand up and begin dribbling the ball. You may move in general space, but you will have to really look where you are going. Of course, you will use your finger pads, push, and keep the ball in front of you. Also, you must move at a slow speed. When the music stops, you must freeze where you are until the music begins again. Do you understand these directions? (Begin music.)

Watch for keeping head up, using pads of fingers, and ball control. Begin and stop music at least five times.

FREEZE. Terrific. You are all doing a wonderful job keeping your head up and watching where you are going. Now I'm going to make it more challenging; you may move at a slow speed or at a medium speed—as long as you can control the ball. (Begin music.)

Watch for ball control, keeping head up, and using pads of fingers. Begin and stop at least five times.

FREEZE. Now let's make it a little harder. When the music stops, you will stop, face me, and do whatever I do while you continue to dribble the ball. Remember to keep your eyes forward and feel for the ball. Do you understand these directions? (Begin music.)

When you stop the music, perform actions such as patting your head, raising one arm up and waving it, scratching your head, and giving a thumbs up.

FREEZE. That was wonderful. I think you're ready for something really hard. When I say GO, each of you should find a partner, locate a personal space for the two of you, and sit back to back. Hold the ball in your lap. GO.

One of you should begin as the leader. Whomever is the younger will be the leader. Your partner will follow you. The two of you may move around the gymnasium at a slow speed and the follower will do everything the leader does, EXCEPT if the leader loses control of the ball, the follower freezes, waiting for the leader to retrieve the ball. Now the person who did not lose control of the ball becomes the leader. (Select a student to follow you and demonstrate moving safely, keeping eyes forward, and changing leaders.) Do you understand? GO.

Begin music and watch for proper skill execution. Repeat the cue words "eyes forward" often. After several minutes, stop the music.

If you have not been the leader yet, you may be the leader until I stop the music again. Do you understand the directions? GO.

Begin the music, repeat "eyes forward," and watch for proper skill performance.

FREEZE. Please sit down where you are and look at (student) and me. (Student) is younger than I am, so she will be the leader first. We are going to face each other and pretend that we are looking in a mirror. I want to do everything she does. We can move around a little, but really should stay close. (Demonstrate with student.) I will tell you when to change leaders. Do you understand the directions? GO.

Begin music, repeat "eyes forward," and watch for proper skill performance. After several minutes, change duties with the leader.

FREEZE. Please return your equipment to the storage bin and line up for your teacher.

Closure:

Students are lined up to leave.

Girls and boys, who can tell me some things I must remember when I dribble a ball with my hands? **(Keep eyes up, or forward and watch where I'm going.)** *Good. Now I can dribble with my fingers being very stiff* (demonstrate). *What's wrong with that?* **(Hard to have control over ball, I should use the pads of my fingers.)** *Excellent! You all are becoming wonderful dribblers. Next time we will concentrate on using either hand to dribble the ball.*

Soccer Dribble

Elementary students enjoy soccer activities because of the continuous movement of the soccer dribble. This skill provides a good cardiovascular workout as well as promoting the development of eye-foot coordination.

Initially children spend as much time chasing the soccer ball as controlling it. To reduce this occurrence, we recommend using partially deflated balls during the early learning period. Large beanbags are also very acceptable replacements for balls when practicing on a wood or tile gymnasium floor. In addition, we recommend stressing the idea of LIGHT FORCE when introducing the skill.

Once students understand the concept of force, the variations that are possible with the soccer dribble make it very motivating for elementary children. The child is not limited to using only one part of the foot. Both the instep and the outside and bottom (sole) of the foot can be used with the soccer dribble. The particular part of the foot used will depend on what the student wants to do with the ball.

Using either foot for the soccer dribble is also essential to developing mastery. To promote this competency, the skill should be introduced in the primary grades before the student begins to form the habit of using only the preferred foot. The NASPE Outcomes Project suggests that fourth grade students should be able to foot dribble a ball and maintain control (outcome 4-5).

Basic Components

Ready Position
—ball on ground directly below head, feet shoulder width apart, knees bent.

Foot Taps Ball
—perform a short series of taps with the inside, outside, or instep of the foot (not the toe). Use of the nondominant foot should be practiced and encouraged.

Keep Ball Close
—the ball should be on the ground directly below the head as it is contacted, with eyes looking forward. Keep the ball within two to four feet while dribbling.

Move With Ball
—the soccer dribble is a movement activity and should be performed at a speed faster than a walk.

Albemarle County Physical Education Curriculum Revision Committee, 1996, 5-6.

Cue Words

The cue words you select for each phase of the skill will depend on the age of the students you are teaching and your areas of emphasis. We have listed, in usable sets, some of the cue words we have used to teach the soccer dribble. You may use each set individually or mix and match the cue words as needed. It is beneficial to have the students say the words out loud as they practice the skill.

EYES UP—ball on ground directly below head, feet shoulder-width apart, knees bent, eyes up.

TAP—perform a short series of taps with the inside, outside, or instep of the foot, and not the toe. Use the nondominant foot when appropriate.

USE THE FLAT PART OF YOUR FOOT—the ball is tapped with either the inside, outside, or instep of the foot.

EASY TAPS—using light force.

GO—the ball should be directly below the head on the ground as the ball is contacted, eyes looking forward. Keep the ball within two to four feet while dribbling. The dribble must be done faster than a walk.

KEEP IT CLOSE—tap the ball lightly so that it goes only two to four feet from the body.

Cue Set 1: EYES UP, TAP, GO

Cue Set 2: USE THE FLAT PART OF YOUR FOOT, EASY TAPS, KEEP IT CLOSE

Suggested Activities for Reinforcing the Components

In the learning process, it is essential that students know how a skill is supposed to look, what its component parts are, and how to perform each individual component correctly. In the preceding section, we furnished pictures and descriptions of the soccer dribble, divided it into its component parts, and provided possible cue words. Since the soccer dribble is a movement skill, it may be difficult to isolate its components completely. You may find it necessary to combine several components when using the activities found in chapter 3. In addition to the material in chapter 3 that reinforces the concepts for all locomotor and manipulative skills, the following section provides specific activities for reinforcing the components unique to the soccer dribble.

Partner Skill Check

Objective: To allow partners to assess each other's progress learning the skill

Equipment: Partner skill check sheets, pencils, and one ball for each set of partners. If the students cannot read or do not speak English, the picture version of the partner skill check sheet may be useful.

Activity:

1. One partner observes the other to see if he has the correct form for the ready position.

2. If the ready position is correct, then the partner places a *Y* in the first box. If the ready position is not correct, he places an *N* in the first box. Non-readers can put a smiling face if the ready position is correct or a sad face if the ready position is not correct.

3. This evaluation continues until each of the components has been assessed five times.

4. A partner skill check sheet is used for each student.

Extensions:

1. You can use the partner skill check sheet to assess the skill development of each student.

2. You can send partner skill check sheets home with report cards or as individual skills develop.

Success Builders

The success builder activities allow you to address individual needs. If students need additional help on individual component parts, the activities listed below will help reinforce correct performance.

Objective: To allow partners to improve areas of deficiency as assessed by the partner skill check

Equipment: See individual stations. We suggest using an unbreakable mirror and a poster of each component of the soccer dribble at each station. The mirror is particularly helpful in these activities because it allows the child to see what she is doing. The easiest way to make the posters would be to photocopy the drawings from this book. Use an opaque projector to enlarge them. Laminating the posters will ensure their use for many years.

Activity:

1. Set up a station for each component in the teaching area. Post a description or a picture of the specific component at the corresponding station.

2. Stations:

Ready

—ball on ground directly below head, feet shoulder-width apart, knees bent.

Equipment: Component poster, mirror (if available), and partner evaluations

Activity: The student assumes the ready position. The partner checks to see if his position matches the poster. The student refers to the mirror for help. The student then walks around and on a signal from his partner assumes the ready position again. When he has had several successful trials, the partners may return to working on the entire skill.

Foot Taps Ball

—using the inside, outside, or instep of the foot (not the toe), strike the ball with a short series of taps. Use the nondominant foot when appropriate.

Equipment: Component poster, mirror (if available), soccer ball, and partner evaluations

Partner Skill Check

Skill: **Soccer Dribble**

Dribbler's name: _____ Watcher's name: _____

1.

   Ready

   1   2   3   4   5

2.

   Foot taps ball

   1   2   3   4   5

3.

   Keep ball close

   1   2   3   4   5

4.

   Move with ball

   1   2   3   4   5

Partner Skill Check

Skill: **Soccer Dribble**

Dribbler's name: _____ Watcher's name:_____

Watch your partner and mark each component of the skill. Let your partner do the skill 5 times. Each time your partner does it right, mark a **Y** in the box. If your partner doesn't do it right, mark an **N** in the box.

START

Ready position

1. Eyes forward
2. Knees bent
3. Feet shoulder-width apart
4. Object in front of body

TRIALS

☐ 1 ☐ 2 ☐ 3 ☐ 4 ☐ 5

ACTION

Foot taps ball

1. Short taps

☐ 1 ☐ 2 ☐ 3 ☐ 4 ☐ 5

2. Use inside, outside, or instep of foot

☐ 1 ☐ 2 ☐ 3 ☐ 4 ☐ 5

Keep ball close

3. Ball stays in dribbler's personal space

☐ 1 ☐ 2 ☐ 3 ☐ 4 ☐ 5

Move with ball

4. Faster than a walk

☐ 1 ☐ 2 ☐ 3 ☐ 4 ☐ 5

Activity: The student demonstrates the soccer dribble while moving in the designated area. The partner checks to see if her position matches the poster. The student refers to the mirror for help. Once the student can successfully demonstrate for her partner the correct part of the foot that taps the ball, the partners may return to practicing the entire skill.

Keep It Close

—the ball should be directly below the head on the ground as the ball is dribbled, eyes looking forward. Keep the ball within two to four feet while dribbling.

Equipment: Component poster, mirror (if available), soccer ball, and partner evaluations

Activity: The student demonstrates the soccer dribble while moving in the designated area. The partner checks to see if the student's body position matches the poster. The partner reminds the student to keep "eyes up." The student looks at the partner's eyes while dribbling. The student can also look at the mirror for help. Once the student can successfully demonstrate to his partner a good dribble with the ball kept close and the eyes looking forward, the partners may return to practicing the entire skill.

Move With Ball

—the dribble must be done faster than a walk.

Equipment: Component poster, mirror (if available), and partner evaluations

Activity: The student demonstrates the soccer dribble while moving in the designated area. The partner checks to see if her position matches the poster. Once the student can successfully demonstrate to her partner a "jog" while dribbling, the partners may return to practicing the entire skill.

Suggested Culminating Activities to Reinforce the Entire Skill

Individual Activities

Color Targets

Objective: To improve dribbling control by dribbling over specified targets

Equipment: Laminated construction paper of different colors and sizes (about 8 to 12 targets of each color) taped to the floor or placed in the activity area and a ball for each student (soccer, playground ball, etc.)

Activity:

1. Create a "color box" in which samples from each color of construction paper have been placed. You will need more samples than you have students.

2. Choose a student to pick a sample color from the color box.

3. The sample color drawn is the color target that all students must find and try to dribble across.

4. Students continue to dribble across the targets of the color selected until you give a stop signal.

5. Designate another student to draw from the color box. The activity continues until all students have been given a chance to select.

Extensions:

1. Instead of using different colors, students could choose different shapes from the "shape box," letters from the "alphabet box," or words from the "word box."

2. Students work with partners. The partner chooses the color, shape, letter, or word that will be used for a target. Partners take turns selecting targets and dribbling.

Create-A-Word

Objective: To create words by stopping the ball on top of the letters while using the soccer dribble

Equipment: One ball per student, four complete sets of alphabet letters scattered and taped to the floor of the gym or play area. It would be advantageous to have extra copies of vowels and selected consonants (e.g., N, R, S, T). You will also need paper and markers or chalkboard and chalk to serve as a "word bank."

Activity:

1. On your signal, students begin to spell words by soccer dribbling to different letters of the alphabet. They must stop the ball on top of the letter they intend to use.

2. The students must have the soccer dribble under control. If the ball is out of control, the student must start the dribble from the point at which he lost control.

3. Once a student has created a word, he goes to the word bank (paper or chalkboard) and writes the word. It will be helpful to have several word banks around the play area so students do not have to wait to record their words.

4. A word may be "banked" or written only once on the paper or chalkboard.

5. If a student dribbles over a letter that she cannot use to form the word being created, she must dribble over that letter again to delete it. Students should be encouraged to dribble *around* the letters they don't need.

Extensions:

1. Students work with partners. The dribbler tells her partner the word she will attempt to spell. The dribbler stops the ball on letters to spell a word while the partner records the letters and evaluates the dribble. If the dribbler has not performed the skill correctly, then she may not use the letter until the dribble is performed properly. When the first partner has spelled a word, the second partner is given a chance to perform the activity.

2. Students work with partners. The partners are given paper and pencil to record the letters they stop the ball on and to write down the words they create. Each partner must dribble over to, and stop the ball on top of, a

vowel and two consonants until the pair has six letters to use to create words. The partners attempt to create six words using one or more of the letters they have collected. Once the partners have created six words and written them down, they attempt to spell the words by dribbling over the letters with the ball. Once a word is spelled, it may be checked off the list. If the students are unable to use a letter they have collected, they must dribble over that letter again to delete it and select another letter.

Partner Activities

Challenges

Objective: To practice the soccer dribble in a variety of situations

Equipment: One ball (soccer, playground, Nerf, or yarn) per pair of students and laminated challenge cards. On a tile or wood floor, large beanbags may be used instead of balls.

Activity:

1. Students select a challenge card.

2. Students perform the task described on the card.

3. Possible challenges could include:

   - Dribble the ball under control using fast speed (slow speed, medium speed).

   - Dribble the ball with the outside of your feet (inside of your feet, inside and outside of your feet).

   - Dribble the ball around cones, two-liter bottles, chairs, etc.

   - Dribble the ball and change direction every time you get to a yellow cone (blue cone, green cone, etc.).

Extensions:

1. Have the partners keep track of their number of correct dribbles and keep a total for the class. A correct dribble occurs when the correct part of the foot is used and the ball stays within two to four feet of the student. Each contact counts as one point. In a follow-up lesson challenge the class to increase the total number of correct dribbles.

2. Place multicolored targets, hoops, cones, or buckets on the floor of the play area, and have the partner tell the dribbler which target to dribble around.

3. Time partners to determine how long they are able to move and keep the ball under control. Next time, challenge the partners to improve their times.

4. Challenge students to dribble successfully for a specific time period (e.g., 15 seconds). The challenges may be for everyone in the class, or students and their partners may take turns.

5. Time partners as they dribble through a set course. Challenge the partners to improve their times on each attempt.

Follow the Leader

Objective: To improve the soccer dribbling skill by working with a partner

Equipment: One ball (soccer, playground, or Nerf) per student

Activity:

1. Everyone has a partner.

2. One partner is the leader and the other is the follower.

3. The leader walks around dribbling his ball while the follower follows, dribbling his ball.

4. After a short period of time the leader becomes the follower and the follower becomes the leader.

Extensions:

1. The leader moves at different speeds (fast, medium, or slow).

2. Make larger groups: for example, groups of four, six, or eight.

Group Activities

Create Your Own Activity

Objective: To allow students to create their own activity to reinforce the soccer dribble

Equipment: One piece of paper and pencil per group and a predetermined list of equipment you will allow the students to use in their activities (e.g., soccer balls, yarn balls, Nerf balls, bowling pins, cones, hula hoops, jump ropes, etc.)

Activity:

1. Form groups with two to five students each. You may select the groups or the students may form their own.

2. Students create their own activity using the soccer dribble as the basic skill. Students are required to have rules that encourage correct performance of the skill, include all players, and address all safety concerns.

3. The groups write their individual names, the rules of the activity, and the equipment needed on their paper and then show the activity to you.

4. Upon approval of their activity, the students may obtain their equipment and begin playing the activity.

5. You must approve all changes to the activity.

Extensions:

1. Groups may teach their activities to other groups.

2. Groups may teach their activities to the entire class.

Rip and Roar

Objective: To dribble the ball while avoiding being tagged

Equipment: One ball and one pinny (or necktie, or flagbelt and flag) for each student dribbler. The two taggers do not need pinnies.

Activity:

1. Select two taggers.

2. Give everyone else a "tail" (pinny). The tails are placed in the back of the pants at the waistline.

3. The taggers start in the center of the gymnasium or play area. Everyone else is scattered throughout the area.

4. The taggers count to five while the other students are dribbling around. After counting to five, the taggers run around trying to pull the tails of the other students.

5. If a student's tail is pulled or his dribble is out of control, he must go to a designated area and dribble for 15 seconds while saying the cue words out loud. The student may then return to the activity.

Extensions:

1. Give the taggers a ball to dribble.

2. Set a time limit for each group of taggers and rotate after that time has expired.

Mine Field

Objective: To practice the soccer dribble while avoiding obstacles

Equipment: One ball (soccer, Nerf, playground, or yarn ball) per student and approximately 20 traffic cones. Two-liter bottles may be substituted for the traffic cones.

Activity:

1. Scatter the cones throughout the gymnasium or play area.

2. Students scatter within the area.

3. On the start signal, students begin to dribble around the mines.

4. If a student hits a mine with her ball, she must go to the designated practice area.

5. Inside the designated practice area, before returning to the activity the student must dribble for 15 seconds while saying the cue words out loud.

Extensions:

1. Play a game of dribble tag. Choose a student or several students to be taggers. Once a student is tagged, he goes to a designated practice area and has a peer evaluate the components of the soccer dribble. You may select a student to go to the designated area as the first watcher when the game begins. When the tagged student finishes demonstrating the soccer dribble, the first watcher returns to the game and the student who was tagged stays in the area and becomes the new watcher. After she watches the next tagged student perform the skill, the watcher returns to the game. This rotation continues as long as the activity is played.

2. If several students are waiting, they may double-up and be watched by the same person. Every effort should be made to minimize time waiting.

3. Place hoops in the mine field with half of the students standing inside them. The remaining students dribble through the mine field and past the hoops trying to control the ball. If a student in a hoop is able to touch a ball with one of her feet, she changes places with the dribbler.

Soccer Madness

Objective: To practice the soccer dribble while avoiding other players.

Equipment: One soccer ball or playground ball per student and a well-defined outside play area

Activity:

1. Select two taggers.

2. The taggers stand in the middle of the play area and the rest of the students stand at one end of the play area.

3. On the start signal, the students begin to dribble a ball to the opposite end of the play area.

4. Each tagger dribbles a ball toward the rest of the students.

5. The taggers try to dribble their soccer balls into other students' soccer balls. (Taggers must be in close proximity to the students they tag.) If this happens before the students reach the opposite end of the play area, the tagged students become taggers and join the original group of taggers. Any student who avoids a tag by kicking the ball away is automatically tagged.

6. After all students have reached the opposite end, the taggers return to the middle of the area. On the start signal, the players not tagged attempt to return to the starting side while avoiding the taggers.

7. This rotation continues until all but two of the students have become taggers. Now a new activity is started with the two untagged students as the first taggers.

Extensions:

1. Start the activity with more than two taggers.

2. If a student has a ball tagged, he must go to a designated area and dribble around five cones before returning to the activity as a tagger.

Courtesy of North American Sports Camps, *Fun and games*. This activity was originally named Dribble Bulldogs.

It's Crowded

Objective: To improve students' ability to keep their eyes focused forward while dribbling

Equipment: One ball per student

Activity:

1. Each student dribbles a ball in general space.

2. Begin to decrease the size of the space in which the students may dribble until movement is limited.

3. Slowly increase the size of the play area.

Extensions:

1. Students dribble a ball smaller than a soccer ball.
2. On a signal students must change directions with the ball.

Summary

Soccer is one of the most popular organized sports that young children play today. In recent years, professional soccer and the World Cup Soccer Championships have received a great deal of media attention. Because of this, children are becoming more and more interested about learning how to play. Probably the most difficult technique for children to master is the soccer dribble.

When young children first learn the soccer dribble, it is a classic case of the ball controlling the child, not the child controlling the ball. Children often mistake a kick, chase, and kick as a soccer dribble; managing the ball has not yet become part of the skill for them. By teaching the mechanics of the soccer dribble and really emphasizing the idea of "light taps," students begin to understand how to successfully control the ball. With this new skill, soccer will be transformed from a kick and chase activity to a challenging yet enjoyable sport that children can play for many years.

Soccer Dribble Troubleshooting Chart

IF YOU SEE	THEN TRY THIS
1. Student using the toe to dribble the ball	• Hang a two-liter soda bottle from a net or rope suspended between two game standards. The bottle should be hung so it is no more than one inch off the ground. The student must tap the bottle from side to side using the inside or outside of the foot. • Have students work in pairs. One partner dribbles the ball a specified distance. The other partner counts the number of times the toe touches the ball. The object is to get a score of zero.
2. Student not using short taps to dribble the ball	• Review the concept of force. • Give each student has a ball to dribble. Walk through the playing area and try to take the ball away from any student who taps it too far away. The object is for the students to keep all balls away from you. • Set up cones approximately two to four feet apart and scattered throughout the playing area. The student must dribble the ball through the cones and tap the ball at least once before passing any one cone.
3. Student always using the same foot	• Have students work in pairs. One partner dribbles the ball a specified distance. The student dribbling must alternate feet during the dribble. The other partner counts every time the feet do not alternate. The object is to get a score of zero. • Hang a two-liter soda bottle from a net or rope suspended between two game standards. The bottle should be hung so it is no more than one inch off the ground. The student must tap the bottle from side to side using the instep or outside of the foot.
4. Eyes focused on the ball	• Students work in pairs. Using an empty milk jug, deflated ball, Nerf ball, etc., one student tries to move the object through the playing area while maintaining eye contact with her partner. • Have the student work with a partner, playing keep away.
5. Student walking while dribbling the ball	• Students work in pairs. One partner is a tagger. The tagger may fast walk to try to catch the dribbler and get the ball. The dribbler may fast walk or run to stay away from the tagger. The object is to keep the ball away from the tagger. • Play the Soccer Madness activity (see page 193).

Soccer Dribble Lesson Plan (First Lesson)

Age group: Second grade

Focus: Keeping control of the soccer dribble

Subfocus: Using different parts of the foot to dribble, moving in general space, and applying the concept of force with a manipulative skill

Objective: To control the ball while performing the soccer dribble on four out of five attempts as measured by teacher observation (**CUES:** "Use the flat part of your foot," "Easy taps," "Keep it close").

Materials/Equipment: One partially deflated playground ball for each student. You will need one floor hockey stick and one tennis ball for a demonstration.

Organization/Management: Students are in personal space for warm-up, instruction, and practice.

Warm-Up:

Students enter the gymnasium and begin moving to music. Call out the different locomotor movements the children should perform, including jog, skip, gallop, and slide.

Watch for students moving safely and performing the locomotor skills correctly. Modify the activity to include the movement concept of force. For example, challenge the children to jog with light force, skip with light force, gallop with light force, and so on.

Watch for students moving safely and performing the skills correctly.

Formation:

Students find personal space in the gymnasium and face you.

Introduction:

Your locomotor skills are wonderful. Besides performing locomotor skills and using different amounts of force, you also had to do something else to be successful with the warm-up. What was it? **(Keeping personal space while moving in general space.)**

Great. Today we're going to work on a skill that also requires us to keep that personal space and use light force. This time we have to keep more than our body under control; we have to keep an object under control, too. We're going to work on a soccer dribble today.

To perform a soccer dribble correctly we have to use our feet to TAP the ball forward, move to it, and TAP it again. It takes a lot of practice to keep the ball from rolling too far. We're going to work with playground balls today that don't have as much air in them as normal. This way, they won't roll too far.

When I call out the color, or something about the shirt you are wearing (if you are wearing a shirt with an animal on it, a shirt with red on it, a shirt with stripes, etc.), you may go get a playground ball and return to your personal space.

GREAT JOB. Everyone stand up where you are and place the ball on the floor. When I put the music on, I want you to move in general space at a slow speed and tap the ball with LIGHT force using only your feet. You must be able to keep the ball close to you, so you don't want to tap it too hard—use LIGHT force. (Begin music.)

Watch for students moving safely and keeping the ball close to them by only tapping lightly. Repeat the cue words "Easy taps" and "Keep it close."

FREEZE. You are doing very well. Now, if I want to really control a ball, should I tap it with a flat surface or a round surface? You think about it while I try an experiment. (Demonstrate using a hockey stick and a tennis ball. Place the ball on the ground. First use the toe of the hockey stick and tap the ball several times. Then use the flat side of the hockey stick to tap the ball several times.)

When did I have the most control over where the ball went? That's right, when I used the flat part of the stick. When we dribble a soccer ball, we need to use the flat part of our foot, too. Everyone show me a flat part of your foot. That's right, we can use the inside or the outside. Our toe is great for kicking and power, but for control, we need that flat part of our foot. (Demonstrate a soccer dribble using the inside and outside of your foot versus the toe for controlling the ball.)

When the music begins, I would like you to move around the gymnasium, dribbling the ball with the flat part of your foot. Again, you want to have EASY TAPS and KEEP IT CLOSE. (Begin music.)

Watch for students using the inside and outside of their feet to dribble. Repeat the cues "Use the flat part of your foot," "Easy taps," and "Keep it close."

FREEZE. When I say GO, I would like everyone to find a partner and sit down side by side with the two balls beside you. GO.

This time, you will play "Follow the Leader." The younger of you will be the leader first. The other partner will follow him or her and keep control of the ball. I will clap my hands when it's time to switch. Now, see who is the younger. Stand up and place the balls on the floor. Do you understand the directions? GO. (Begin music.)

Watch for students using the inside and outside of their feet to dribble, keeping control of the ball, and "following the leader." Repeat the cues "Use the flat part of your foot," "Easy taps," and "Keep it close." (After two to three minutes, the other partner is the leader.)

FREEZE. When I say GO, I would like you and your partner to find another pair of students and sit near each other. GO.

Now, you have a group of four. I would like you to stand up in height order with the shortest person in front. Moving SLOWLY so as not to lose anyone, you will pretend that you are a train. The first person will be the locomotive and the rest of you will be cars on the train. You must dribble your ball and stay behind the locomotive. Do you understand these directions? Stand up with your group. When the music starts, you may begin. (Begin music.)

Watch for control of the ball and following the leader. Repeat the cue words "Easy taps" and "Keep it close" often. (After two minutes the locomotive is rotated so that everyone has a turn.)

FREEZE. Please put your equipment away and line up.

Closure:

Let's review the key ideas we learned today.

1. *What part of my foot do I use to dribble a soccer ball?* ***(The flat part.)***

2. *What kind of force did we use today when dribbling a ball?* ***(Light force.)***

3. *Which foot do I use to dribble with?* ***(Either foot.)*** *That's right, and next time we will work on dribbling with our right foot and our left foot.*

chapter 9

Striking

Striking is an integral part of many sport activities. The strike can take the form of an underhand strike as in a volleyball serve, a side-arm strike as in a tennis forehand, or a two-hand side-arm strike as in batting.

Children's first attempts at striking tend to be uncontrollable "swats" or "hits" *at* an object. As children develop their skills, the swat becomes more recognizable as a strike. Unfortunately, when first learning the strike, children tend to hit an object as hard as they can. The challenge for teachers is to provide adequate cues and activities to help children control the striking movement. This allows them to control the force of the strike and the direction of the object being struck.

In this chapter, we will examine all three of the primary striking patterns: the underhand strike (volleyball serve), the side-arm strike (tennis forehand), and the two-hand side-arm strike (batting). Due to the complexity of each skill and the use or nonuse of equipment, the age for mastery of each skill varies. The NASPE Outcomes Project suggests that a second grade student should be able to strike a ball with three different body parts toward a target (outcome 2-13), repeatedly strike a ball with a paddle (outcome 2-14), and use the correct grip and stance to bat a ball off a tee (outcome 2-15). By fourth grade, NASPE suggests that the student should be able to strike a softly thrown ball with either a bat or a paddle (outcome 4-7).

Underhand Strike

The underhand throwing components are very similar to the underhand serve in volleyball. Once a child becomes proficient with the underhand throw, it is easier for him to develop the underhand strike skill. When this movement pattern is set, the addition of implements can transform the skill into a serve in badminton.

We have found that mastery of the underhand strike may not occur until the second or third grade. It should, however, be introduced in kindergarten.

Basic Components

Ready Position
—face the direction of the strike, feet shoulder-width apart, eyes looking forward, ball held in non-dominant hand in front of the body at waist level.

Step and Swing
—pull striking arm back past the midline of the body to waist level, lean forward, step forward with nondominant foot while dominant hand strikes the ball in front of the body at waist level or below.

Hit
—strike the underside of the ball with the heel of the hand while continuing the step with the foot opposite the striking hand.

Follow Through
—hand continues in the direction of the ball but does not go beyond the height of the shoulder.

Cue Words

The cue words you select for each phase of the skill will depend on the age of the students you are teaching and your areas of emphasis. We have listed, in usable sets, some of the cue words we have used to teach the underhand strike. You may use each set individually or mix and match the cue words as needed. We have found that it is beneficial to have the students say the words out loud as they practice the skill.

READY—face the target, feet shoulder-width apart, eyes looking forward, ball held in nondominant hand in front of the body at waist level.

START—face the direction of the strike, feet shoulder-width apart, eyes looking forward.

HOLD IT LOW and EXTEND—ball is held in nondominant hand, arm is extended and in front of the body at waist level.

STEP—step forward with foot opposite the striking hand.

HIT—strike the ball on the underside.

ARM BACK—pull striking arm back in a straight pathway behind the body about waist level.

STEP AND SWING and STEP AND HIT—step forward with nondominant foot while dominant hand strikes the ball in front of the body at waist level or below. Hit ball on the underside with the heel of the hand.

FOLLOW THROUGH—hand continues in the direction of the ball but does not go beyond the height of the shoulder.

Cue Set 1: READY, STEP, HIT

Cue Set 2: HOLD IT LOW, STEP, HIT

Cue Set 3: START, EXTEND, STEP AND SWING, FOLLOW THROUGH

Cue Set 4: READY, ARM BACK, STEP AND HIT, FOLLOW THROUGH

Suggested Activities for Reinforcing the Components

In the learning process, it is essential that students know how a skill is supposed to look, what its component parts are, and how to perform each individual component correctly. In the preceding section, we furnished pictures and descriptions of the underhand strike, divided it into its component parts, and provided possible cue words. In addition to the material in chapter 3 that reinforces the concepts for all locomotor and manipulative skills, the following section provides specific activities for reinforcing the components unique to the underhand strike.

Partner Skill Check

Objective: To allow partners to assess each other's progress learning the skill

Equipment: Partner skill check sheets, pencils, and one ball for each set of partners. If the students cannot read or do not speak English, the picture version of the partner skill check sheet may be useful.

Activity:

1. One partner observes the other to see if she has the correct form for the ready position.

2. If the ready position is correct, then the partner places a *Y* in the first box. If the ready position is not correct, she places an *N* in the first box. Non-readers can put a smiling face if the ready position is correct or a sad face if the ready position is not correct.

3. This evaluation continues until each of the components has been assessed five times.

4. A partner skill check sheet is used for each student.

Extensions:

1. You may use the partner skill check sheet to assess the skill development of each student.

2. You may send the partner skill check sheet home with report cards or as individual skills develop.

Skill: **Underhand Strike**

Striker's name: _____ Watcher's name: _____

 **1.**

1   2   3   4   5

Ready

 **2.**

1   2   3   4   5

Step and swing

 **3.**

1   2   3   4   5

Hit

 **4.**

1   2   3   4   5

Follow through

Partner Skill Check

Skill: **Underhand Strike**

Striker's name: _____   Watcher's name:_____

Watch your partner and mark each component of the skill. Let your partner do the skill 5 times. Each time your partner does it right, mark a **Y** in the box. If your partner doesn't do it right, mark an **N** in the box.

START

TRIALS

Ready position

1. Eyes on target
2. Feet shoulder-width apart
3. Ball held in nonhitting hand
4. Ball to front and side of body, waist level

1	2	3	4	5

ACTION

Step and swing

1. Swing hitting hand back

1	2	3	4	5

2. Body leans forward a little

1	2	3	4	5

3. Step forward with foot opposite the striking hand

1	2	3	4	5

Hit

4. Swing hitting hand forward, heel of hand hits lower half of ball

1	2	3	4	5

STOP

Follow through

1. Hand swings to shoulder height

1	2	3	4	5

© A.Y. Colvin, N.J. Markos, and P.J. Walker, 2000, *Teaching the Nuts and Bolts of Physical Education* (Champaign, IL: Human Kinetics).

Success Builders

The success builder activities allow you to address individual needs. If students need additional help on individual component parts, the activities listed below will help reinforce correct performance.

Objective: To allow partners to improve areas of deficiency as assessed by the partner skill check

Equipment: See individual stations. We suggest using an unbreakable mirror and a poster of each component of the underhand strike at each station. The mirror is particularly helpful in these activities because it allows the child to see what he is doing. The easiest way to make the posters would be to photocopy the drawings from this book. Use an opaque projector to enlarge them. Laminating the posters will ensure their use for many years.

Activity:

1. Set up a station for each of the four components in the teaching area. Post a description or a picture of the specific component at the corresponding station.

2. Stations:

Ready

—face target, feet shoulder-width apart, eyes looking forward, object held in nondominant hand at waist level in front of the body.

Equipment: Component poster, mirror (if available), and partner evaluations

Activity 1: The student assumes the ready position. The partner checks to see if her position matches the poster. The student refers to the mirror for help. The student pretends to strike a ball and on a signal from her partner assumes the ready position again. Once the student can successfully demonstrate the ready position to the partner, partners may return to practicing the entire skill.

Activity 2: Sometimes children will bend the arm that is holding the ball, which will cause an improper hit. An elbow pad can help the student feel the elbow bend during practice and cue him to keep that arm straight. As soon as possible, remove the elbow pad and encourage the student to practice without it.

Step and Swing

—pull striking arm back past midline of the body to waist level, step forward with nondominant foot while dominant hand strikes the ball in front of the body at waist level or below.

Equipment: Component poster, tape (floor or masking) on floor, and partner evaluations

Activity: The student assumes a stride position with the leg opposite the striking hand forward. (If necessary, use floor or masking tape on the floor or other visual cues that will assist the student in stepping in opposition.) The student should begin practice from this position, then progress to starting with feet together and then stepping with the opposite foot. Once the student can successfully demonstrate a good step and swing to the partner, the partners may return to practicing the entire skill.

Hit

—strike the ball on the underside with the heel of the hand while continuing to step with the foot opposite the striking hand.

Equipment: Component poster, balls, chalk eraser, and partner evaluations

Activity 1: Use a magic marker to draw a three-inch diameter circle on the ball. The student holds the ball so that she can easily hit the circle with the striking hand. Have the student practice striking the ball so that she can see the heel of the striking hand hitting the circle drawn on the ball.

Activity 2: Using a dusty eraser from the classroom, put some chalk dust on the lower half of the ball. Have the children strike the ball so that they have chalk dust on the heel of their striking hand after the hit.

Follow Through

—hand continues in the direction of the ball but does not go beyond the height of the shoulder.

Equipment: Component poster, overhead projector, unbreakable mirror, and partner evaluations

Activity 1: The student stands so that he is between the overhead projector and a wall. It should be possible for the student to cast a shadow on the wall when he practices. The student practices the underhand strike, and his partner places a piece of tape on the wall showing how far his hand went after the strike. The partners continue the drill until the student consistently stops the follow-through before reaching the shoulder level.

Activity 2: The student faces the mirror and practices the underhand strike without a ball. The student watches the mirror to determine where she ends the follow-through. The partner may also evaluate the student.

Suggested Culminating Activities to Reinforce the Entire Skill

Individual Activities

Color Targets

Objective: To improve the underhand strike by hitting a specific target

Equipment: Laminated construction paper of different colors and sizes (about 8 to 12 targets of each color) taped to the wall of the gymnasium or activity area and a ball for each student (volleyball, playground ball, eight-inch Nerf ball, etc.)

Activity:

1. Create a "color box" in which samples from each color of construction paper have been placed. You will need more samples than you have students.

2. Select a student to draw a sample color from the color box.

3. The sample color chosen is the color target all students must hit using the underhand strike.

4. Students continue to strike the targets of the selected color until you give a stop signal.

5. The activity continues until all students have been given an opportunity to draw from the color box.

Extensions:

1. Instead of using different colors, students could select different shapes from the "shape box," letters from the "alphabet box," or words from the "word box."

2. Students work with partners. The partner chooses the color, shape, letter, or word that will be used for a target. The student must hit the selected target using the underhand strike. Partners take turns selecting targets and striking.

Create-A-Word

Objective: To create words by hitting letters using the underhand strike

Equipment: One ball (volleyball, playground ball, eight-inch Nerf ball, etc.) per student and four complete sets of laminated alphabet letters scattered and taped to the wall of the gymnasium or activity area. It would be advantageous to have extra copies of vowels and selected consonants (e.g., N, R, S, T). You will also need paper and markers or a chalkboard and chalk to serve as a "word bank."

Activity:

1. On your start signal, students begin to spell words by striking different letters of the alphabet.

2. Once a student has created a word, he goes to the word bank (paper or chalkboard) and writes the word. It will be helpful to have several word banks so students will not have to wait in line to write their words.

3. A word may be "banked" or written only once on the paper or chalkboard.

4. If a student strikes a letter that cannot be used to form the word being created, she must strike the letter again to delete it.

Extensions:

1. Students work with partners. One student hits letters to spell a word while his partner records the word and evaluates the underhand strike. The striker may not use the letter until the underhand strike is performed properly. When the striker has spelled a word, the partner is then given an opportunity to collect letters using the underhand strike.

2. Students work with partners. Partners are given paper and pencil to record the letters they hit and to write down the words they create. Each partner must strike a vowel and two consonants until the pair has six letters to use to create words. The partners attempt to create six words using one or more of the letters they have hit. Once the partners have created six

words and written them down, they attempt to spell the words by using the underhand strike to hit the letters with the ball. Once a word is spelled, it may be checked off the list. If the students are unable to use a letter they have hit, they must strike that letter to delete it and select another letter.

Partner Activities

Challenge

Objective: To practice the underhand strike in a variety of settings

Equipment: One ball per pair of students and laminated challenge cards

Activity:

1. Students select a challenge card.
2. Students perform the task described on the card.
3. Possible challenges may include:
   - Strike the ball using hard force (light force, medium force).
   - Strike the ball to hit targets at different levels (high, medium).
   - Strike the ball at the same time your partner does.

Extensions:

1. Place multicolored targets on the wall and have the partner tell the striker which target to hit.
2. Set up game standards with a volleyball net or rope between them. The striker must strike the ball over the net/rope. Use different heights for the net/rope.
3. Suspend a rope between two game standards. Attach various objects (e.g., empty two-liter plastic bottles, hoops, aluminum pie pans) to the rope. Students must call out which object they will hit before they strike the ball.

Wall Ball

Objective: To improve the underhand striking skill by hitting a ball to a wall

Equipment: One ball (playground or volleyball) per student pair

Activity:

1. Partners stand at least 15 feet from the wall.
2. One partner uses the underhand strike to hit the ball against the wall.
3. Her partner has to catch the ball after it comes off the wall but before it hits the ground.
4. When the partner has caught the ball, she must underhand strike the ball back to the wall from the place it was caught.
5. Partners count how many successful strikes and catches they have in a row.

Extensions:

1. Allow the ball to bounce once before it is caught.

2. Place a target on the wall and challenge the partners to strike it.

Back It Up

Objective: To improve the underhand striking skill by hitting a ball to a partner from varying distances

Equipment: One ball (volleyball, playground ball, eight-inch Nerf ball, etc.) per student pair

Activity:

1. Students stand approximately 10 feet apart and face each other.

2. The student with the ball underhand strikes the ball to his partner, who must catch it.

3. After the partner catches it, he underhand strikes it back to the partner, who must catch it.

4. Once the ball has been hit and caught twice, one of the partners takes a step backward and the process is repeated.

5. If the ball is not hit correctly or caught, the partners must return to their original location.

Extensions:

1. After a correct strike, you may allow the ball to bounce once before it is caught without any penalty.

2. A volleyball net (or rope) may be used so that the students have to strike the ball over it to a partner.

From *Complete elementary physical education guide* by Rosalie Bryant and Eloise McLean Oliver. Copyright © 1975. Reprinted with permission of Prentice Hall Direct.

Through the Hoop

Objective: To improve underhand striking accuracy by hitting a ball through a suspended hoop

Equipment: A large hula hoop suspended from an overhead structure (e.g., game standards, basketball backboards, etc.) and one ball per student pair

Activity:

1. Partners stand on each side of the hoop.

2. Partners take turns trying to hit the ball using the underhand strike so that it goes through the hoop.

Extensions:

1. Partners may count how many successful strikes they have in a specified time period (e.g., one minute).

2. Partners may be required to have a correct underhand strike and a successful catch before the strike is counted.

Group Activities

Create Your Own Activity

Objective: To allow students to create their own activity to reinforce the underhand strike

Equipment: One piece of paper and pencil per group and a predetermined list of equipment you will allow the students to use in their activities (e.g., bowling pins, cones, ropes, hula hoops, volleyballs, Nerf balls, etc.)

Activity:

1. Form groups with two to five students each. You may select the groups or the students may form their own.

2. Students create their own activity using the underhand strike as the basic skill. Students are required to have rules that encourage correct performance of the skill, include all players, and address all safety concerns.

3. The groups write their individual names, the rules of the activity, and the equipment needed on their paper and then show the activity to you.

4. Upon approval of their activity, the students obtain the necessary equipment and begin playing the activity.

5. You must approve all changes to the activity.

Extensions:

1. Groups may teach their activities to another group.

2. Groups may teach their activities to the entire class.

Cycle/Recycle

Objective: To improve the underhand strike by striking balls over a net

Equipment: Two game standards and a net at volleyball height, and one soft ball (e.g., Super Safe, Gator Skin, beach ball, or Nerf ball) per student

Activity:

1. Divide the class in half.

2. Place half the class on either side of the net.

3. On the start signal, everyone strikes the balls over the net.

4. Students count the number of balls they strike over the net.

Extensions:

1. Have the students total the number of correct strikes (strikes over the net) the entire group made over the net. These results can be recorded and later charted or graphed to show class improvement.

2. Each time a student strikes the ball over the net, she goes around the standards and becomes a member of the other group.

Adapted, by permission, from J.A. Wessell, PhD, 1974, *Project I CAN* (Northbrook, IL: Hubbard).

Underhand Strike Troubleshooting Chart

IF YOU SEE	THEN TRY THIS
1. Ball not held in front of body	• Place a mirror in front of the student so he can see his arm and hand placement. • The student works with a partner. The student gets into the correct position, and the partner places the ball into his hand.
2. Arm not going back far enough	• Hang a balloon from a net or rope suspended between two game standards. Have the student stand in front of the balloon and swing her arm back until it hits the balloon. This can also be done with the student standing with her back to the wall and swinging her arm back to touch the wall. • Place a large piece of paper on the wall. Have the student stand sideways to the paper and mark the student's waist height. Swing the student's arm back and draw the arc of the backswing on the paper for the student to see.
3. Student not stepping, or stepping forward on the wrong foot	• Place a spot or footprint in front of the student. He must step onto the spot or footprint before hitting the ball. • Place a small whoopee cushion in front of the student. The student must step onto the cushion before hitting the ball.
4. Student throwing the ball up in the air before striking	• Have a partner touch the arm holding the ball. The partner needs to apply enough resistance so the student can feel the arm remaining stationary. • Hang a balloon from a net or rope suspended between two game standards. Have the student hold the balloon and strike it. If the student tosses the balloon he will see a bend in the balloon rope.
5. Student not using the heel of the hand to strike the ball	• Hang a damp sponge from a volleyball net or rope suspended between two game standards. Have the student hit the sponge with the heel of her hand. Check to see where the water is on the hand. • Partners face each other; one has her hand outstretched with the palm down. Using light force and an underhand motion, the other partner swings her arm and strikes the first partner's outstretched hand with the heel of her hand.
6. Swing arm not following through	• Suspend a net or rope between two game standards so the bottom of it is at the student's shoulder height. Have the student perform the skill without a ball, continuing the arm swing until the heel of the hand touches the net. • Partners face each other; one has his hand outstretched with the palm down at shoulder height. Using light force and an underhand motion, the other partner swings his arm and strikes the first partner's outstretched hand with the heel of his hand.

Summary

Playing a game of volleyball can be a very frustrating experience for older students who are poorly skilled in the underhand strike technique. When it becomes their turn to serve, many are unable to execute even a basic underhand serve. In our experience, we have learned that these students do not hold the ball low before contact and the resulting hit goes up to the ceiling. Another major problem happens when children bend their holding arm and a mis-hit occurs. While both of these mechanical problems are easy to correct in elementary school, the motor pattern may be difficult to alter in later years. During initial instruction, the elementary school-aged child does not need the challenge of hitting a ball over a net. Proper instruction and plenty of practice opportunities while working with a wall or a partner will ensure improved mechanics and better participation in later grades.

Underhand Strike Lesson Plan (Second Lesson)

Age group: Second grade

Focus: Extension of the nonstriking arm

Subfocus: Bending and extending body parts, and stepping in opposition

Objective: To fully extend the nondominant arm before the ball is contacted during the underhand strike four out of five times as measured by teacher observation. (**CUES:** "Extend your arm," "Arm straight," "Keep it low.")

Materials/Equipment: One Super Safe ball or beach ball (or similar ball) per student

Organization/Management: Students are in personal space for warm-up, instruction, and practice. Set up teaching stations with one ball beside the wall and a line parallel to and at least 15 feet from the wall.

Warm-up:

Today we're going to warm up with music. When the music starts, I would like you to jog in general space. When the music stops you will FREEZE in your own personal space.

Watch for students moving safely.

(Stop music.) *Everyone stand where you are and look toward me. I would like to make your warm-ups more challenging by teaching you the words BEND and EXTEND. Watch as I bend my arm, now I extend the arm to make it straight. Can you bend one leg? Can you extend that leg to make it straight? Can you bend your wrist? Can you extend your wrist? Excellent.*

This time, I'm going to use the words we just learned to make our warm-ups more challenging. Use the locomotor movement that I call out and when the music stops, freeze in a position where you will either bend or extend the body part I name. (Select two students to demonstrate the skip and on FREEZE tell the students to fully extend their arms.) *Do you understand what you are to do? GO.*

Watch for students performing the locomotor skills correctly and using the bending and extension commands correctly. Stop the children several times to change the locomotor movement and the limb to bend or extend.

Formation:

Students find personal space in the gymnasium and face you.

Introduction:

Today, we will be putting the EXTEND and BEND words to use with the underhand strike. Who can tell me how to do this underhand striking skill? (Using the "teach the teacher" technique, review the key components of READY, SWING, STEP AND HIT, and FOLLOW-THROUGH, placing particular emphasis on stepping in opposition.) *Excellent. Everyone stand up. Let's pretend that we have an imaginary ball in our hand. Get ready, swing your arm back, step with your stepping foot, hit, and follow through.* (Children practice several times.)

Watch for stepping in opposition and following through.

Excellent. When we did our warm-ups today, I had you practice bending and extending different parts of your body. To do the underhand strike correctly, we have to really extend one arm, and that's what we are going to stress today. Everyone stand up in your personal space. Face me. Hold your striking arm (dominant arm) high in the air. Take your other arm and extend it downward in front of you so that your hand makes an **L** *(see figure).*

It is very important that the arm be almost straight. Excellent.

Watch for straight arms extended in front of the body.

Pretend you have a ball in that hand. Really extend that arm—keep it straight. Can you step, hit the ball, and follow through? Let's try that a few times with our imaginary ball.

Watch for straight arms extending in front of the body, stepping in opposition, and following through.

FREEZE. You are doing very well. Help me remember, how do I hold the ball? **(Straight arm.)** *Excellent. Now you are ready to work with a ball. Watch as I strike the ball.* (Demonstrate several times.) *Who can tell me where I strike the ball?* **(Bottom half.)** *Excellent! What can you tell me about my feet?* **(They're stepping in opposition or you're using the stepping foot.)** *What about the arm that holds the ball?* **(Extend it.)**

It's time to practice. There are balls placed against the walls and there are lines marked off in front of them. When I tell you to GO, you will find a station, pick up the ball, and stand on your line, but still face me. (Dismiss students by groups.)

Terrific. When I say "GO," you may begin striking the ball toward the wall. Remember to extend your arm and hold the ball low. GO.

Watch for arm extension and stepping in opposition. Children practice for three to five minutes.

FREEZE. Everyone find a partner and sit down side by side on one of your lines. GO. Now, we will only need one ball for the two of you. One of you return a ball and then come back to your line. GO.

This time you are going to help each other with the skill. Your partner will underhand strike the ball against the wall and you will really watch to make sure he or she is holding the ball low to begin with and is stepping with the correct foot. YOU have to make sure your partner can do those things. I will tell you when to change jobs. Do you understand these directions? GO.

Watch for arm extension and stepping in opposition. Children practice for two to three minutes, then change jobs.

FREEZE. All of you are doing very well. This time you and your partner are going to play a cooperative activity. It is called Wall Ball. Watch as (student) and I demonstrate. I will underhand strike the ball to the wall and when it comes off the wall, (student) will catch it. It's okay to let it bounce once. But I have to strike it so (student) can be there to catch it. Then (student) will strike the ball and I'll catch it. We want to count how many times we can do this in a row. You must really work together. Do you understand the directions? GO.

Watch for arm extension, stepping in opposition, and good catching techniques. If any skill problems occur, stop the class and reteach the skills. Children practice for five to seven minutes.

Closure:

Line up the students to leave.

*Girls and boys, who can tell me how to hold the ball in my hand? (**Make an L and really extend the arm.**) Where do I strike the ball? (**On the bottom half.**) Which foot do I step with when I strike the ball? (**My opposite foot or my stepping foot.**) Next time we are going to practice striking the ball to a target.*

Side-Arm Strike

The side-arm strike can be performed by striking the ball out of the hand as in the side-arm volleyball serve or off a bounce as in handball. When equipment is added, the side-arm strike can become the forehand stroke used in racket sports. For young children, using an implement to strike an object may be difficult. They can, however, become proficient in using the side-arm strike technique to hit a bounced playground ball. The following section will focus on the mechanics of the side-arm strike without using an implement. Later, as the child's eye-hand coordination improves, you can add smaller balls, paddles, and rackets successfully.

Basic Components

Ready Position
—front of the body toward the target, eyes on the target, feet shoulder-width apart, knees bent, hands parallel with palms facing each other and fingers pointing forward.

T
—body turns as the feet pivot in place, side to target, arms extended in the shape of a **T**. Extend the striking hand away from the intended line of travel with the palm facing outward. Hold the ball toward the target in the nonstriking hand. Drop the ball. Eyes are on the ball throughout the movement.

Step and Hit
—step toward the target with the foot opposite the striking arm, arm swings through as the hip and shoulder rotate toward the target allowing the front body surface to face the target.

Follow Through
—hand continues in the direction of the strike.

Cue Words

The cue words you select for each phase of the skill will depend on the age of the students you are teaching and your areas of emphasis. We have listed, in usable sets, some of the cue words we have used to teach the side-arm strike. You may use each set individually or mix and match the cue words as needed. We have found that it is beneficial to have the students say the words out loud as they practice the skill.

READY—face the target, feet shoulder-width apart, weight evenly distributed on both feet, ball is held in nondominant hand

START and DROP—nondominant side toward the target, feet shoulder-width apart, and weight evenly distributed on both feet. Bring the striking hand back parallel to the ground. Drop the ball from the nondominant hand. Eyes are on the ball throughout the movement.

T—body turns as the feet pivot in place, side to target, arms extended in the shape of a **T**. Extend the striking hand away from the intended line of travel with the palm facing outward. Hold the ball in the nonstriking hand toward the target. Drop the ball from the nondominant hand. Eyes are on the ball throughout the movement.

STEP—step toward the target with the foot opposite the striking arm, arm swings through as the hip and shoulder rotate toward the target, allowing the front body surface to face the target (use the cue "bellybutton" to help reinforce correct body position).

GO—step forward with opposite foot while bringing striking hand forward.

STEP AND HIT—step toward the target with the nondominant foot, hips and spine rotate as the arm is brought forward. Strike object with hand.

HIT and WHACK IT—strike ball with dominant hand.

FOLLOW THROUGH—striking hand continues in the direction of the hit.

REACH HIGH—hand continues in the direction of the strike.

Cue Set 1: READY, T, STEP, FOLLOW THROUGH

Cue Set 2: START, GO, HIT

Cue Set 3: DROP, GO, WHACK IT

Cue Set 4: START, STEP AND HIT, REACH HIGH

Suggested Activities for Reinforcing the Components

In the learning process, it is essential that students know how a skill is supposed to look, what its component parts are, and how to perform each individual component correctly. In the preceding section, we furnished pictures and descriptions of the side-arm strike, divided it into its component parts, and provided possible cue words. In addition to the material in chapter 3 that reinforces the concepts for all locomotor and manipulative skills, the following section provides specific activities for reinforcing the components unique to the side-arm strike.

Partner Skill Check

Objective: To allow partners to assess each other's progress learning the skill

Equipment: Partner skill check sheets, pencils, and one ball for each set of partners. If the students cannot read or do not speak English, the picture version of the partner skill check sheet may be useful.

Activity:

1. One partner observes the other to see if he has the correct form for the ready position.

2. If the ready position is correct, then the partner places a *Y* in the first box. If the ready position is not correct, he places an *N* in the first box. Non-readers can put a smiling face if the ready position is correct or a sad face if the ready position is not correct.

3. This evaluation continues until each of the components has been assessed five times.

4. A partner skill check sheet is used for each student.

Extensions:

1. You may use the partner skill check sheet to assess the skill development of each student.

2. You may send partner skill check sheets home with report cards or as individual skills develop.

Success Builders

The success builder activities allow you to address individual needs. If students need additional help on individual component parts, the activities listed below will help reinforce correct performance.

Objective: To allow partners to improve areas of deficiency as assessed by the partner skill check

Equipment: See individual stations. We suggest using an unbreakable mirror and a poster of each component of the side-arm strike at each station. The mirror is particularly helpful in these activities because it allows the child to see what she is doing. The easiest way to make the posters would be to photocopy the drawings from this book. Use an opaque projector to enlarge them. Laminating the posters will ensure their use for many years.

Activity:

1. Set up a station for each of the four components in the teaching area. Post a description or a picture of the specific component at the corresponding station.

2. Stations:

Ready

—front of the body toward the target, eyes on the target, feet shoulder-width apart, knees bent, ball is held in nondominant hand.

Equipment: Component poster, mirror (if available), and partner evaluations

Activity: The student assumes the ready position. The partner checks to see if his position matches the poster. The student refers to the mirror for help. The student pretends to strike a ball and on a signal from his partner assumes the ready position again. Once the student can successfully demonstrate the ready position to the partner, partners may return to practicing the entire skill.

Striker's name: _____ Watcher's name:_____

1.

    1   2   3   4   5

Ready

2.

    1   2   3   4   5

T

3.

    1   2   3   4   5

Step and hit

4.

    1   2   3   4   5

Follow through

Partner Skill Check

Skill: **Side-Arm Strike**

Striker's name: _____ Watcher's name:_____

Watch your partner and mark each component of the skill. Let your partner do the skill 5 times. Each time your partner does it right, mark a **Y** in the box. If your partner doesn't do it right, mark an **N** in the box.

START

Ready position

1. Eyes on the target
2. Knees bent
3. Feet shoulder-width apart
4. Hands apart in front of the body

TRIALS

1 2 3 4 5

ACTION

T

1. Side to target

1 2 3 4 5

2. T—hitting hand back, other hand pointing at target

1 2 3 4 5

Step and hit

3. Step forward on opposite foot

1 2 3 4 5

4. Hip and shoulder turn to target, palm of hand points in direction of hit

1 2 3 4 5

STOP

Follow through

1. Arm continues across body after the release, bellybutton points toward target

1 2 3 4 5

—body turns as the feet pivot in place, side to target, arms extended in the shape of a T. Extend the striking hand away from the intended line of travel with the palm facing outward. Hold the ball in the nonstriking hand toward the target. Drop the ball from the nondominant hand. Eyes are on the ball throughout the movement.

Equipment: Component poster, tape (floor or masking) on floor, and partner evaluations

Activity 1: The student turns his nondominant side toward the target and assumes a stride position with the leg opposite the striking hand stepping forward. (If necessary, use floor or masking tape on the floor or other visual cues that will assist the student in stepping in opposition.) The arms extend to make a T. The student should begin practice from this position, then progress to starting with feet together (READY) and then pivoting to the T (READY, T). Once the student can successfully demonstrate a good turn to the T position to the partner, the partners may return to practicing the entire skill.

Activity 2: Sometimes children will bend the arm that is to strike the ball, which will cause an improper hit. An elbow pad can help the student feel the elbow bend during practice, cueing her to keep that arm straight when striking the ball. As soon as possible, remove the elbow pad and encourage the student to practice without it.

Step and Hit

—step toward the target with the foot opposite the striking arm, arm swings through as the hip and shoulder rotate toward the target allowing the front body surface to face the target (use the cue "bellybutton" to help reinforce correct body position).

Equipment: Component poster, mirror, pie plate with duct tape on the bottom (allows plate to be attached to the student's shirt), PVC pipe or wooden dowel three to four feet in length, and partner evaluations.

Activity 1: The student begins this activity from the T position, nondominant side to the mirror or partner. The student holds the PVC pipe (or dowel) behind the neck with both hands at the end of the PVC pipe that faces the target. The student rotates the hips and shoulders, turning so the length of pipe is parallel to the mirror or partner. The student practices this several times before returning to practicing the entire skill.

Activity 2: The student attaches the pie plate to his shirt and works with a partner. He begins this activity from the T position with the nondominant side to the partner. On a signal from the partner, the student swings the striking arm while rotating the hips and shoulders. The student should finish the movement with the pie plate facing the partner. If a mirror is used, it should be placed in the same position as the partner. The student practices this several times before returning to practicing the entire skill.

Follow Through

—hand continues in the direction of the strike.

Equipment: Component poster, unbreakable mirror, and partner evaluations

Activity: The student faces the mirror and practices the side-arm strike without a ball. The student watches the mirror to determine when she ends the follow-through. A partner may also evaluate the student.

Suggested Culminating Activities to Reinforce the Entire Skill

Individual Activities

Color Targets

Objective: To provide students opportunities to practice the side-arm strike while hitting a specific target

Equipment: Laminated construction paper of different colors and sizes (about 8 to 12 targets of each color) taped to the wall of the gymnasium or activity area and a ball for each student (volleyball, beach ball, Nerf ball, etc.)

Activity:

1. Create a "color box" in which samples from each color of construction paper have been placed. You will need more samples than you have students.
2. Select a student to draw a sample color from the color box.
3. The sample color chosen is the color target all students must locate and strike using a side-arm strike.
4. Students continue to strike the target until you give a stop signal.
5. The activity continues until all students have been given an opportunity to draw from the color box.

Extensions:

1. Instead of using different colors, students could select different shapes from the "shape box," letters from the "alphabet box," or words from the "word box."
2. Students work with partners. The partner chooses the color, shape, letter, or word that will be used for a target. The student must strike the selected target. Partners take turns selecting targets and striking.

Create-A-Word

Objective: To create words by hitting letters using the side-arm strike

Equipment: One ball (volleyball, beach ball, Nerf ball, etc.) per student and four complete sets of laminated alphabet letters scattered and taped to the wall of the gymnasium or activity area. It would be advantageous to have extra copies of vowels and selected consonants (e.g., N, R, S, T). You will also need paper and markers or a chalkboard and chalk to serve as a "word bank."

Activity:

1. On your start signal, students begin to spell words by striking different letters of the alphabet.

2. Once a student has created a word, he goes to the word bank (paper or chalkboard) and writes the word. It will be helpful to have several word banks so students will not have to wait in line to write their words.

3. A word may be "banked" or written only once on the paper or chalkboard.

4. If a student strikes a letter that cannot be used to form the word being created, he must strike the letter again to delete it.

Extensions:

1. Students work with partners. One student hits letters to spell a word while the partner records the word and evaluates the side-arm strike. The striker may not use the letter until the side-arm strike is performed properly. When the first partner has spelled a word, the other partner is given an opportunity to strike letters.

2. Students work with partners. Partners are given paper and pencil to record the letters they hit and to write down the words they create. Each partner must perform a side-arm strike and hit a vowel and two consonants until the pair has six letters to use to create words. The partners attempt to create six words using one or more of the letters they have hit. Once the partners have created six words and written them down, they attempt to spell the words by using the side-arm strike to hit each letter. Once a word is spelled, it may be checked off the list. If the students are unable to use a letter they have hit, they must strike that letter to delete it and select another letter.

Partner Activities

Challenges

Objective: To practice the side-arm strike in a variety of settings

Equipment: One ball (beach ball, Nerf ball, or volleyball) per pair of students and laminated challenge cards

Activity:

1. Students select a challenge card.

2. Students perform the task described on the card.

3. Possible challenges may include:

   • Strike the ball using hard force (light force, medium force).

   • Strike the ball at targets at different levels (medium, low).

   • Strike the ball at the same time your partner does.

Extensions:

1. Place multicolored targets on the wall and have the partner tell the striker which target to hit.

2. Suspend a rope between two game standards. Attach various objects (e.g., empty two-liter plastic bottles, hoops, aluminum pie pans) to the rope. Students must call out which object they will hit before they strike the ball.

Back It Up

Objective: To side-arm strike the ball to a partner from different distances

Equipment: One ball (volleyball, beach ball, Nerf ball, etc.) per student pair

Activity:

1. Students stand approximately 10 feet apart and face each other.

2. The student with the ball side-arm strikes it to his partner, who must catch it after one bounce.

3. After the partner catches it, he side-arm strikes it back to the student, who must catch it after only one bounce.

4. Once the ball has been hit and caught twice, one of the partners takes a step backward and the process is repeated.

5. If the ball is not struck correctly or caught, the partners must return to their original location.

Extensions:

1. After it is struck correctly, the ball may bounce more than once before it is caught without any penalty.

2. A volleyball net (or rope) may be used so that the students have to strike the ball over the net and to their partners.

From *Complete elementary physical education guide* by Rosalie Bryant and Eloise McLean Oliver. Copyright © 1975. Reprinted with permission of Prentice Hall Direct.

Through the Hoop

Objective: To improve the accuracy of the side-arm strike by hitting a ball through a suspended hoop

Equipment: One large hula hoop, and one ball (beach ball, Nerf ball, or volleyball) per student pair. Suspend the hula hoop from an overhead structure (for example, volleyball standards or basketball goals) approximately four feet above the floor.

Activity:

1. Partners stand on each side of the hoop.

2. Partners take turns trying to hit the ball using the side-arm strike so that the ball goes through the hoop.

Extensions:

1. Partners may count how many successful strikes they have in a specified time period (e.g., one minute).

2. Partners may be required to have a successful catch before the strike is counted.

Group Activities

Create Your Own Activity

Objective: To allow students to create their own activity to reinforce the side-arm strike

Equipment: One piece of paper and pencil per group and a predetermined list of equipment you will allow the students to use in their activities (e.g., bowling pins, cones, ropes, hula hoops, beach balls, volleyballs, Nerf balls, tennis balls, etc.)

Activity:

1. Form groups with two to five students each. You may select the groups or the students may form their own.

2. Students create their own activity using the side-arm strike as the basic skill. Students are required to have rules that encourage correct performance of the skill, include all players, and address all safety concerns.

3. The groups write their individual names, the rules of the activity, and the equipment needed on their paper and then show the activity to you.

4. Upon approval of their activity, the students obtain the necessary equipment and begin playing.

5. You must approve all changes to the activity.

Extensions:

1. Groups may teach their activities to other groups.

2. Groups may teach their activities to the entire class.

Cycle/Recycle

Objective: To practice the side-arm strike by hitting all of the balls over a net

Equipment: Two volleyball standards and a net placed at tennis height, and one soft ball (e.g., Super Safe, Gator Skin, or Nerf ball) per student

Activity:

1. Divide the class in half.

2. Place half the class on either side of the net.

3. On the start signal, everyone strikes the balls over the net.

4. Students count the number of balls they strike over the net.

Extensions:

1. Students total the number of correct strikes the entire group made over the net. These results can be recorded and later charted or graphed to show class improvement.

2. Each time a student strikes the ball over the net, he goes around the standards and becomes a member of the other group.

3. Place an additional net at volleyball height and challenge the students to strike the balls between the two nets.

Adapted, by permission, from J.A. Wessell, PhD, 1974, *Project I CAN* (Northbrook, IL: Hubbard).

Keep It Going

Objective: To practice the side-arm strike while hitting the ball over a net

Equipment: Two volleyball standards, a net placed at tennis height, and one soft ball (e.g., Super Safe, Gator Skin, or Nerf ball) per group of four students

Activity:

1. Divide the students into groups of four.

2. Gather the students in a shuttle formation: make one line with two students standing front to back on one side of the net and a line of two students standing front to back on the other side of the net.

3. The first student in line starts with a ball.

4. As soon as the first student in line strikes the ball over the net, she moves and stands behind the second student on the same side of the net.

5. After the ball goes over the net it must bounce. The first student in line on the opposite side of the net must strike it back.

6. That student then moves behind the second student on the same side of the net.

7. The striking continues until the ball cannot be struck after one bounce.

Extensions:

1. Students total the number of properly performed side-arm strikes the entire group made. These results can be recorded and later charted or graphed to show class improvement.

2. Students are placed in groups of six to eight. Each time a student strikes the ball over the net, he goes around the standards and becomes a member of the other group. If the ball does not go over the net, the student tries the strike again.

Summary

Perhaps the area of biggest concern with the side-arm strike is the inability of the student to pivot or turn his side to the target. When that first action is omitted, the rest of the skill deteriorates. Unfortunately that may be a result of the way in which he was taught the skill. During initial instruction it helps to have the students already assume a side orientation while they practice the other components. As soon as the students begin to grasp the skills, however, make sure to include the pivot. Once the student is successful with this addition, increase the distance he has to move in order to strike the ball. This sequence will ensure a logical skill progression and make the practice more "game-like," and provide a better transition into future sport participation.

Side-Arm Strike Troubleshooting Chart

IF YOU SEE	THEN TRY THIS
1. Student not keeping eyes on ball	• Place a two-liter bottle on top of a cone and have the student try to knock it off. • Draw a picture on the ball and have the student focus on this as he watches the ball. If the ball has words on it, just use the words. • The student's partner bounces a ball to him using light force. He must move so the ball will touch his bellybutton.
2. Student not turning side to the target	• Draw two arrows perpendicular to each other in front of both of the student's feet as she is standing in the ready position. Have the student practice rotating on the balls of her feet to turn her side to the target. • Have the student's partner give a verbal cue to "turn" as the ball comes toward the student. • Have the student's partner bounce a ball to her. The student must rotate so the ball will touch the side of her body.
3. Student not pulling the striking arm back	• Have the student turn and touch a wall located behind him with the striking arm. • The student's partner stands behind him with one hand held in the traffic cop stop position. The student turns and pulls his arm back until it touches the palm of the partner's hand.
4. Student not taking a step forward	• Use spots placed on the floor to indicate to the student where the stepping foot should be placed during the strike. • Have the student step over a line or flat object with the opposite foot before striking. • Use a small, non-skid "bug" (floor spot) in front of the stepping foot and ask the student to "squash the bug" as she strikes the ball.
5. Limited hip and shoulder rotation	• Have the student check his bellybutton position after the strike. It should be facing in the direction of the target. • Have a partner hold rubber tubing or Dynabands to add resistance while the student goes through the rotation motion.
6. Striking arm not coming through in an extended position	• Hang an object (small wind chimes, sheet, pie plates, etc.) from a net or rope suspended between two game standards. Have the student touch the object as the striking arm moves forward. • Have the student's partner hold an object (hula hoop, bean bag, two-liter bottle, etc.). The student takes the object out of the partner's hand as the student moves her arm forward.
7. Student not continuing the follow-through	• Hang a balloon from a basketball goal. Have the student perform the striking skill and touch the balloon with her hand as she finishes.

Side-Arm Strike Lesson Plan (First Lesson)

Age group: First grade

Focus: Dropping the ball and then contacting it

Subfocus: Stepping with appropriate foot, force, and catching

Objectives: To drop a playground ball and contact it with the dominant hand four out of five times as measured by teacher observation (**CUE:** "Drop, step, and hit"), and to step in opposition as measured by teacher evaluation (**CUE:** "Use your stepping foot").

Materials/Equipment: One beach ball or Super Safe ball per student

Advance preparation: A learning station for each child may be helpful. Place two pieces of floor tape or masking tape on the floor. Use as many pairs of tape as you have students. These pieces of tape should be approximately one foot apart and placed parallel to and approximately 15 feet from the wall. This will enable each child to have her own place to practice. To facilitate distribution of equipment, place a playground ball or volleyball at each station (see figure).

Organization/Management: Students are in personal space for warm-up, instruction, and practice.

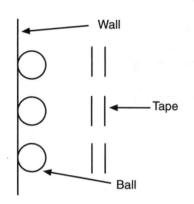

Warm-up:

(Students enter gymnasium and find their own personal space.) *Today we're going to review two of our locomotor skills, the gallop and a slow run, which is also called a jog. Let's start with the gallop. Who can show me a good gallop?* (Choose two students to demonstrate the gallop. Stress the key components of keeping one lead foot and the irregular "step-together" pattern.)

When I put the music on, I would like you to gallop in general space. When the music stops, you will wait for further directions. Do you understand? (Begin music.)

Watch for lead foot and step-together pattern. (Stop music.)

FREEZE. Now, who can show me how to run slowly? (Choose two students to demonstrate the jog. Stress the key components of "eyes forward" and "pump your arms.")

When I put on the music, I would like you to jog in general space. When the music stops, you will freeze where you are and wait for more directions. Do you understand? (Begin music.)

Watch for eyes forward and the proper use of arms. (Stop music.)

FREEZE. Your galloping and jogging are wonderful. Now, I'm going to try to trick you. When I put the music on, you will gallop. When the music stops, you will keep moving, but this time you will jog as I re-start the music. When the music stops again, you will gallop. You will change locomotor skills each time the music stops. Now, which skill will we start with? **(Gallop.)** *Excellent. Do you have any questions?* (Begin music.)

Watch for proper skill performance and stop the music several times to allow the students to change skills.

Introduction:

FREEZE. Everyone find their personal space and sit down. Excellent.

Today we are going to learn how to strike a ball with our hands. Now, pretend you are in a parade. Wave with one hand. Excellent. Before, when we learned to roll and throw, we called this our throwing arm or strong arm. This same arm is our striking arm.

Now hitting or striking a ball is a little different from the underhand roll. This time we have to turn our side to the target so that our striking arm is away from the wall (demonstrate).

To do this we turn our side to the wall and hold the ball in one hand and strike it with the other. Which arm would be the best for striking? **(The strong arm.)**

Notice that we have stations around the gymnasium. At each station we have a ball and there are two pieces of tape on the floor. Right now I do not need the ball, but watch as I practice. (Stand on the tape and then extend your dominant hand back.) *Girls and boys, notice that my striking arm is toward the middle of the gymnasium and away from the wall. I have one foot on each piece of tape. I bring back my striking arm and step toward the wall with the foot that is closest to the wall. As I step, I bring my striking arm forward.* (Repeat actions and the cues of "Step" and "Hit" several times.)

I need some helpers. (Select about five students, one of which should be left handed.) *Each of you find a station and stand on the tape with your striking arm toward the middle of the gymnasium.* (Watch for extension of the proper hand.) *Excellent. Now girls and boys, notice that (student) has a striking arm that is different from the other students'. That's fine. What's important is that each of us use our striking arm. We do not have to be exactly like everyone else. It's OUR striking arm.*

Let's see how well these students step and strike the ball. (Children repeat the action three or more times.)

Excellent. It's time for everyone to practice. When I call out a color you are wearing, I would like you to find a station and stand on the tape so that your striking arm is toward the middle of the gymnasium. (Call out colors until all children are at a station.) *Make sure you have your striking arm toward the middle of the gymnasium.*

Look for extension of the correct arm and children standing on the pieces of tape.

Very well done. Now, let's all practice stepping and striking the ball. Just like in the underhand roll and the throw, we have to step with our stepping foot. As I say the words STEP and HIT, you will step toward the wall with your foot that is closest to the wall—that's your stepping foot—and bring your striking arm forward. (Repeat the cues "Step" and "Hit" at least five times.)

Look for extension of the correct arm and children stepping toward the wall.

Excellent. Now I think you're ready to try something a little harder. I want you to pretend that there is a ball in your other hand. You are going to pretend to drop it, then step and hit. Watch as I do this. (Demonstrate and say the cues "Drop" and "Step and hit.") *Remember that we have to step and strike the ball at the same time. Everyone stand up and try this as I say the words.*

Repeat the cues "Drop" and "Step and Hit" several times as you look for dropping the "ball," extension of the correct arm, and children stepping toward the wall.

FREEZE. Now I think you're ready to put everything together. Watch as I take the ball, hold it in one hand, and bring my striking arm back. I still have my feet on the tape and now I'm going to DROP (not throw or bounce) the ball and then STEP and HIT it with my striking arm. (Demonstrate several times and repeats the cues "Drop" and "Step and Hit.")

Let's see if some of you are ready. (Select about five children to practice the skill of dropping, stepping, and hitting as the cues are repeated. Correct actions are noted and problem areas addressed.)

Notice that some of the balls are bouncing off the wall too hard. How can we fix that problem? **(Use less force.)** *That's right. In fact, let's make it a rule that the ball must bounce ONCE before it gets back to you. That way you will use light force.*

When I say GO, I would like each of you to pick up the ball next to the wall, stand on your pieces of tape, bring your striking arm back, and hold the ball in your other hand. Do NOT drop the ball yet. Do you understand these directions? GO.

Watch for striking arm extended, side to the wall.

Now, when I say GO, I would like you to drop the ball you are holding, step, and hit it. Make sure it bounces once before you catch it. GO.

Watch for striking arm extended, side to the wall, dropping (not throwing or bouncing) the ball, and contacting the ball with the extended arm.

FREEZE. That was very well done. Now, I would like you to say the words DROP, STEP, and HIT out loud as you practice. You may keep striking the ball, catching it, and striking it again as long as you keep repeating the words DROP, STEP, and HIT out loud each time. Remember to use LIGHT FORCE, and the ball must bounce once before it returns to you and the tape. Do you understand these directions? GO.

FREEZE. This time I would like you to count how many times you can strike the ball against the wall AND catch it. Remember, the ball has to bounce once. GO.

Watch for striking arm extended, side to the wall, dropping (not throwing or bouncing) the ball, and contacting the ball with the extended arm.

FREEZE. How many of you were able to catch it five times? Eight times? Ten times? Terrific. If you were able to catch it ten times, you may play wall ball. Find a partner. Watch as (student) and I play. (Demonstrate as he gives directions.) *I strike the ball to the wall, it bounces, and then (student) catches it. Then he strikes the ball and I catch it. We still have to have our side to the wall, use our stepping foot, and drop the ball. We want our partner to be able to catch it, so we still use light force.*

If you weren't able to catch it ten times, you should keep practicing by yourself for the next few minutes. Does everyone understand these directions? GO.

Watch for cooperative play as well as striking arm extended, side to the wall, dropping (not throwing or bouncing) the ball, and contacting the ball with the extended arm.

FREEZE. If you have been working alone, I would like you to find a partner and play wall ball. GO.

Activity continues for three to five minutes.

FREEZE. Time is up. Please return the balls to their place near the wall and line up for your teacher.

Closure:

Children are lined up to leave.

(Student), tell me one thing I should do to get ready to strike the ball. (Do what the child instructs. Call on another student and continue to do EXACTLY what the children explain. Keep modifying the movement and asking questions until the side-arm strike is performed correctly.

Now, help me remember some of the cues we have used. **(DROP, STEP and HIT.)** *Excellent. Next time, we will work on hitting a target with our two-hand side-arm strike.*

Two-Hand Side-Arm Strike

The two-hand side-arm strike is used when batting a ball. Equipment should always be of an appropriate weight and size, especially when the child is first learning the skill. When children use bats that are so heavy they must use an open grip (hands apart), they often fatigue after only a few swings. Because children should practice striking with bats they can control, we recommend using plastic bats initially and then using heavier bats when students are ready for them.

Safety concerns must be addressed with this skill. Besides using plastic bats, we suggest using yarn, foam rubber, rag (cloth), or *soft* rubber balls. "Real" softballs and baseballs are inappropriate for physical education classes.

Safety must be taught and practiced. Often young children become so excited about retrieving balls that have been hit that they do not look where they are moving. Teachers must continuously remind children to hold the bat securely, look before they swing, and to look where they are moving. We recommend setting up clearly marked areas around the batter so that children are prevented from walking in front of or behind the batter. By properly planning their lessons, teachers can substantially reduce the risk of injuries. The NASPE Outcomes Project suggests that a second grader be able to consistently strike a ball with a bat from a tee and use correct grip and side orientation (outcome 2-15). By the fourth grade, the student should be able to use a level swing to hit a softly thrown ball (outcome 4-7). Since this skill requires many repetitions, all of our suggested drills and activities assume the use of a batting tee.

Basic Components

Ready Position
—nondominant side toward the intended target, chin placed over the nondominant shoulder, hands gripping the bat are level with the armpit with the dominant hand above the nondominant hand, bat is held behind the dominant shoulder, and dominant elbow is parallel to the ground.

Step and Swing
—step forward with nondominant foot while dominant foot remains stationary. Weight transfers from the back foot to the front foot as the hip and shoulder begin to rotate.

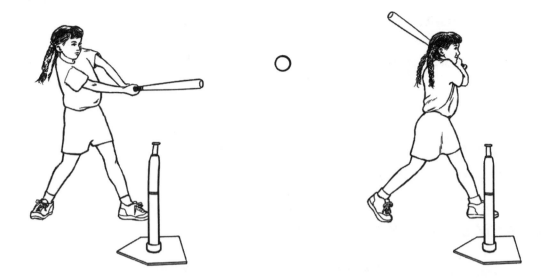

Hit

—arms extend and ball is contacted in front of the body and in line with the front foot. Use the upper half of the bat when striking the ball.

Follow Through

—bat continues past the point of the strike, dominant shoulder moves to position under the chin, and both hands remain on the bat.

(Albemarle County Physical Education Curriculum Revision Committee, 1996, 3-1).

Cue Words

The cue words you select for each phase of the skill will depend on the age of the students you are teaching and your areas of emphasis. We have listed, in usable sets, some of the cue words we have used to teach the two-hand side-arm strike. You may use each set individually or mix and match the cue words as needed. It is beneficial to have the students say the words out loud as they practice the skill.

READY and BAT BACK—stand with the nondominant side toward the intended target, the chin over the nondominant shoulder, the hands gripping the bat so that the dominant hand is above the nondominant hand, the hands holding the bat are level with the armpit, the bat is held behind the dominant shoulder, and the dominant elbow is parallel to the ground.

STEP AND SWING—step forward with the nondominant foot while the dominant foot remains stationary. Weight transfers from the back foot to the front foot as the hip and shoulder begin to rotate.

STEP—step forward with the foot closest to the target.

SWING—As hips and shoulders rotate, bat is brought forward and strikes ball with arms fully extended.

STEP AND HIT—step with foot closest to target, hips and shoulders rotate, and bat contacts the ball.

HIT—arms extend and ball is contacted in front of the body and in line with the front foot using the upper half of the bat.

FOLLOW THROUGH—the bat continues past the point of the strike, the dominant shoulder moves to position under the chin, and both hands remain on the bat.

SHOULDER—bat continues past the point of the strike, dominant shoulder moves to a position under the chin, both hands remain on the bat.

SWING THROUGH THE BALL—step with foot closest to target, hips and shoulders rotate, and bat contacts the middle of the ball. Bat continues past the point of the strike, dominant shoulder moves to a position under the chin, both hands remain on the bat.

Cue Set 1: READY, STEP AND SWING, HIT, FOLLOW THROUGH

Cue Set 2: READY, STEP, SWING

Cue Set 3: BAT BACK, STEP AND HIT, SHOULDER

Cue Set 4: READY, SWING THROUGH THE BALL

Suggested Activities for Reinforcing the Components

In the learning process, it is essential that students know how a skill is supposed to look, what its component parts are, and how to perform each individual component correctly. In the preceding section, we furnished pictures and descriptions of the two-hand side-arm strike, divided it into its component parts, and provided possible cue words. In addition to the material found in chapter 3 that reinforces the concepts for all locomotor and manipulative skills, the following section provides specific activities for reinforcing the components unique to the two-hand side-arm strike.

Partner Skill Check

Objective: To allow partners to assess each other's progress learning the skill

Equipment: Partner skill check sheets, pencils, and one bat and ball for each set of partners. If the students cannot read or do not speak English, the picture version of the partner skill check sheet may be useful.

Activity:

1. One partner observes the other to see if she has the correct form for the ready position.

2. If the ready position is correct, then the partner places a *Y* in the first box. If the ready position is not correct, she places an *N* in the first box. Nonreaders can put a smiling face if the ready position is correct or a sad face if the ready position is not correct.

3. This evaluation continues until each of the components has been assessed five times.

4. A partner skill check sheet is used for each student.

Extensions:

1. The teacher may use the partner skill check sheet to assess the skill development of each student.

2. The teacher may send partner skill check sheets home with report cards or as individual skills develop.

Partner Skill Check Skill: **Two-Hand Side-Arm Strike**

Batter's name: _____ Watcher's name:_____

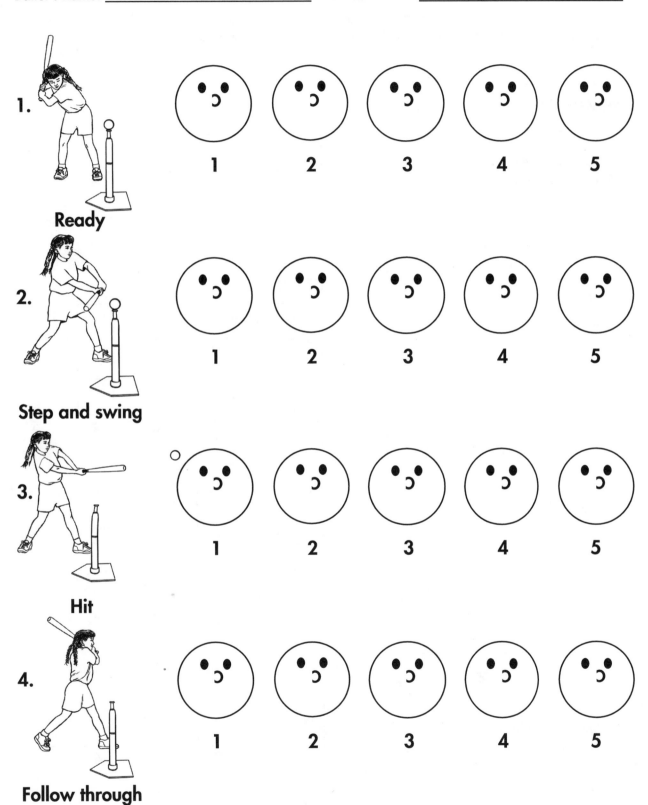

1.

1 2 3 4 5

Ready

2.

1 2 3 4 5

Step and swing

3.

1 2 3 4 5

Hit

4.

1 2 3 4 5

Follow through

Partner Skill Check Skill: **Two-Hand Side-Arm Strike**

Batter's name: _____ Watcher's name:_____

Watch your partner and mark each component of the skill. Let your partner do the skill 5 times. Each time your partner does it right, mark a **Y** in the box. If your partner doesn't do it right, mark an **N** in the box.

START	TRIALS

START

TRIALS

Ready position

1. Side to target
2. Chin over shoulder
3. Hands together on bat
4. Elbow up

☐ 1 ☐ 2 ☐ 3 ☐ 4 ☐ 5

ACTION

Step and swing

1. Step toward target

☐ 1 ☐ 2 ☐ 3 ☐ 4 ☐ 5

2. Bellybutton turns to face target

☐ 1 ☐ 2 ☐ 3 ☐ 4 ☐ 5

Hit

3. Bat hits ball

☐ 1 ☐ 2 ☐ 3 ☐ 4 ☐ 5

4. Arms stretched out when bat hits ball

☐ 1 ☐ 2 ☐ 3 ☐ 4 ☐ 5

STOP

Follow through

1. Shoulder under chin

☐ 1 ☐ 2 ☐ 3 ☐ 4 ☐ 5

Success Builders

The success builder activities allow the teacher to address individual needs. If students need additional help on individual component parts, the activities listed below will help reinforce correct performance.

Objective: To improve areas of deficiency as assessed by the partner skill check

Equipment: See individual stations. We suggest using an unbreakable mirror and a poster of each component of the two-hand strike at each station. The mirror is particularly helpful in these activities because it allows the child to see what he is doing. The easiest way to make the posters would be to photocopy the drawings from this book. Use an opaque projector to enlarge them. Laminating the posters will ensure their use for many years.

Activity:

1. Set up a station for each of the four components in the teaching area. Post a description or a picture of the specific component at the corresponding station.

2. Stations:

Ready

—stand with the nondominant side toward the intended target, hands gripping the bat so that the dominant hand is above the nondominant hand, and the bat is held behind the dominant shoulder.

Equipment: Component poster, bat, mirror, and partner evaluations

Activity: The student assumes the ready position. The partner checks to see if her position matches the poster. The student refers to the mirror for help. The partner then tells the student to put the bat down, get ready, etc., until the student can successfully perform the ready position five times in a row. When the student is successful, she may return to the rest of the group.

Step and Swing

—step forward with the nondominant foot while the dominant foot remains stationary. Weight transfers from the back foot to the front foot as the hip and shoulder rotate.

Equipment: Component poster, bat, tape on floor, and partner evaluations

Activity: The student stands on tape that is shoulder-width apart with the non-dominant side facing the target. On his partner's command, he steps toward the target with the front foot, placing it on a piece of tape placed in the appropriate spot. After this can be accomplished without problems, the swing is added. The student assumes the ready position while holding a bat. On his partner's command, he steps toward the target and swings the bat.

Hit

—arms extend and ball is contacted in front of the body and in line with the front foot. Use the upper half of the bat when striking the ball.

Equipment: Component poster, batting tee (target is to wall), bats, cloth softballs, and partner evaluations

Activity: The student approaches the tee and extends the bat to determine where she must stand in order for the bat to strike the tip of the tee. The partner evaluates the student as she practices the ready, step, and swing, and then strikes the very tip of the tee. The partner provides feedback so that the student strikes the tee in the proper location. When this can be completed at least five times in a row, a cloth ball is added, and the partner continues to evaluate. The student may return to the rest of the class after this activity can be accomplished five times in succession.

Follow Through

—bat continues past the point of the hit and both hands remain on the bat.

Equipment: Bat, component posters, and partner evaluations

Activity: Using the mirror, the student attempts to swing at an imaginary ball and concentrate on having the bat go through the ball and on finishing with the dominant shoulder under the chin. After the partner indicates that this has been accomplished five times in succession, the pair may return to the rest of the class.

Suggested Culminating Activities to Reinforce the Entire Skill

Individual Activities

Batting Tee Challenges

Objective: To improve the two-hand side-arm strike by hitting balls from a batting tee

Equipment: Each student pair will need a batting tee (or traffic cone), a bat, one Wiffle ball, and three targets attached to the wall.

Activity: Tees are placed approximately 15 feet from the wall and students attempt to strike the ball toward the wall. Using the batting tee (traffic cone), students use correct form to:

- Strike the ball to the wall without touching the tee.
- Hit the ball to a target on the wall that is directly in front of the tee.
- Adjust her stance in order to strike the ball to one of three targets that are placed on the wall.

Extensions:

1. Suspend a net between two game standards. Have the students try to strike the ball into the net.
2. Suspend two ropes between two game standards with approximately two feet between them. Have the students attempt to strike the ball so that it travels between the two ropes.

Whack It

Objective: To improve the two-hand side-arm strike by hitting a suspended ball

Equipment: One bat and one Wiffle ball suspended by a heavy string from an overhead structure (e.g., basketball goal). The ball should hang within the student's strike zone.

Activity:

1. The ball is stationary.
2. The student goes through the READY, STEP AND SWING, HIT, and FOLLOW THROUGH components while striking the Wiffle ball.

Extensions:

1. A partner may evaluate the student's technique.
2. The student attempts to strike the ball as it gently swings toward her.

Partner Activities

Challenges

Objective: To practice the two-hand strike in a variety of settings

Equipment: One ball, one bat, and one batting tee (or traffic cone) per pair of students and laminated challenge cards

Activity:

1. Students select a challenge card.
2. Students perform the task described on the card.
3. Possible challenges may include:
   - Strike the ball using hard force (light force, medium force).
   - Strike the ball to hit targets at different levels (high, medium, low).

Extensions:

1. Place three targets on the wall side by side (different colors of construction paper work well). Partners challenge each other to strike specific targets.
2. Increase the distance between the targets so that students are challenged to hit in a variety of directions.

Moving Target

Objective: To strike a moving ball that a partner is swinging

Equipment: A bat and one tennis ball inside of one leg of a pair of panty hose

Activity:

1. One partner swings the panty hose and ball over her head (like a lasso) so that it is in the strike zone of her partner.
2. The student attempts to strike the ball.
3. Students change positions after five hits.

Extensions:

1. Use the panty hose with a soft rag ball.

2. Count how many times the batter can strike the ball in a row. Have the partners total the strikes and add these to the rest of the class's scores.

Group Activities

Create Your Own Activity

Objective: To allow students to create their own activity to reinforce the two-hand side-arm strike

Equipment: One piece of paper and pencil per group and a predetermined list of equipment you will allow the students to use in their activities (e.g., cloth softballs or soft rag ball, bats, cones, ropes, hula hoops, Nerf balls, etc.)

Activity:

1. Form groups with two to five students each. The teacher may select the groups or the students can form their own.

2. Students create their own activity using the two-hand strike as the basic skill. Students are required to have rules that encourage correct performance of the skill, include all players, and address all safety concerns.

3. The groups write their individual names, the rules of the activity, and the equipment needed on their paper and then show the activity to the teacher.

4. Upon approval of the activity, the teacher allows the students to obtain the necessary equipment and begin playing.

5. Changes to the activity are allowed but must be approved by the teacher.

Extensions:

1. One group may teach the activity it designed to another group.

2. Groups may teach their activities to the entire class.

Summary

The increasing number of tee ball and peewee baseball and softball teams have made learning the skill of batting (two-hand side-arm strike) very important to young children. As teachers we will inevitably compete with the advice of coaches, parents, and grandparents when we teach this skill. We'll also encounter children who want to use a bigger bat (as they use in practice) or possibly even practice prebatting rituals like the big league players do. While these outside influences can be challenging to work with, our focus should remain on proper mechanics and form.

With proper organization of your lesson plans, children will receive many more opportunities to practice the two-hand side-arm strike in physical education than they will on recreational teams. Classrooms can act as the batting clinics that will provide the foundation for later success on the athletic field.

Two-Hand Side-Arm Strike (Batting)
Troubleshooting Chart

IF YOU SEE	THEN TRY THIS
1. Dominant elbow not parallel to ground	• Have the student demonstrate the ready position (without bat) with the teacher or partner lifting the elbow to the correct position, if needed. • Set up a mirror and have the student demonstrate the ready position.
2. Student not stepping forward on nondominant foot	• Place a footprint or spot where the student should step. • Have the student practice the swing a set number of times while the partner counts the number of times the student does not step. The object is to get a score of zero.
3. Limited hip and shoulder rotation	• Have the student check the position of his bellybutton. After hitting the ball, the bellybutton should be pointing in the direction of the target. • Use rubber tubing or Dynabands and have a partner hold the tubing adding resistance while the student goes through the rotation motion.
4. Arms not coming through in an extended position	• Hang an object (small wind chimes, sheet, pie plates, etc.) from a net or rope suspended between two game standards. Have the student touch the object as the arms swing forward. • Have the student's partner hold an object (hula hoop, bean bag, two-liter bottle, etc.). The student takes the object out of the partner's hand as he swings his arms forward.
5. Head moving during the swing or student not keeping eyes on ball	• See the success builder activities. Place a baseball/softball glove on the student's head. The student swings the bat. The object is for the student to keep the head stationary, which will keep the glove on her head. • Color half of a six-inch ball one color and the other half a different color (you can use marker, paint, chalk). After hitting a pitched or tossed ball, the student must be able to tell the teacher or a partner what color he hit.
6. Student not continuing the follow-through	• Have the student practice swinging an imaginary bat. The student should focus on keeping the head still and rotating the shoulders so that the rotation progresses from the nondominant shoulder under the chin to the dominant shoulder under the chin.

Two-Hand Side-Arm Strike Lesson Plan (Second Lesson)

Age group: Second grade

Focus: Attaining a level swing

Subfocus: Proper step

Objective: To swing the bat in a horizontal plane three out of five times as measured by teacher evaluation (**CUE:** "Swing THROUGH the ball.")

Materials/Equipment: One plastic bat or piece of PVC plastic pipe, two traffic cones, a hula hoop, and one small Nerf ball per child

Advance preparation: If possible, set up a learning station for each child. Attach a construction paper target to the wall about 24 inches above the floor. Approximately 10 feet from the wall place an 18-inch traffic cone with a Nerf ball balanced on it. Place another cone against the wall for later use.

To prepare for the warm-up, scatter hula hoops throughout the gymnasium. Place a plastic bat or piece of PVC pipe that is 1 inch in diameter and approximately 3 feet long inside each hoop.

Organization/Management: Students are in personal space for warm-up, instruction, and practice. Teaching stations are set up as described in the advance preparation.

Warm-up:

Today we're going to review two of our locomotor skills, the gallop and the skip. Let's start with the gallop. Who can show me a good gallop? (Choose two students to demonstrate the gallop while stressing the key components of keeping one lead foot and the irregular "step-together" pattern.)

Excellent. When I put the music on, I would like everyone to gallop in general space. The hula hoops will be used later, so just go around them now. Do you understand these directions? GO.

Teacher watches students gallop to determine if they are performing the skill correctly and to make sure students are using the general space appropriately.

(Music stops.) FREEZE. Stand quietly where you are. Now, let's review the skip. It is a STEP, HOP. (Select two students to demonstrate the skip.) *When the music begins, I would like you to skip in general space. When it stops, you will then gallop. When it stops again, you will skip. Now, which locomotor skill will we begin with?* **(SKIP.)** *Good.* (Begin music. Stop the music several times for the students to change locomotor skills.)

Watch students for correct execution of the skill.

(Stop music.) FREEZE. I would like each of you to find the nearest hula hoop, place the equipment outside of the hoop, and sit inside the hoop. GO.

Introduction:

Yesterday we learned how to hold a bat correctly. Who can tell me how I place my hands? **(Dominant hand is above the other hand and they are on the end of the bat.)**

Pretend I am the pitcher or your target. I would like each of you to stand up INSIDE your hula hoop, pick up the bat or PVC pipe, hold it correctly, and turn your side toward me. GO.

Watch for correct hand placement on the bat and side orientation.

How far back should I bring my hands? **(So they are even with the armpits.)** *Excellent. Everyone pull your bat back to where it should be.*

Walk around the gymnasium to make sure the students are holding the bat correctly and point out correct student performance.

Everyone stand outside of your hoop. (Demonstrate as you give directions.) Bring the bat back even with your armpits. Swing the bat forward as you step. Remember, we use some of the same ideas we used with the overhand throw— we step with our stepping foot (stepping in opposition) and make sure we squash the bug (pivot) on our back foot.

As I repeat the cues "Ready" and "Step and swing," each of you show me your swing. Remember to stay NEAR your hoop but not IN it. This way we can really spread out and won't trip on the hoop.

Repeat the cues "Ready" and "Step and swing" as you watch for hand position, step, and swing.

FREEZE. Now, this time when you swing, I want you to think about swinging so that your bat is level. You have to swing THROUGH THE BALL. Watch as I show a level swing. (Demonstrate swinging level.) See how different that is than if I swing like this? (Demonstrate a swing that finishes upward.) If I strike the ball, where would it go? **(Up.)** *That's right. I want to swing level. (Demonstrate again.) Now, if I chop down (demonstrate), where will the ball go?* **(Down.)** *That's right, I want to swing LEVEL. I need to SWING THROUGH THE BALL. Everyone practice your swing on your own and think about swinging THROUGH THE BALL. GO.*

Watch for correct execution of the skill.

FREEZE. I think you're ready to put your skills to use. When I call out a color you are wearing, I would like you to take your bat and sit beside one of the traffic cones away from the walls. (Dismiss children by color of clothing.)

This time you will be hitting off a batting tee or, for us, a traffic cone. Watch as I place the Nerf ball on the tee. I need to stand so that my side is toward the target. I bring my bat back, step, and swing. If I stand too far in front of the cone, can I have a level swing? (Demonstrate.) **(No.)** *I need to stand so that my front foot (the foot closest to the wall) is even with the cone. Everyone stand up, place the ball on the cone, and stand as if you were going to hit it but DON'T STRIKE IT YET.*

Walk around the group to make sure students are holding the bat correctly and standing beside the cone properly. If necessary, masking tape can be placed on the floor to assist students in finding their ready position.

Excellent. Now, as I repeat the cues, I would like you to say the cues with me—"Ready," "Swing through the ball"—as you hit the ball off the tee or cone.

Repeat the cues with the students as they perform the skill. Students should repeat the activity at least five times with you telling them when to retrieve the balls and when to strike.

*You're doing very well. I would like you to practice your swing by your-
selves. Try to swing so that you can hit the construction paper in front of your
cone. GO.*

Students repeat this drill for about three minutes as you walk around making
corrections. After three minutes instruct the students to stop, and then point
out several children who are showing the correct form. Students then resume
practice.

*FREEZE. This time, I am going to walk around the gymnasium and give
each of you different things to do. So if you see someone doing something
different from what you are doing, it's all right. Resume practicing.*

Help each student with problem areas. If the student is coming under the ball,
place a traffic cone in front of the other cone. To strike the ball, the student
will have to swing level. If a student is chopping down on the ball, place the
cone in front of the other cone (nearer the wall). If the student is having no
difficulty, place the other cone in front of the first cone and put a ball on top
of it. Challenge the student to strike both balls.

*FREEZE. Everyone return your equipment to where you found it when class
began—bats in hoops, extra cones and balls against the wall—and line up.*
(Line up students to leave.)

Closure:

*I am going to pretend to strike a ball with the bat. I will call on several
students to tell me if I am performing the skill correctly.* (Use a reverse grip,
step with wrong foot, hold bat too low or too high, chop the ball, etc.) *How
does it look?* (Students correct each problem.)

Now, tell me the cues we used today for the two-hand side-arm strike.
("Ready," "Swing through the ball," "Hit," and "Follow through.") *How
do I swing through a ball?* **(Hit it in the middle, swing level).** *Excellent.
Tomorrow we will move our cones farther back and continue to work on
hitting the targets.*

chapter 10

Kicking and Punting

Soon after children begin walking, they begin propelling objects with their feet either by kicking them off the ground or holding them and punting. Later, the skills of kicking and punting are found in such diverse activities as "kick the can," kickball, and soccer. Without proper instruction, children often learn to kick and punt with the wrong part of their foot or develop such poor mechanics that a mature pattern is impossible to attain.

While the NASPE Outcomes Project does not address punting, it does deal with kicking. It suggests that a kindergartner should be able to kick a stationary ball smoothly (outcome K-12). By second grade, a student should be able to kick a rolling ball (outcome 2-9), and a mature kicking pattern should be evident by fourth grade (outcome 4-12).

Kick

Children begin kicking by standing still and kicking a nonmoving object. Far more advanced is the skill of traveling toward a moving ball and skillfully kicking it. Between these two skills are several intermediate phases that children must master.

After a child can kick a stationary ball while standing still, he will attempt to move toward and kick a stationary ball. In the next phase the child remains stationary and attempts to kick a moving ball. Finally the child advances to the last phase in which he moves toward and kicks a moving ball. Clearly, the final and most difficult skill can only be attained after the other phases have been mastered (Harrison and Blakemore 1992). Unfortunately, educators sometimes attempt to teach the final skill before the earlier skills are understood. In this chapter, we emphasize the basic components of a good kick when the ball is stationary and the child's movement is limited to his approach steps. We have included extensions for the child and the ball in motion where appropriate.

To increase practice time and promote safety, we recommend using one of the following suggestions for each activity:

- Use partially deflated balls so that students do not spend a lot of time chasing the balls they kick.

- Have students work with partners, but be sure they are a safe distance apart in case one child kicks a playground ball excessively hard.

- Use a wall or fence as the "partner."

Of course, physical education catalogs today are filled with softer balls that are safer for kicking. Some of these include inexpensive beach balls, Nerf balls, Gator Skin balls, Softi, and Super Safe balls. Your equipment budget and facilities will dictate what precautions you use.

Basic Components

Ready Position
—stand behind the ball, focus eyes on the ball.

Step and Leap
—step forward on the kicking foot to generate power for the kick, leap forward on the nonkicking foot placing the toes beside the ball, lean forward with the kicking foot off the ground.

Kick
—contact the ball at or slightly below the center with either the toe or the instep.

Follow Through
—arm opposite the kicking leg swings forward, kicking foot continues forward in the direction of the kick.

(Albemarle County Physical Education Curriculum Revision Committee, 1996, 5-1).

Cue Words

The cue words you select for each phase of the skill will depend on the age of the students you are teaching and your areas of emphasis. We have listed, in usable sets, some of the cue words that we have used to teach the kick. You may use each set individually or mix and match the cue words as needed. We have found that it is beneficial to have the students say the cue words out loud as they practice.

READY—focus eyes on the stationary ball.

STEP—step forward with the kicking foot.

APPROACH—watch the ball and step forward with the kicking foot.

LEAP—leap onto the nonkicking foot.

PLANT—plant the nonkicking foot beside the ball while bringing the kicking leg forward.

AND—step forward with nonkicking foot and place it beside the ball.

LEG BACK—bring the kicking leg back.

KICK—contact the ball below its center with either the toe or instep.

BOOM—swing the kicking leg forward and contact the ball below the center with either the toe or instep.

FOLLOW THROUGH and HIGH—kicking foot continues in the direction of the kick with the opposing arm stretched forward for balance.

Cue Set 1: READY, STEP, LEAP, KICK, FOLLOW THROUGH

Cue Set 2: APPROACH, LEAP, PLANT, KICK, FOLLOW THROUGH

Cue Set 3: READY, LEAP, KICK, HIGH

Cue Set 4: READY, AND, KICK

Cue Set 5: LEG BACK, BOOM

Suggested Activities for Reinforcing the Components

In the learning process, it is essential that students know how a skill is supposed to look, what its component parts are, and how to perform each individual component correctly. In the preceding section, we furnished pictures and descriptions of the kick, divided it into its component parts, and provided possible cue words. In addition to the material found in chapter 3 that reinforces the concepts for all locomotor and manipulative skills, the following section provides specific activities for reinforcing the components unique to the kick.

Partner Skill Check

Objective: To allow partners to assess each other's progress learning the kick.

Equipment: Partner skill check sheets, pencils, and one ball for each set of partners. If the students cannot read or do not speak English, the picture version of the partner skill check sheet may be useful.

Activity:

1. One partner observes the other to see if she has the correct form for the ready position.

2. If the ready position is correct, the partner places a *Y* in the first box. If the ready position is not correct, she places an *N* in the first box. Nonreaders can put a smiling face if the ready position is correct or a sad face if the ready position is not correct.

3. This evaluation continues until each of the components has been assessed five times.

4. A partner skill check sheet is used for each student.

Extensions:

1. You can use the partner skill check sheet to assess the skill development of each student.

2. You can send partner skill check sheets home with report cards or as individual skills develop.

Partner Skill Check

Skill: **Kick**

Kicker's name: _____ Watcher's name: _____

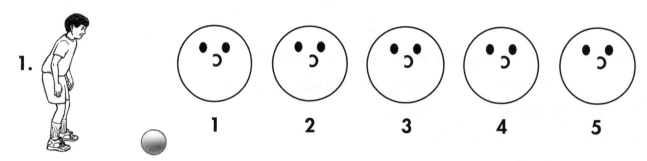

1.

1 2 3 4 5

Ready

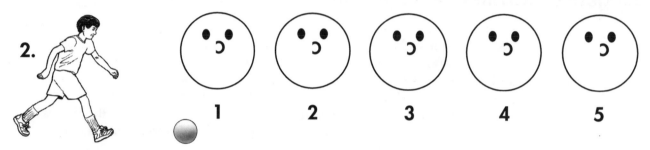

2.

1 2 3 4 5

Step and leap

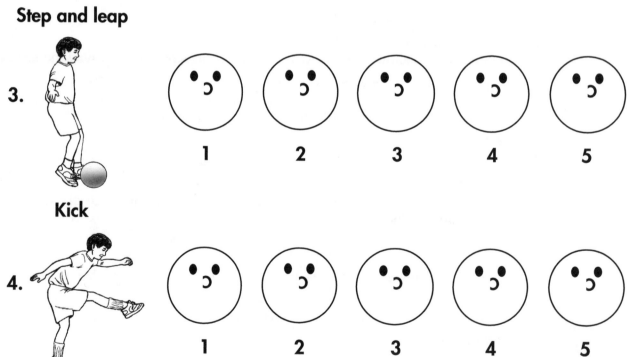

3.

1 2 3 4 5

Kick

4.

1 2 3 4 5

Follow through

Partner Skill Check

Skill: **Kick**

Kicker's name: _____ Watcher's name: _____

Watch your partner and mark each component of the skill. Let your partner do the skill 5 times. Each time your partner does it right, mark a **Y** in the box. If your partner doesn't do it right, mark an **N** in the box.

START   TRIALS

Ready position

   1. Eyes on target
   2. Knees bent
   3. Facing target
   4. Feet shoulder-width apart

☐ 1 ☐ 2 ☐ 3 ☐ 4 ☐ 5

ACTION

Step and leap

   1. Step forward on the kicking foot

☐ 1 ☐ 2 ☐ 3 ☐ 4 ☐ 5

   2. Leap with nonkicking foot, toes only are placed beside the ball

☐ 1 ☐ 2 ☐ 3 ☐ 4 ☐ 5

Kick

   3. Foot contacts the ball just below the center

☐ 1 ☐ 2 ☐ 3 ☐ 4 ☐ 5

   4. Use toe or instep to kick

☐ 1 ☐ 2 ☐ 3 ☐ 4 ☐ 5

STOP

Follow through

   1. Kicking foot and body continue toward target

☐ 1 ☐ 2 ☐ 3 ☐ 4 ☐ 5

Success Builders

The success builder activities allow you to address individual needs. If students need additional help on individual component parts, the activities listed below will help reinforce correct performance.

Objective: To allow partners to improve areas of deficiency as assessed by the partner skill check

Equipment: See individual stations. We suggest using an unbreakable mirror and a poster of each component of the kick at each station. The mirror is particularly helpful in these activities because it allows the child to see what he is doing. The easiest way to make the posters would be to photocopy the drawings from this book. Use an opaque projector to enlarge them. Laminating the posters will ensure their use for many years.

Activity:

1. Set up a station for each of the four components in the teaching area with a description or a picture of the specific component posted at the corresponding station.

2. Stations:

Ready

—focus eyes on the ball.

Equipment: Component poster, mirror (if available), and partner evaluations

Activity: The student assumes the ready position. The partner checks to see if her position matches the poster. The student then walks around and on a signal from her partner assumes the ready position again. When she has had several successful trials, the partners may return to working on the entire skill.

Step and Leap

—step forward on the kicking foot to generate power for the kick, leap forward on the nonkicking foot placing the toes beside the ball, lean forward with the kicking foot off the ground.

Equipment: Component poster, mirror (if available), tape (floor or masking) on floor marking where the student's feet are to start and where they should be on the step and leap, and partner evaluations

Activity: The student starts in the ready position with both feet on the tape. The student steps forward onto the "stepping tape" and leaps onto the "leaping tape." The partner watches and gives feedback. Once the student can do this three times in a row, she goes to another area and attempts the skill without the tape. When she has had several successful trials, the partners may return to working on the entire skill.

Kick

—foot contacts the ball at or below its center.

Equipment: Component poster, mirror (if available), partially deflated ball (this limits how far the ball will travel) with a line drawn around the middle of the ball, partially deflated ball without any markings, and partner evaluations

Activity: The student works with a partner. The partner stands to the side and slightly in front of the student's starting position. The student leaps onto the nonkicking foot and brings the kicking foot forward to contact the ball. The student should contact the ball below the marked center line. Once the student is successful three times, he tries the kick with a partially deflated ball that has no markings. When he has completed several successful trials, the partners may return to working on the entire skill.

Follow Through

—arm opposite the kicking leg swings forward, kicking foot continues forward in the direction of the kick.

Equipment: Component poster, mirror (if available), partially deflated ball, and partner evaluations

Activity: The student may work with a partner. The student practices swinging the kicking leg forward and bringing the opposite arm forward at the same time. The mirror and partner evaluations should give essential feedback. When the student has had several successful trials, she attempts to kick a partially deflated ball placed on the floor. The partner checks again to make sure the follow-through is correct. When the student is successful on several trials, the partners may return to working on the entire skill.

Suggested Culminating Activities to Reinforce the Entire Skill

Individual Activities

Hit the Corners

Objective: To improve kicking accuracy by hitting a specific target

Equipment: One playground or soccer ball per student

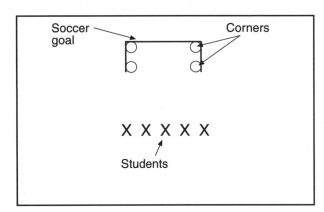

Activity:

1. Students stand 10 yards from a soccer goal (or other well-defined, four-corner area). Students take turns kicking and retrieving balls only on your instruction (see figure).

2. Students practice kicking the ball into each of the four corners of the goal.

Extensions:

1. The student must call out which corner he will hit on each kick.

2. The second person in line tells the student which corner to hit. If successful, he is given another challenge. If unsuccessful, the second student gets to kick.

3. You may challenge each group to hit a specific area.

Hit the Wall

Objective: To improve kicking distance by kicking a ball so that it hits a wall 25 feet away before it touches any other surface

Equipment: One playground or soccer ball per student

Activity:

1. Have students form lines of three approximately 35 feet from one wall of the gymnasium (or play area).

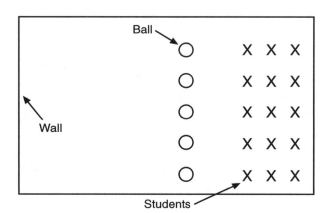

2. Place a playground ball approximately 10 feet in front of each line (see figure).

3. On your signal, the first student in each line attempts to kick the ball so that it hits the wall before it touches any other surface.

4. Due to safety concerns, students should be allowed to kick and retrieve the ball only on your signal.

Extensions:

1. When the students are first learning the skill, move the lines closer to the wall to ensure success. Move the start line back as the students' skills improve.

2. The second student in line tells the first what she is doing well with the kick and what she needs to do to improve the kick.

3. Use a baseball backstop or fence as the wall if playing outside.

4. Hang hoops at different levels for targets on the backstop or fence.

Magic Fence

Objective: To practice the kicking action while emphasizing the leap

Equipment: 24 six-inch cones, 12 jump ropes. You can also use weighted two-liter bottles to raise the rope off the floor.

Activity:

1. Set up six magic fences. Each fence consists of four cones and two ropes. Place the handles of one rope in the top of two cones and have the handles stick out of the bottom of the cones to anchor the rope. Place the cones as far apart as the rope allows so the rope is off the ground. Do the

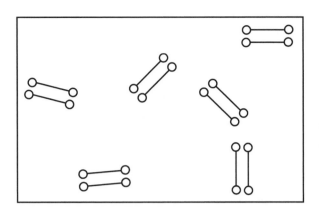

same to the second rope and set the two sections of the fence parallel to each other and about 12 inches apart.

2. Scatter the magic fences throughout the play area (see figure).

3. Assign groups of students to each magic fence.

4. On your signal, the students leap over their twelve-inch fences.

5. Upon landing, the students perform the kicking action.

6. The students continue to leap over their fences until you give a stop signal.

Extensions:

1. The students travel around the gymnasium or play area leaping over all the fences.

2. Change the widths of the magic fences.

3. Put all of the magic fences end to end creating one long fence. Place a ball at each fence, but have the students leap over the fence without using the ball so they can judge the proper ball placement. (Ball placement is an important safety issue. The ball must be placed on the opposite side from the leaper. For other safety reasons, each fence should have only one student leaping at a time.) Upon landing, the leaper tries to kick the ball. The partner retrieves the ball and then takes a turn.

Cone Kick

Objective: To practice the kick while emphasizing the leap

Equipment: One cone (six-inch or lightweight) and three footprints (laminated paper or footprints) per student. If inside, the footprints should be securely taped to the floor for safety.

Activity:

1. Each student sets up her footprints and cone: two footprints must be shoulder-width apart. Have the student leap, making sure she lands on her nonkicking foot, and place the third footprint where she lands. Then place the cone to the side and slightly in front of the toe of the third footprint. The cone is now in place to be kicked.

2. When the equipment is appropriately set, the student takes off on the kicking foot and lands on the third footprint with the nonkicking foot.

3. The kicking foot kicks the cone.

Extensions:

1. Use a Nerf ball or a slightly deflated ball.

2. Use the footprints and add the Magic Fence activity from this section.

Partner Activities

Challenges

Objective: To practice the kick in a variety of situations

Equipment: One playground or soccer ball per pair of students and laminated challenge cards. Different types of challenges may require additional equipment.

Activity:

1. Students select a challenge card.

2. Students perform the task as described on the card.

3. Possible challenges may include:

   • Kick the ball using hard force (light force, medium force).

   • Kick the ball to a medium target (low target, high target).

   • Kick the ball high in the air (low to the ground).

   • Kick a ball at the same time as your partner kicks one and try to make them go the same height and land at the same time.

Extensions:

1. Attach multicolored targets, pictures, hoops, bowling pins, cones, or empty two-liter bottles to a wall or fence in the play area and have the partner tell the kicker which target to hit.

2. Set up game poles or volleyball standards and tie a rope between them. Suspend different objects from the rope (at a variety of levels) and challenge the students to hit them. Possible targets could include hoops, aluminum pie pans, and empty two-liter plastic bottles.

2-4-6-8

Objective: To practice the kick by using different amounts of force

Equipment: One playground or soccer ball per pair of students and enough cones to set up the play area. The play area consists of a space defined by five rows of cones placed approximately 10 feet apart. Jump ropes mark the start area and are placed 10 feet in front of the first row of cones (see figure).

Activity:

1. One partner (the receiver) enters the play area while the kicker stays in the start area behind the ropes. For safety, the receiver should position herself in the six-point area.

2. The kicker first tries to kick the ball only into the first area, which is worth two points. The receiver in the field kicks the ball back.

3. The kicker then tries to kick the ball into the second area (for four points), then the third area (for six points), and finally the last area (for eight points).

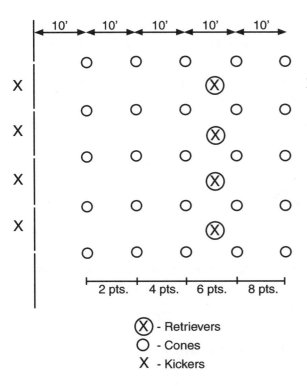

2 pts. 4 pts. 6 pts. 8 pts.

Ⓧ - Retrievers
O - Cones
X - Kickers

4. If the kick is executed correctly and lands in the targeted area, the partners may add the points to their score.

5. After four kicks, the partners change places.

Extensions:

1. The students try to score the most amount of points in their four kicks.

2. The pairs keep track of the points scored for each properly executed kick. Later the class can use math skills (addition) to figure their total score.

3. The pairs keep track of their number of correct kicks and keep a total for the class. In a follow-up lesson challenge the class to increase the total number of correct kicks. You may choose to chart these numbers to motivate the students and reinforce the skill.

4. The kickers start in the eight-point area and kick back to their receivers standing behind the ropes. The kickers then move up and kick from the six-point, four-point, and two-point areas. Then the partners change areas.

Group Activities

Keep the Balls Out of the Middle

Objective: To practice kicking and trapping a ball

Equipment: A very large play area and one to four Nerf balls (eight inches in diameter) or other soft balls (e.g., Super Safe). The number of balls needed will vary based on the skill level of the students.

Activity:

1. Divide the class into two groups.

2. Place one group in the center of a large circle and the other group outside of the circle.

3. On your start signal, the students on the outside roll the balls into the circle. The students inside the circle must stop (trap) the balls and then kick them back outside of the circle.

4. The students on the outside retrieve the balls, return to their positions, roll the balls into the circle again, and the activity continues.

5. Have the two groups change places after one to two minutes.

Extensions:

1. Tally the total number of correct kicks for each group. You may choose to chart these or record them to serve as a target to improve upon in a later lesson.

2. Tally the total number of correct kicks for the entire class. The class should try to increase their total correct kicks each time they play the activity.

3. Observe the students while they are playing. Tell any student having trouble kicking correctly to go to the practice area and work with a partner.

4. Have the students kick the balls without stopping them.

Create Your Own Activity

Objective: To allow students to create their own activities to reinforce the skill of kicking

Equipment: One piece of paper and pencil per group and a predetermined list of equipment you will allow the students to use in their activities (e.g., playground balls, cones, hoops, etc.)

Activity:

1. Form groups with two to five students each. You may select the groups or the students may form their own.

2. Students create their own activity using the kick as the basic skill. Students are required to have rules that encourage correct performance of the skill, include all players, and address all safety concerns.

3. The groups write their individual names, the rules of the activity, and the equipment needed on their paper and then show the activity to you.

4. Upon approval of their activity, the students obtain their equipment and begin playing.

5. You must approve all changes to the activity.

Extensions:

1. Groups may teach their activities to other groups.

2. Groups may teach their activities to the entire class.

Kick and Go

Objective: To kick balls of various sizes

Equipment: A variety of balls that may be kicked (e.g., playground balls of different colors, soccer balls of different sizes, Super Safe balls, etc.). No two balls should be identical.

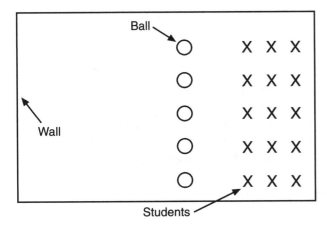

Activity:

1. Place students in lines of three with a ball in front of each line (see figure).

2. On the start signal, the first student in each line stands up, approaches the ball, and kicks it as far as he can. For safety, a start command must be used for each rotation.

3. The student then runs to retrieve a kicked ball. He may NOT return with the same ball that he kicked.

4. The student hands the ball to the next student in line.

5. The activity continues through several rotations.

Extensions:

1. The students soccer dribble the ball back to the line.

2. The student must name the type of ball he retrieved. Other members of the line are allowed to help if needed.

From *Complete elementary physical education guide* by Rosalie Bryant and Eloise McLean Oliver. Copyright © 1975. Reprinted with permission of Prentice Hall Direct.

Summary

Children enjoy using their feet to move objects on the ground. As with all skills, logical progressions are necessary for skill mastery. When introducing the kick, the ball and the child should be stationary. Once the student has demonstrated an ability to perform the kick from a stationary position, the movement part of the kick can be introduced. The kicker's movement will eventually become a run, leap, and kick. With proper instruction and logical progressions, your students can become skillful kickers.

Kick Troubleshooting Chart

IF YOU SEE	THEN TRY THIS
1. Eyes not looking at the ball	• Have the student draw a face on the ball or use any word(s) already on the ball for a focus point. • Place three different types of balls in front of the student (playground, Nerf, and soccer). Call out the ball the student is to approach and *touch* (not kick).
2. Student not stepping forward on the kicking foot, or not taking a large enough step	• Place an object (footprint, color spot, etc.) in front of the student for her to step on. • Place an object (jump rope) in front of the student for her to step over.
3. Student stepping onto the nonkicking foot instead of leaping	• Have the student practice the leap skill before she tries to use it with the kick. • Place two ropes parallel to each other on the ground for the student to leap over.
4. No forward lean	• Have the student check his shadow for the forward lean. • Have the student pretend to be a runner leaning forward to win a race. Once the student can lean forward, have him practice leaping and leaning.
5. Toes of the nonkicking foot not placed beside or diagonally to the ball	• Place a footprint next to the ball and have the student practice the leap and land on the footprint. • Have the student's partner check to see if part of the foot is hidden by the ball.
6. Knee of the kicking leg straight as it swings behind the body, or the kicking leg not off the ground behind the body	• Place a six-inch cone so that the student must leap and the knee of the kicking leg travels over the top of the cone. • Have the student watch her shadow to check the position of the kicking leg. • Have the student's partner check the position of the kicking leg.
7. Toe or instep of the kicking foot not contacting the ball below the center of the ball	• Place baby powder or chalk below the center of the ball. Have the student kick the ball and then check the ball and the foot to see where contact was made. • Set up two six-inch cones with a strip of tape or string across the top of the cones. Have the student place the ball on the side opposite him and try to kick the ball while keeping the foot below the tape or string.
8. Arm opposite the kicking leg not swinging forward, or the kicking foot not continuing in the direction of the ball	• Have the student stand and practice swinging the kicking leg forward to touch the fingers of the outstretched opposite hand. • Set up a rope at waist level to the student and have him practice the kick without a ball. He must follow through on the kick so that the kicking foot and the opposite arm touch the bottom of the rope.

Kick Lesson Plan (Second Lesson for Upper Elementary Grades)

Age group: Upper elementary

Focus: Leaping into the kick

Subfocus: Technique and power

Objectives: To execute a correct leap four out of five times as measured by teacher and partner observation (**CUES:** "Take off on one foot," "Get airborne," "Land on the other foot"); and approach the ball, leap, plant the foot, and contact the ball four out of five times as measured by teacher observation (**CUES:** "Approach, leap, kick").

Materials/Equipment: One playground ball for each student

Advance preparation: Tape a line to the floor that divides the gymnasium in half. In addition, place nonparallel lines throughout the teaching area. Indoors, floor tape (or masking tape) is useful. Outdoors, white shoe polish works well on blacktop. The nonparallel lines should be in varying widths and lengths (see figure).

Organization/Management: Students are in personal space for instruction and warm-up. Later, students will find their own practice areas in the gymnasium.

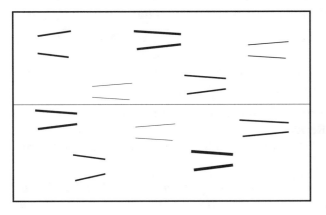

Warm-up: Music is playing as students enter the gymnasium. They move in general space according to your locomotor directions, for example, slide, gallop, jog, walk, and skip. Later, challenge the students to "freeze" where they are and pretend to kick an imaginary ball. After warming up, students find their personal space and sit on the floor facing you.

Introduction:

Today we are going to work on our kicking again. We need to really think about generating power—or kicking harder. Of course, we will remember our safety rules while we learn. Now to generate power, we need to run up to the ball, get in the air, and kick. Watch how I approach the ball. I'm NOT going to kick it, just approach it. (Approach the ball, leap onto nonkicking foot, and stop.) *Girls and boys, who can tell me the type of locomotor movement I just did?* **(Leap.)** *Excellent. When we want to kick correctly and generate more power, we need to approach correctly, and the leap is VERY important.*

Before we begin our kicking today, we're going to practice our leaping. Who can tell me the parts of a good leap? **(Take off on one foot and land on the other.)** *That's correct. Now we do those same things—take off on one foot and land on the other—when we run. What are some differences between the leap and the run?* **(In the air longer and the step or stride is longer for** *the leap.) Great. (Select two students.) Can you demonstrate a leap for everyone? Use the lines next to you. Try to leap from one line to the other. Think of the cue words "Take off on one foot, get airborne, and land on the other foot." Everyone watch to see how they take off and land. Excellent. Now everyone watch their arms. Notice that the arm opposite the leaping leg stretches out. This gives them balance.*

Girls and boys, when I say GO, I would like you to find a set of lines and sit down. There may be no more than three people at each set of lines. GO.

Excellent. I would like you to take turns leaping across the lines. We are going to pretend that the area between the lines is water, and you really don't want to get your feet wet. You will take off behind one line and land across the other line. Before we begin, who can tell me some safety rules we should have? (Students generate ideas. They should include **take turns** and **watch where you are going**. You can also limit the distance the children may run from.) *When I say GO, you will begin. GO.*

When you are satisfied that the activity is being performed safely, watch for skill performance. Ensure that the students are taking off on one foot and landing on the other. Repeat the cue words "Take off on one foot, get airborne, and land on the other foot" throughout. If students are not getting enough height, challenge them to move farther down the lines so that the distance they have to leap is greater.

FREEZE. Excellent. You are doing well with your approach and leap. Now, I would like you to take turns helping each other. Two students will watch, while the third student performs the skill. The watchers must look for taking off on one foot, getting airborne, landing on the other foot, and using the arms to help. The arm opposite the leaping leg is stretched out for balance.

Can you remember those things? Great. Now when a member of your group leaps over the lines, you must be able to say what he or she is doing right and what he or she needs to work on. Then let that person practice it a few more times. I'll tell you when to change duties. Select your first leaper. Now GO.

Watch to make sure the leapers are performing the skill correctly and the watchers are giving good feedback. Repeat cue words out loud. After several minutes, students rotate duties. Rotations continue until everyone has had an opportunity to work on the leap with feedback from a peer.

FREEZE. Everyone sit down where you are. Your leaping is terrific. When I say GO, I would like you to find your personal space, practice taking one step, leap onto the foot you DON'T kick with, and then pretend to kick. You should step with the foot you kick with first. Watch me as I demonstrate. I kick with my RIGHT foot, so I will step right, leap to my left, and then pretend to kick. Do you have any questions? GO.

Watch for approach, leap, and kick.

Excellent. We are ready to REALLY kick a ball. When I call on each group, I would like those students to pick up a playground ball and sit on the line in the middle of the gymnasium with the ball in your lap. Now, since it would be very dangerous to have balls bouncing all over the gymnasium, I have let a lot of the air out of them. They will still kick fine, but won't bounce off the walls so hard. (Dismiss groups individually.)

This time we are going to practice our approach, leap, and really kick a ball. Watch me as I demonstrate: Ready, step, leap, kick, and follow through. We have to watch the ball the entire time and then let our kicking foot follow in the direction of the kick. Notice that the arm opposite the kicking leg comes forward. This gives us balance.

Have every other student kick toward an opposite wall (see figure).

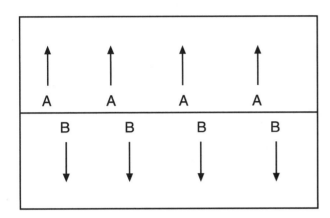

Here are the safety rules: You may kick only when given the GO signal, and you will go get your playground ball only when told to. Do you understand these rules?

Let's all kick together the first time: Ready, step, leap, kick, follow through.

Students practice kicking while you repeat the cues out loud. Watch specifically for the approach and the leap. Encourage students to contact the ball below its center and to follow through.

Allow students to retrieve the balls and give the GO command again. This continues for at least five repetitions. Reteach problem areas that arise and point out students using correct technique for the other students.

FREEZE. Now I want to teach you a new activity. It's called Hit the Wall. First, we must put away the deflated balls and sit in five lines at the end of the gymnasium (see figure).

Place a properly inflated playground ball 10 feet in front of each line of students.

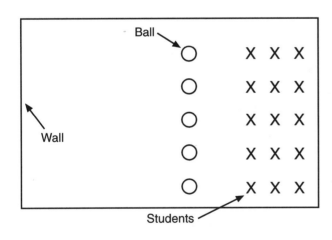

When I say GO, the first person will approach the ball, step, leap, kick, and follow through. The goal is to have the ball hit the wall before it hits the ground. After all of the students who are first in line have kicked, I will let those students retrieve the balls. You will return it to where you kicked it from and then go talk to the second person in line. That person must tell you what you did well and what you should work on next time. Now, watchers, you have to tell them how to get better. What are some of the things we are looking for? ***(Watching the ball, getting airborne, kicking the ball below its middle, etc.)*** *Does everyone understand? GO.*

Watch for proper performance and good feedback from the watchers. To decrease waiting time, add more lines if it can be done safely.

FREEZE. We're out of time. Please put away your equipment and line up for your teacher.

Closure:

1. *Who can tell me how to leap?* ***(Take off on one foot, get airborne, and land on the other foot.)***

2. *How is a leap different from a run?* **(In the air longer, longer stride.)**

3. *So why is a leap so important to a kick?* **(Gives more power.)**

4. *Now we talked a little bit about the follow-through today. Who remembers some important parts to the follow-through?* **(Arm opposite the kicking leg is extended for balance, watch the ball the entire time, let the leg continue toward the target after the kick.)**

Your approach, leap, and kick are great. Tomorrow we will work on improving your follow-through.

Punt

Punting is much more difficult to master than kicking since it involves two distinct but necessary skills—dropping the ball and kicking it as it falls. Because of the difficulty of coordinating these two movements, we have found that children rarely master the punt before the fourth grade.

As with the kick, we recommend using one of the following suggestions for each punting activity:

1. If students are working with partners, be sure they are a safe distance apart in case one child punts the ball excessively hard.

2. Use a wall or fence as the "partner."

You should practice this skill outside unless you have the softer balls that are safer for indoor punting, such as inexpensive beach balls, Nerf balls, Gator Skin balls, and Super Safe balls. Your equipment budget and facilities will dictate what precautions you use.

Basic Components

Ready Position
—stand in a stride position with the nonpunting foot slightly in front of the punting foot, feet shoulder-width apart. Distribute weight equally on both feet, bend knees, hold ball with both hands in front of the body at waist level.

Leap
—leap onto the nonpunting foot in the direction of the punt, lifting the punting foot off the ground behind the body.

Drop and Punt
—drop the ball from outstretched hands. Bring the punting leg forward, and contact the ball on top of the punting foot (shoelaces). Leg and foot should be at full extension on contact.

Follow Through
—leg continues in the direction of the punt as the opposite arm comes forward for balance.

Cue Words

The cue words you select for each phase of the skill will depend on the age of the students you are teaching and your areas of emphasis. We have listed, in usable sets, some of the cue words we have used to teach the punt. You may use each set individually or mix and match the cue words as needed. We have found that it is beneficial to have the students say the cue words out loud as they practice.

READY—stand in a stride position with the nonpunting foot slightly in front of the punting foot, feet shoulder-width apart. Distribute weight equally on both feet, bend knees, hold ball in front of the body at waist level with both hands.

LEAP—leap onto the nonpunting foot in the direction of the punt, lifting the punting foot off the ground behind the body.

DROP AND PUNT—drop the ball from outstretched hands. Bring the kicking leg forward and contact the ball on top of the punting foot (shoelaces). Leg should be at full extension on contact.

DROP—drop the ball from waist level.

PUNT and POW—contact the ball on the shoelaces. Leg should be at full extension on contact.

FOLLOW THROUGH—leg continues in the direction of the punt as the opposite arm comes forward for balance.

Cue Set 1: READY, LEAP, DROP AND PUNT, FOLLOW THROUGH

Cue Set 2: READY, DROP, PUNT

Cue Set 3: READY, DROP, POW

Suggested Activities for Reinforcing the Components

In the learning process, it is essential that students know how a skill is supposed to look, what its component parts are, and how to perform each individual component correctly. In the preceding section, we furnished pictures and descriptions of the punt, divided it into its component parts, and provided possible cue words. In addition to the material found in chapter 3 that reinforces the concepts for all locomotor and manipulative skills, the following section provides specific activities for reinforcing the components unique to the punt.

Partner Skill Check

Objective: To allow partners to assess each other's progress learning the skill of punting

Equipment: Partner skill check sheets, pencils, and one ball for each set of partners. If the students cannot read or do not speak English, the picture version of the partner skill check sheet may be useful. If the assessment is to be performed inside, appropriate safety considerations should be made; for example taking turns, using softer balls, etc.

Activity:

1. One partner observes the other to see if she has the correct form for the ready position.

2. If the ready position is correct, the partner places a *Y* in the first box. If the ready position is not correct, she places an *N* in the first box. Nonreaders can put a smiling face if the ready position is correct or a sad face if the ready position is not correct.

3. This evaluation continues until each of the components has been assessed five times.

4. A partner skill check sheet is used for each student.

Extensions:

1. You can use the partner skill check sheet to assess the skill development of each student.

2. You can send partner skill check sheets home with report cards or as individual skills develop.

Success Builders

The success builder activities allow you to address individual needs. If students need additional help on individual component parts, the activities listed below will help reinforce correct performance.

Objective: To allow partners to improve areas of deficiency as assessed by the partner skill check

Equipment: See individual stations. We suggest using an unbreakable mirror and a poster of each component of the punt at each station. The mirror is particularly helpful in these activities because it allows the child to see what he is doing. The easiest way to make the posters would be to photocopy the drawings from this book. Use an opaque projector to enlarge them. Laminating the posters will ensure their use for many years.

Activity:

1. Set up a station for each of the four components in the teaching area. Post a description or a picture of the specific component at the corresponding station.

2. Stations:

Ready

—stand in a stride position with the nonpunting foot slightly in front of the punting foot. Distribute weight equally on both feet. Hold the ball with both hands in front of the body at waist level.

Equipment: Component poster, mirror (if available), and partner evaluations

Activity: The student assumes the ready position. The partner checks to see if her position matches the poster. The student then walks around and on a signal from her partner assumes the ready position again. When she has had several successful trials, the partners may return to working on the entire skill.

Leap

—leap onto the nonpunting foot in the direction of the punt, lifting the punting foot off the ground behind the body.

Equipment: Component poster, mirror (if available), tape (floor or masking) on floor marking where the student's feet are to start and where they should be on the step and leap, and partner evaluations

Punter's name: _____ Watcher's name: _____

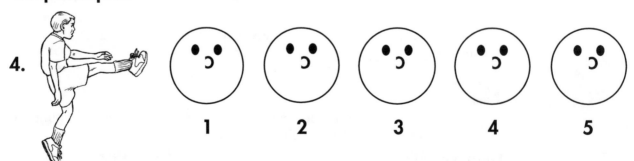

1. 1 2 3 4 5

Ready

2. 1 2 3 4 5

Leap

3. 1 2 3 4 5

Drop and punt

4. 1 2 3 4 5

Follow through

Partner Skill Check

Skill: **Punt**

Punter's name: _____ Watcher's name: _____

Watch your partner and mark each component of the skill. Let your partner do the skill 5 times. Each time your partner does it right, mark a **Y** in the box. If your partner doesn't do it right, mark an **N** in the box.

START

TRIALS

Ready position

1. Eyes on target
2. Knees bent
3. Feet shoulder-width apart
4. Object held in front of body

☐ 1 ☐ 2 ☐ 3 ☐ 4 ☐ 5

ACTION

Leap

1. Leap onto the nonpunting foot in the direction of the punt

☐ 1 ☐ 2 ☐ 3 ☐ 4 ☐ 5

2. Punting foot is off the ground behind the body

☐ 1 ☐ 2 ☐ 3 ☐ 4 ☐ 5

Drop and punt

3. Drop the ball from waist level

☐ 1 ☐ 2 ☐ 3 ☐ 4 ☐ 5

4. Shoelaces contact the ball

☐ 1 ☐ 2 ☐ 3 ☐ 4 ☐ 5

STOP

Follow through

1. Punting leg, opposite arm continue in the direction of the punt

☐ 1 ☐ 2 ☐ 3 ☐ 4 ☐ 5

Activity: The student starts in the ready position with both feet on the tape. The student steps forward onto the "stepping tape" and leaps onto the "leaping tape." The partner watches and gives feedback. Once the student can do this three times in a row, he goes to another area and attempts the skill without the tape. When he has had several successful trials, the partners may return to working on the entire skill.

Drop and Punt

—extend arms forward at waist level. Step forward on the nonpunting foot, lean forward with the punting foot off the ground, and contact the ball below the center with the top of the foot (shoelaces).

Equipment: Component poster, mirror (if available), a variety of slow-moving balls (for example, large beach balls, smaller beach balls, and volleyball trainers), and partner evaluations

Activity: The student practices extending her arms and dropping the ball. She should begin with the large beach ball and attempt to punt it. When she is successful at contacting the ball on the top of her foot with the leg extended five times in a row, she may attempt a smaller beach ball. Later a volleyball trainer is used, then a Super Safe ball (or its equivalent). In each instance the partner provides feedback. When the student has had several successful trials, the partners may return to working on the entire skill.

Follow Through

—punting foot continues forward in the direction of the punt.

Equipment: Component poster, mirror (if available), and partner evaluations

Activity: The student practices swinging the punting leg forward and bringing the opposite arm forward at the same time. The mirror and partner evaluations should give essential feedback. When she has had several successful trials, she attempts to punt a partially deflated ball. The partner checks again to make sure the follow-through is correct. When the student is successful on several trials, the partners may return to working on the entire skill.

Suggested Culminating Activities to Reinforce the Entire Skill

Individual Activities

Over the Net

Objective: To practice punting over a target

Equipment: Outdoor or large indoor play area, one ball (playground, Super Safe ball, football, etc.) per student and two or more volleyball nets

Activity:

1. Divide the class into two groups with each group on one side of the net. Set up a start line approximately 10 to 15 feet away from the net. On your start signal, students attempt to punt the balls over the net from behind the start line.

2. When a ball goes over the net, the student must run around the net, retrieve the ball, and return to the start line.

3. When all of the students have returned, give another start signal for the students to punt again.

Extensions:

1. The students punt immediately once they return to the start line, not on command.

2. Perform the activity inside with a volleyball net if you have sufficient slow-moving, soft balls (e.g., beach balls, volleyball trainers, etc.).

3. The student change sides every time the ball goes over the net. (You may choose to use a back stop if there is enough space on the other side to play). The student must change sides by going around the end of the net.

Partner Activities

Challenges

Objective: To practice the punt in a variety of situations

Equipment: One playground or soccer ball per pair of students and laminated challenge cards. Different types of challenges may require additional equipment.

Activity:

1. Students select a challenge card.

2. Students perform the task as described on the card.

3. Possible challenges may include:

   • Punt the ball using hard force (light force, medium force).

   • Punt the ball to a medium target (low target, high target).

   • Punt the ball high in the air.

   • Punt the ball as far as you can.

   • Punt the ball into a target (e.g., into the enclosed tennis courts).

   • Punt a ball at the same time as your partner does and try to make them go the same height and land at the same time.

Extensions:

1. Attach multicolored targets, pictures, hoops, bowling pins, cones, or empty two-liter bottles to a wall or fence in the play area and have the partner tell the punter which target to hit.

2. Have the students punt over a volleyball net, soccer goal, or fence from approximately 30 feet away.

Keep It Going

(This activity should be played outside in an open area.)

Objective: To improve punting accuracy by punting to a partner

Equipment: One playground (or other appropriate) ball per pair of students

Activity:

1. Partners spread out in an open space.

2. Students punt the ball back and forth.

3. The punter attempts to punt the ball so that her partner can catch it easily. The catcher attempts to catch the ball before it hits the ground.

4. Partners tally how many successful punts-to-catches they make.

Extensions:

1. Use groups of three and form triangles for punting.

2. Challenge the students to improve the number of successful punts and catches they can perform in a row.

2-4-6-8

Objective: To practice the punt by using different amounts of force

Equipment: One playground or soccer ball per pair of students and enough cones to set up the play area. The play area consists of a space defined by five rows of cones approximately 10 feet apart. Place jump ropes 10 feet in front of the first row of cones to mark the start area (see figure).

Activity:

1. One partner goes in the play area and the punter stays in the start area behind the ropes.

2. The punter tries to punt the ball into the first area, which is worth two points. The partner in the field punts the ball back to his partner.

3. The punter then tries to punt the ball into the second area (for four points), then the third area (for six points), and finally the last area (for eight points).

4. If the ball lands in the targeted area and the punt is executed correctly, the partners add the points to their score.

5. After four punts, the partners change places.

Extensions:

1. Students try to score the most points in their four punts.

2. The pairs keep track of the points scored for each properly executed punt. Later the class uses math skills (addition) to figure their total points.

3. The pairs keep track of their number of correct punts and keep a total for the class. In a follow-up lesson challenge the class to increase the total number of correct punts. You may choose to chart these numbers to motivate the students and reinforce the skill.

4. Rather than start close, the punter may begin at the maximum distance (eight point area) and punt back to their partners behind the ropes. The

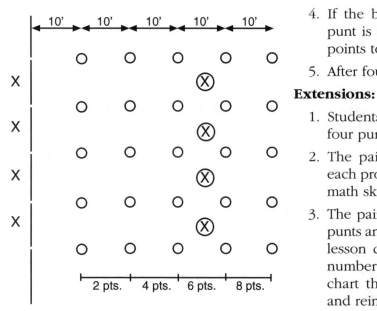

⊗ - Retrievers
O - Cones
X - Kickers

punters then move up and punt from the six-point area, the four-point area, and the two-point area. Then the partners change places. The idea is to get the ball to your partner so he can catch it.

Group Activities

Over the Fence

(This activity should be played outside.)

Objective: To practice punting over a target from a variety of distances

Equipment: One playground ball per student

Activity:

1. Divide the class into two groups and place the groups on either side of a fence (or wall or volleyball net).

2. On your start signal, students attempt to punt the playground balls over the "fence."

3. When a ball comes over the fence, another student must try and catch it and then stand still.

4. On your signal, the students who have caught balls will punt the balls back over the fence from the spot where they were caught. Be sure that the students closest to the fence are out of the way of those punting behind them. Students *must* call for balls before attempting to catch them.

Extensions:

1. Have a definite line for students to stand on when punting and to return to after each catch.

2. Allow the students to punt immediately after the ball is caught.

3. You may perform the activity inside with a volleyball net if you have sufficient slow-moving, soft balls (e.g., beach balls, volleyball trainers, etc.). You may wish to have the students remove their shoes when punting these softer balls.

Adapted, by permission, from J.A. Wessell, PhD, 1974, *Project I CAN* (Northbrook, IL: Hubbard).

Create Your Own Activity

Objective: To allow students to create their own activities to reinforce the skill of punting

Equipment: One piece of paper and pencil per group and a predetermined list of equipment you will allow students to use in their activities (e.g., playground balls, cones, footballs, Nerf balls, etc.)

Activity:

1. Form groups with two to five students each. You may select the groups or the students may form their own.

2. Students create their own activity using the punt as the basic skill. Students are required to have rules that encourage correct performance of the skill, include all players, and address all safety concerns.

3. The groups write their individual names, the rules of the activity, and the equipment needed on their paper and then show the activity to you.

4. Upon approval of their activity, the students obtain their equipment and begin playing.

5. You must approve all changes to the activity.

Extensions:

1. Groups may teach their activities to other groups.

2. Groups may teach their activities to the entire class.

Punt and Go

(This activity is best played outside.)

Objective: To punt balls of various sizes

Equipment: A variety of balls that may be punted (e.g., playground balls of different colors, soccer balls of different sizes, footballs, etc.). No two balls should be identical.

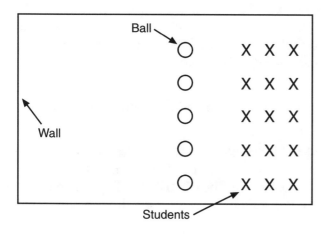

Activity:

1. Place students in lines of three with a ball in front of each line (see figure).

2. On the start signal, the first student punts it as far as he can. For safety, a start command must be used for each rotation.

3. The student then runs to retrieve a punted ball. He may NOT return with the same ball that he punted.

4. The student hands the ball to the next student in line.

5. The activity continues for several rotations.

Extensions:

1. The student must name the type of ball he retrieves. Other members of the line are allowed to help if needed.

2. Students are in lines of three. Make a very large circle using one cone for each group. Have each group stand behind one of the cones. The groups now look like the spokes of a wagon wheel. Have the students do the activity as described above. Students are punting into the center of the circle area.

3. Divide the class into two groups. Each group stands behind a restraining line. The lines are approximately 30 feet apart. Each student in Group A starts with a ball and punts the ball toward Group B's restraining line. On a signal from the teacher each student in Group B finds a ball he has not punted and returns to the Group B restraining line to wait for the signal to punt. Students may not punt the same type of ball twice in succession.

Summary

When children are holding an object and punting it, they are again demonstrating that they enjoy using their feet to move objects on the ground. As with all skills, logical progressions are necessary for skill mastery—therefore, punting movement should be limited to just a ball drop during initial instruction. As with kicking, once the student has demonstrated an ability to perform the punt from a stationary position, the movement part of the punt can be introduced. The punter will leap, plant her foot, and punt. With proper instruction and logical progressions, your students can become skillful punters.

Punt Troubleshooting Chart

IF YOU SEE	THEN TRY THIS
1. Arms not extended	• Have the punting student take a step forward, extend the ball out, and give it to her partner. The partner takes the ball. • Have the student watch her shadow to check for the arm extension.
2. Student not stepping forward on the punting foot, or not taking a large enough step	• Place an object (footprint, color spot, etc.) in front of the student to step on. • Place a jump rope in front of the student for him to step over.
3. Student stepping onto the nonpunting foot instead of leaping	• Have the student practice the leap skill before he tries to use it with the punt. • Place two ropes parallel to each other on the ground for the student to leap over.
4. No forward lean	• Have the student watch her shadow to check for the forward lean. • Have the student pretend to be a runner leaning forward to win a race. Once the student can lean forward, have her practice leaping and leaning.
5. Knee of the punting leg straight as it swings behind the body, or the punting leg not off the ground behind the body	• Place a six-inch cone so that the student must leap and the knee of the punting leg travels over the top of the cone. • Have the student look at his shadow to check the position of the punting leg. • Have the student's partner check the position of the student's punting leg.
6. Student tossing the ball into the air	• Have the student stand and practice dropping the ball. • Have the student step, leap, then drop the ball into a box or hula hoop. • Have the student's partner watch to see if the ball is dropped or tossed.
7. Top of the punting foot (shoelaces) not contacting the ball	• Place baby powder or chalk on the ball. Have the student kick the ball and then check the ball and the foot to see what part of the foot contacted which part of the ball. • Suspend a beanbag, Nerf ball, etc., from a rope strung between two game standards. Have the student practice touching the top of her foot to the suspended object.
8. Arm opposite the punting leg not swinging forward, or the punting foot not continuing in the direction of the ball	• Have the student stand and practice swinging her punting leg forward to touch the fingers of her outstretched opposite hand. • Set up a rope at waist level to the student punting and have her practice the punt without a ball. She must follow through on the punt so that the punting foot and opposite arm touch the bottom of the rope.

Punt Lesson Plan (First Lesson)

Age group: Upper primary

Focus: Executing a proper drop and punt

Subfocus: Keeping your own space

Objectives: To say the cue words for the punt every time (**CUES:** "Ready, drop and punt, follow through"), and execute a correct drop and punt of a small beach ball four out of five times as measured by teacher observation (**CUE:** "Let it drop from your hands").

Materials/Equipment: One small beach ball per student

Advance preparation: Place a line down the center of your teaching area.

Organization/Management: Students are in personal space for instruction and warm-up. Later, students will find their own space on the center line of the gymnasium for practice.

Warm-up:

Today, we are going to learn a different type of kick. It is called a punt. To practice this skill, we have to really warm up the muscles in our legs. When I put on the music, I would like you to begin moving in general space with a locomotor skill of your choice. Who can name a locomotor skill? (Repeat the question several times until **skip, slide, gallop, run,** and **walk** are all mentioned.)

Now when the music stops, I would like you to freeze on the spot and perform a stretching exercise for your legs. How long should we hold a stretch? **(At least 10 seconds.)** *That's right. You will count to yourself and hold the stretch for 10 seconds, rest, and return. After about three times (or reps), I will call out "switch" and you will begin stretching the other leg. Do you understand?*

Just in case you can't think of one, who can show me a stretching exercises that will really warm up your legs? (Call on several children.)

Begin music. Watch to make sure students are performing the locomotor skills correctly, that they are using a variety of skills, and that the leg stretching exercises are held for at least 10 seconds for each leg and are sufficient for the day's activity.

Formation:

Students find their own personal space and sit down.

Introduction:

The special kick we will be doing today, the punt, is used in soccer and football and just for fun. We are going to practice three parts today. They are ready, drop and punt, and follow through. I am going to demonstrate how to punt. (Call on a student to retrieve the balls you punt. Punt several balls while repeating the cue words "ready, drop and punt, and follow through" each time.)

Now this is VERY important. The hardest part of the punt is dropping the ball to kick it. You have to stretch your arms in front and hold the ball with BOTH hands. The foot you don't punt with is in front. You drop the ball and punt it with the same foot you kick with. The ball is dropped, not thrown. Contact the ball on your shoelaces and really stretch your leg out in front.

You will be able to practice this today. Since we are inside, it would be very dangerous to have footballs or soccer balls or even playground balls punted all over the gymnasium. Today we are going to practice punting small beach balls. Watch me as I punt the beach ball. Notice that I drop the ball and contact it where my shoelaces are on my shoes (see figure).

When I call on each group, I would like those students to pick up a small beach ball and sit on the line in the middle of the gymnasium with the ball in your lap. (Have every other student face an opposite wall as in the kicking lesson plan, on page 259).

Here are the safety rules: You may punt only when given the GO signal, and you will go get your beach ball only when told to. Do you understand these rules?

Let's all punt together the first time. Ready—hold the ball in front of you. Now the next two parts come together quickly. Remember, they are drop and punt and follow through. Okay, let's say them out loud together: **Ready, drop and punt, follow through.**

Students continue practicing and the teacher repeats the cues out loud. Watch specifically for dropping the ball and contacting it on the top of the foot. After students retrieve their balls, give the GO command again. This continues for at least 10 repetitions. Reteach problem areas that arise and point out which students have correct technique so the other students can watch and learn.

FREEZE. Sit down where you are. Now you will be able to practice your punting again. This time, you may retrieve the ball after you punt it and then punt it again without me telling you to GO. Of course, I expect you to watch where you are punting and where you are running. Do you understand these rules? Remember to let the ball drop from your hands, don't throw it. GO.

Watch the students for safety and correct performance, especially on dropping the ball to punt it. Repeat the cue words "Let it drop" often.

FREEZE. Please sit down. Now who can tell me differences between the beach balls we were punting and a soccer ball or football? **(The beach ball is lighter.)** *Right. Does a lighter ball drop faster or slower than a heavier ball?* **(Slower.)** *That's right, using the beach ball gives us time to react and punt the ball. What other kind of ball can you think of that would drop or travel more slowly than a soccer ball?* **(Gator Skin balls, balloons, volleyball trainers, etc.)** *Great.*

This time when you are punting, I will be watching for the drop of the ball and that you contact the ball on the top of your foot. If you can do this correctly five times in a row, you may exchange your beach ball for a Gator Skin ball. You should not make this change until you are ready; in other words, five successful punts in a row. Do you understand? GO.

Walk around as students are punting and encourage students who are ready to change to Gator Skin balls. Correct performance is required. Activity continues for five minutes.

FREEZE. I would like you to find a partner who is using a ball that is the same as you are using (Gator Skin ball or beach ball) and sit back to back. GO. Now one of you return your ball and your partner keeps his or hers. GO.

We are going to use the entire length of the gymnasium. You will be on one side of the gym and your partner will be on the other. (Choose a student who has performed very well on the punt.) (Student), would you be my partner to demonstrate? (Student), you stand on the other side of the gymnasium. When I say GO, I will punt to my partner. She (or he) will try to catch it, then return to the end line. When I say GO again, she (or he) will punt it back to me. Now really watch how your partner is performing the punt. After a few minutes you will need to talk to your partner and say something he or she is doing right and something to work on. Watch my partner and me practice punting.

Tell students to watch for step, drop and punt, using the top of the punting foot, and the follow-through, emphasizing the drop and using the top of the foot. After each demonstrator has performed twice, stop the demonstration, then perform the skill correctly.

Girls and boys, do you have any questions? Now one of you line up on the baseline that has the posters (or American flag or drawings, etc.) on it. The ball should be with that partner. The other partner lines up across from the first partner. (Make sure students are spread out.) Again, you may only punt when I say GO. GO.

Watch students for step, drop and punt, using the top of the punting foot, and the follow-through, emphasizing the drop and using the top of the foot. After each partner has performed twice, stop the practice and have the partners meet to discuss problem areas.

Have the students practice again for three repetitions and give feedback to each other again.

FREEZE. Girls and boys, we have run out of time. Those of you holding a ball should walk over, put it away, and line up for your teacher. GO. The rest of you may walk over and line up too. GO.

Closure:

As students are lined up to leave, ask the following questions:

1. *Now who can tell me the cue words for the punt?* **(Ready, drop and punt, follow through.)**

2. *Why do you think we drop the ball rather than throw it for a punt?* **(More likely to contact it, more control, etc.)**

3. *Tell me about the foot and leg of our punting leg when we contact the ball.* **(Leg is extended and the top of the foot contacts the ball.)**

4. *What are some of the safety precautions we used today to make our punting lesson safe?* **(Softer balls, only punt when told to.)**

Great job. Next time we will work on punting for accuracy and the follow-through.

References

Albemarle County Physical Education Curriculum Revision Committee. 1996. Albemarle County Physical Education Curriculum Guide. Unpublished manuscript, Albemarle County Public Schools, Charlottesville, VA.

Buschner, C.A. 1994. *Teaching Children Movement Concepts and Skills: Becoming a Master Teacher.* Champaign, IL: Human Kinetics.

Fitts, P.M. & Posner, M.I. 1967. *Human Performance.* Pittsburgh, PA: University of Pittsburgh Press.

Franck, M., et al. (The Outcomes Committee of NASPE). 1992. *Outcomes of Quality Physical Education Programs.* Reston, VA: National Association for Sport and Physical Education.

Gabbard, D. 1992. *Lifelong Motor Development.* Dubuque, IA: William C. Brown.

Graham, G., Holt-Hale, S., and Parker, M. 1998. *Children Moving: A Reflective Approach to Teaching Physical Education.* Mountain View, CA: Mayfield Press.

Harrison, J.M., and Blakemore, C.L. 1992. *Instructional Strategies for Secondary School Physical Education.* Dubuque, IA: William C. Brown.

Pangrazi, B., Chomokos, N., and Massoney, D. 1981. "From Theory to Practice: A Summary." Pp. 65–71 in *Motor Development: Theory into Practice* (Monograph 3 of *Motor Skills: Theory into Practice*), edited by A. Morris. (ERIC Document Reproduction Service No. ED 225 939)

Seefeldt, V. 1979. "Developmental Motor Patterns: Implications for Elementary School Physical Education." In *Psychology of Motor Behavior and Sport,* edited by C. Nadeau, W. Halliwell, K. Newell, and C. Roberts. Champaign, IL: Human Kinetics.

Smith, T. K. 1997. Authentic Assessment: Using a Portfolio Card in Physical Education. *Journal of Physical Education, Recreation and Dance* 68(4): 46-52.

About the Authors

Vonnie Colvin, EdD, is an assistant professor at the University of Kentucky in the Department of Kinesiology and Health Promotion. In addition to her teaching duties, she works with student teachers in the schools and is co-coordinator of student teaching for her department. She was the 1999 recipient of the College of Education's Exceptional Achievement Award for Teaching for nontenured faculty at Kentucky.

Colvin is a member of both the American Alliance for Health, Physical Education, Recreation and Dance (AAHPERD) and the Kentucky Association for Health, Physical Education, Recreation and Dance. She served as Vice President of Physical Education for her state organization in 1999.

Vonnie Colvin

Before coming to the University of Kentucky in 1995, Colvin taught physical education in Louisa County, Virginia, for 21 years, including 8 in elementary school, 2 in middle school, and 11 at the high school level. During this time she also worked with student teachers from Norfolk State University and Virginia Tech.

Colvin earned her BS in Health, Physical Education, Recreation and Dance at Radford University in 1973, her MS in Physical Education at James Madison University in 1981, and both her MEd (in Counselor Education) in 1991 and her EdD (in Physical Education Pedagogy) in 1995 at the University of Virginia. She lives in Lexington, Kentucky, and enjoys camping, gardening, and reading.

Nancy Markos, MEd, has been an elementary physical education and health specialist in the Albemarle County school system in Charlottesville, Virginia, for 16 years. She is also a clinical instructor at the University of Virginia, where she mentors students in the Physical Education and Adapted Physical Education Programs. Prior to coming to Virginia, Markos taught physical education at the elementary level for three years in Maryland, and at the middle school level for five years in Maryland and Rhode Island.

Markos is a member of the National Education Association, AAHPERD, the Virginia Association of Health, Physical Education, Recreation and Dance, and the education

Nancy Markos

sorority Delta Kappa Gamma. She is also on the editorial board of *Strategies*, an AAHPERD Publication, and is a member of the Curry School of Education's Clinical Instructor Advisory Board at the University of Virginia.

Markos earned her BS from Springfield College in 1971 and her MEd from the University of Virginia in 1994. She lives in Earlysville, Virginia, and enjoys spending time with her family as well as playing racquetball and golf.

Pam Walker

Pam Walker, MEd, has been an elementary physical education and health specialist in the Albemarle County School system in Charlottesville, Virginia, for 21 years. She has spent the last 16 years at Red Hill Elementary in North Garden, Virginia. She is also a clinical instructor at the University of Virginia, where she works with practicum students and student teachers. Walker was named the 1995 Elementary Physical Education Teacher of the Year by the Virginia Association of Health, Physical Education, Recreation and Dance.

In addition to her membership in the state association, Walker is a member of AAHPERD, the National Education Association, and the education sorority Delta Kappa Gamma.

In 1997, along with coauthor Nancy Markos, Walker cofounded Physical Education for All Kids (PEAK), an organization committed to educating parents, teachers, and administrators on the importance of providing quality daily physical education to all students.

Besides her work in physical education, Walker is the Instructional Technology Lead Teacher and Technology Troubleshooting Specialist for her school.

Walker earned her BS in Physical Education from Longwood College in Farmville, Virginia, in 1975 and her MEd in Physical Education, Motor Learning and Pedagogy in 1981 from the University of Virginia. Walker's hobbies include swimming, golfing, and camping.

Other books from Human Kinetics

Authentic Assessment Strategies
for Elementary Physical Education
Suzann Schiemer, MS
1999 • 168 pp • Item BSCH0569
ISBN 0-88011-569-6 • $23.00 ($34.50 Canadian)

A practical resource that shows physical educators how to design and implement assessment strategies.

Physical Education for Lifelong Fitness
The Physical Best Teacher's Guide
American Alliance for Health, Physical Education, Recreation and Dance
1999 • Paperback • Approx 400 pp • Item BAAH0983
ISBN 0-88011-983-7 • $39.00 ($58.50 Canadian)

A guide that presents a framework for implementing health-related physical fitness education effectively.

Physical Education Methods for Classroom Teachers
Human Kinetics
1999 • Paperback • 360 pp • Item BHKP0842
ISBN 0-88011-842-3 • $25.00 ($37.50 Canadian)

This book shows non-specialists how to develop a realistic and workable approach
to teaching physical education.

Interdisciplinary Teaching Through Physical Education
Theresa Purcell Cone, MEd, Peter Werner, PED, Stephen L. Cone, PhD, and Amelia Mays Woods, PhD
1998 • Paperback • 280 pp • Item BCON0502
ISBN 0-88011-502-5 • $27.00 ($40.50 Canadian)

The text makes learning more meaningful, fun, and rewarding for students
by bridging the gap between physical education and other subjects.

Teaching Children Movement Concepts and Skills
Becoming a Master Teacher
Craig A. Buschner, EdD
1994 • Paperback • 160 pp • Item BBUS0480
ISBN 0-87322-480-9 • $16.00 ($23.95 Canadian)

Strategies for teaching children fundamental movements they can use for a lifetime.

To request more information or to order, U.S. customers call 1-800-747-4457, e-mail us at humank@hkusa.com, or visit our website at www.humankinetics.com. Persons outside the U.S. can contact us via our website or use the appropriate telephone number, postal address, or e-mail address shown in the front of this book.

HUMAN KINETICS
The Information Leader in Physical Activity
P.O. Box 5076, Champaign, IL 61825-5076
2335